CIVIL
DISOBEDIENCE

CIVIL DISOBEDIENCE

THEORY AND PRACTICE

EDITED BY

HUGO ADAM BEDAU

PEGASUS / NEW YORK

Library of Congress Catalogue Card Number 69-27984

In Memory Of

MARTIN LUTHER KING, JR.

(January 15, 1929–April 4, 1968)

*who labored
in the tradition of these words:*

"We hold these truths to be self-evident, that all Men are created equal, that they are endowed by their Creator with certain unalienable Rights, that among these are Life, Liberty, and the Pursuit of Happiness—That to secure these Rights, Governments are instituted among Men, deriving their just Powers from the Consent of the Governed, that whenever any Form of Government becomes destructive of these Ends, it is the Right of the People to alter or to abolish it, and to institute new Government, laying its Foundation on such Principles, and organizing its Powers in such Form, as to them shall seem most likely to effect their Safety and Happiness."

PREFACE

"Human history," Erich Fromm has observed, "began with an act of disobedience, and it is not unlikely that it will be terminated by an act of obedience." The extermination camps of the Nazis, the incineration of Hiroshima and Nagasaki, not to mention more recent and (if measured by the scale of these ghastly deeds) less extensive violence waged by governments against their own citizens—what can such events suggest but that men are entirely capable of committing yet greater catastrophes in the name of "superior orders"? Disobedience of duly constituted authority and such justifications as can be marshaled for it, therefore, deserve to be pondered by all reflective men. An unyielding "No!" may yet prove to be our sole password to the future. It is the purpose of this volume of essays to explore that negative by providing a critical perspective on civil disobedience, its actual practice by men of conscience in our midst today, and its theory as interpreted by philosophers of various persuasions.

The plan of this volume of essays is quite simple. In Part I, which serves as the general introduction, I have chosen to orient the reader to the entire subject through the study of Thoreau's celebrated essay on civil disobedience. I have stressed in my introductory comments those issues raised in his essay which will prove most instructive to the reader in light of the subsequent selections in this book. The truly classic quality of his essay is attested by the ease with which this can be readily managed, for the issues central to his discussion turn out to be equally crucial for understanding civil disobedience in contemporary America.

Expansionist warfare and racist institutions (specifically, the Mexican War and slave-holding in the South) prompted Thoreau to refuse to pay taxes to a government that cooperated in such outrages. In our time, five generations later, these same two issues have caused major convulsions in our national life and have provoked every form of individual and mass protest, including civil disobedience. A definite path leads from Thoreau in Concord jail to Albert Bigelow behind bars in Honolulu in 1959 and Martin Luther

King, Jr., in the city jail of Birmingham in 1963. Accordingly, the essays, manifestos, letters, and other documents in Parts II and III explore the acts and campaigns of civil disobedience in America in the civil rights and peace movements during the past decade. As these selections show, the civil disobedient and his critic are divided over a series of questions, the most fundamental of which are whether the particular act of disobedience was effective and justified, and whether any dissent at all was warranted. The answers to these questions in turn invariably hinge upon the particular facts of the grievance in question, on which there may be room for reasonable men to disagree, but which in any case is not to be settled merely by an arbitrary and willful appeal to conscience. It is to be expected, therefore, that most of the essays in Parts II and III would, as they do, devote considerable space to developing the factual background on the issues of race and war in contemporary America.

Thoreau and his spiritual heirs are, of course, partisan and polemical. Their arguments and the rebuttals of their critics also raise more questions than they solve. Any number of concepts, principles, and inferences are assumed and employed in the selections reprinted in Parts II and III, but the authors frequently lack the caution and thoroughness necessary to instruct the unpersuaded. Or so the sceptical reader will conclude. What is needed are discussions by philosophical thinkers willing to explore the major considerations relevant to defining, appraising, and justifying civil disobedience under whatever circumstances it may occur, without regard to the details and merits of specific controversies. The essays in Part IV, some of which appear here for the first time, are intended to provide such a perspective.

A book of this relative brevity cannot offer a definitive or exhaustive treatment of civil disobedience. Hopefully, however, the writings collected here will suffice to illustrate the actual course of debate in recent years and to provoke intelligent discussion of the aims, achievements, methods, and legitimacy of acts of civil disobedience. Social scientists owe us testable hypotheses concerning the political effectiveness of mass civil disobedience; so far, they have provided too little information of this sort; the topic seems not to have aroused their interest as it deserves. It presents complex empirical questions, and I have tried to avoid speculating on their answers.

Except for Thoreau's essay, classic thinkers on civil disobedience such as Tolstoy and Gandhi are not represented in this volume. Several other anthologies are available which will provide anyone interested with a wide range of selections on pacifism, conscientious objection, nonviolence, direct action, and related topics.[1] Thanks to these collections, I have felt justified in isolating the specific issue of civil disobedience from much else with which it is typically and properly connected in the minds of many, and also in concentrating attention on some of the most recent writings on civil disobedience by including them to the exclusion of older favorites.

Civil disobedience in fact, if not in theory, is usually practiced alongside other, more legal, and less disruptive tactics aimed at reforming the same social ills, as study of the civil rights and peace movements will quickly show. Adequate treatment of this important fact would have required an extensive account of contemporary strategies of social reform. I have chosen to concentrate instead on the special qualities of civil disobedience alone. Some readers may be misled thereby into thinking that civil disobedience has been the main or even the only form of protest practiced on behalf of equal rights and peace. Nothing, of course, could be further from the truth, as anyone can testify who knows the effective work of such groups as the National Association for the Advancement of Colored People and the American Friends Service Committee, organizations nowhere mentioned in this book because they do not work through civil disobedience campaigns. Likewise, groups such as the Student Nonviolent Coordinating Committee and the Committee for Nonviolent Action, who have organized mass civil disobedience on many occasions, have also undertaken as part of their continuing program to achieve their larger aims much protest, demonstration, and education that is wholly within the law. The selections in Parts II and III do not fully reveal this. It is also true that civil disobedience is often accompanied by violence, both incidentally and unintentionally, and sometimes as the deliberate act of those who share the discontent of the civil disobedient but not his commitment (whether it be principled or merely tactical) to nonviolent methods. This, too, is an important effect of the social injustices which provoke civil disobedience, but it is not developed in the essays comprising this volume.

I am grateful to all the authors and publishers who have allowed me to reprint their work here, and due acknowledgment in each case is given elsewhere in the volume. I especially appreciate the generosity of John Rawls and Bruce Pech in making available unpublished essays of theirs for inclusion here. John Jensen was enthusiastic and encouraging from the start over this project and helped prod me to an early completion. Joseph Ellin, Walter Harding, and David McReynolds are among those who have put their knowledge at my disposal on various points I raised with them. Without the steady help and independent criticism of my wife, Jan, however, there would be no book; she has shared the toil and pleasure of editing and writing; and without her contribution these tasks would have been more tedious than they were.

Finally, it would be impossible not to mention that a few days before work on this book of readings was completed, Martin Luther King, Jr., was killed by an assassin's bullet. I believe that all the authors whose writings appear with Dr. King's in this volume would join me in dedicating it to his memory and to the fulfillment of his vision.

Hugo Adam Bedau

April 1968
Acton, Massachusetts

CONTENTS

Part One

———

CIVIL
DISOBEDIENCE

———

INTRODUCTION

Thoreau's essay on civil disobedience was first given to the public as a lecture before the Concord Lyceum in January 1848, under the title, "On the Relation of the Individual to the State."[1] He spoke to the Lyceum to justify his successive refusals to pay state taxes, which, as he explains, began in 1842 and culminated in his arrest and confinement to the county jail in Concord in July 1846.[2] He was under lock and key only one night because his tax arrears were paid immediately by an anonymous friend. The tax he refused to pay was the generally unpopular poll or head tax imposed by the Commonwealth of Massachusetts. Thoreau does not mention in his essay that in refusing to pay this tax, and in suffering arrest for it, he was following the lead of others (notably, his friend Bronson Alcott). What insured Thoreau's unrivaled position as spokesman to later generations for the resistance of his day was his vindication of himself to his neighbors and then to the world through this published lecture. Even though civil disobedience is as old as Antigone and Socrates, it is Thoreau to whom, especially in this country, we return again and again to take our bearings as we confront a government or a law we judge to be immoral. Thoreau, as one critic has said:

> . . . seems to stand at a pivotal point in the history of the movement. In one way or another the concept of Civil Disobedience has been voiced and acted upon for at least 2,400 years, but never has it received such mass support, never has it been the object of so much public attention as during the century since Thoreau laid down in such clear intellectual terms the reasons why men should seek to govern their own actions by justice rather than legality.[3]

Despite the familiarity of Thoreau's essay and the act it endeavors to explain and justify, a number of features of his argument continue to perplex critics. Controversy and obscurity in interpreting Thoreau tend to cluster around four questions, questions which inevitably arise in all current discussions of civil disobedience as well: What, exactly, is civil disobedience? What degree of commitment to methods of nonviolence does it imply? What purpose characterizes the intention of those who commit it? By appeal to what considerations is it thought to be justified? Provisional answers to these questions will not only make the study of Thoreau's essay more informed, they will also prepare the reader for the selections that follow.

Did Thoreau Really Commit Civil Disobedience? Gandhi once said of civil disobedience that "The expression was, so far as I am aware, coined by Thoreau . . ."[4] Curiously, Thoreau nowhere used the term in his essay, and he seems not to have used it in referring to it in his other writings. The essay first appeared as "Civil Disobedience" when it was republished in a volume of his writings titled *A Yankee in Canada,* four years after his death. There seems, therefore, little reason to doubt that Thoreau's tax refusal was a clear-cut act of civil disobedience.

Nevertheless, some recent commentators have put this conclusion in doubt. One philosopher of law has said that "Thoreau was mixed-up and confused and . . . his action was not disobedience, but an act of lawbreaking that cannot be condoned even though it was not a criminal act in the full sense of that term."[5] A far more radical inference is contained in the remark of a lawyer who recently claimed, "If civil disobedience means willful breaking of an existing law, then how can it be civil disobedience? It would seem to me . . . to be criminal disobedience, for we have the criminal mind."[6] According to the first objection, Thoreau did not commit civil disobedience because his act "cannot be condoned"; according to the second, Thoreau's act was not civil disobedience because it was "criminal." These are extraordinary conclusions to reach; they have their source in widespread but elementary confusion over what the term "civil disobedience" means and how it is to be used.

Perhaps the tangle of semantic issues involved can best be unravelled by means of a hypothetical debate over whether someone has committed civil disobedience. We could imagine partisans arguing as follows:

   A. Socrates committed civil disobedience, but I think he acted unreasonably, unjustifiably.

   B. No, Socrates' act was a clear case of justifiable civil disobedience.

C. You're both wrong—it wasn't justifiable, and it wasn't civil disobedience either.

D. I agree that it wasn't civil disobedience, but it certainly was justifiable, nevertheless.

In the absence of further information, it would be impossible, of course, to say which of the four has the better argument.[7] What I hope this imaginary dialogue brings out is that there are two apparently independent sets of possibilities to be determined: (a) whether the act in question is or is not civil disobedience, and (b) whether the act is or is not justifiable. The former is essentially a question of proper description, classification, or identification; the latter is clearly a different kind of question altogether, and calls for a complex moral, normative, or evaluative judgment. The distinction between (a) and (b), and the foregoing sketch of dialogue, confirm the opinion that it is possible to classify Thoreau's act as civil disobedience without therewith approving of it, and possible to deny that Thoreau's act is justified without implying that it really wasn't civil disobedience after all.

Now, the difficulty with the two passages quoted a paragraph earlier is that each blurs (but in opposite ways) this point. The first writer uses "civil disobedience" so that it means "non-criminal but justifiable disobedience." This usage, if imposed upon the imaginary dialogue above, renders A's judgment self-contradictory and makes B's trivially true. Surely, such an outcome is absurd and unnecessary. It can be avoided only by resolutely preventing the adjective "civil" from connoting justification. The error of the second critic above is somewhat more complex. In his usage there simply cannot be anything properly called "civil disobedience." For him, this follows because disobedience if willful is always criminal (and therefore, unjustifiable), or else it is not criminal; in which case, it is not illegal (and there is no disobedience involved). This usage transforms the hypothetical dialogue involving A and B in the reverse direction: it makes A's judgment trivial and B's a patent self-contradiction. Once again, the critic cannot or will not use "civil disobedience" as a term of neutral description and classification in application to a class of acts whose ultimate legitimacy and justifiability is not implicitly already decided from the onset. In this instance, however, the confusion is especially perverse. If civil disobedience is "criminal" because it involves intentional and presumptive lawbreaking, we may grant that it is *prima facie* in need of justification (in contrast to conformity to law, which is not *prima facie* unjustified). But it is misleading to convey this point by claiming that civil disobedience is really criminal disobedience. For this suggests that the act, being criminal, is in violation of a criminal law, i.e., involves committing a crime, is not only *prima facie* but is once and for all unjustified, and that the civil disobedient acts selfishly and with the disregard for the principles of law and order typical of "the criminal mind." None of these is usually true, as subsequent essays will show.

The analysis so far does not quite explain, however, Thoreau's precise intention in calling his act and his essay "civil disobedience." Should we take him to be saying, in effect, "Here is my act of tax refusal; I call it and acts like it 'civil disobedience,' and I regard them as justified"? Or did he rather say this: "Here is my act of justifiable resistance to government; let us call it and other such justifiable acts 'civil disobedience' "? As scholars have observed, Thoreau may well have intended to tease the reader with this ambiguity.[8] Without attempting, therefore, to press the pun out of his use of the word "civil," and without conceding anything by way of its implied justification, I think we must accept Thoreau's refusal to pay taxes as indeed a paradigm of civil disobedience.

Is Thoreau a Pacifist? The true place of nonviolence in Thoreau's understanding of his act also affects our interpretation of the term "civil disobedience." There are, of course, other ways to disobey, other things to disobey, other reasons for disobeying, than Thoreau's, any of which could make an act of disobedience not civil at all. There is, for instance, the contrast suggested with the position of a soldier and superior orders (military disobedience) and of religious men and doctrinal authorities (ecclesiastical disobedience). By contrast, civil disobedience is a *civic* act, the disobedience of a person in his capacity as a *citizen* under government. In addition, there is the contrast suggested with all forms of violence, intentional and otherwise. Civil disobedience is disobedience which is "passive," "nonviolent," "courteous," "not uncivil." (Note, too, that the transition from a purely classificatory use of "civil disobedience" into its justificatory or commendatory use may now be underway.) Thoreau's act of tax refusal obviously qualifies under both of these sets of contrasts as an act of civil disobedience. But was it expressive of any profound or consistent pacifism on his part? How essential to Thoreau's own understanding of what he has done is its nonviolence?

It is mainly pacifists who have used civil disobedience over the centuries and developed its tactics and strategy, since it is the one form of direct action which goes beyond legal protest without consisting of (or inevitably resulting in) violence. Not surprisingly, several of the essays elsewhere in this volume advocating civil disobedience are by avowed pacifists. Thoreau's essay itself has appeared in more than one pacifist anthology. However, he nowhere calls himself a pacifist, nor does he speak of the nonviolent character of his act as an essential (or redeeming) feature of it. Moreover, when the nation was alarmed by Captain John Brown's daring raids to free slaves, bloody forays from their beginning on the Kansas border in 1856 to the final assault at Harper's Ferry in 1859, Thoreau spoke and wrote in support of Brown openly and without reservations.[9] Thoreau, in short, was not a pacifist, and the nonviolence of his refusal to pay taxes seems not to have been a crucial consideration to him in committing it or in calling it "civil disobedience."

Thoreau's willingness to go to jail for his convictions is equally subject to qualification. Gandhi often demonstrated, both in his writings and his actions, that the person who commits civil disobedience must "cheerfully suffer imprisonment," and show "the strictest and willing obedience to gaol discipline."[10] (Some have gone so far as to say Gandhi's willing acceptance of the lawful punishment for his acts "is why it is called *civil* disobedience rather than *criminal* disobedience.")[11] Yet, as one commentator has noted of Thoreau, he "says nothing about what some of us take as a special morality in civil disobedience—the need to accept the punishment. He goes to jail, but he goes because he cannot figure out any way of getting out of going. He offers no theory about the propriety of going or not going to jail; it just happens."[12]

We should not forget, however, that imprisonment does play a role in Thoreau's interpretation of his act. He says, ". . . if one thousand, if one hundred, if ten men . . . ay, if *one* honest man . . . were actually to . . . be locked up in the county jail . . . it would be the abolition of slavery in America." The context of this remark shows that he thinks the effect of arresting, prosecuting, and imprisoning civil disobedients would jolt the government into awareness of the immorality of its position, then shame the authorities into refusing to perform these duties, and thereby alter the attitude of society as a whole. No doubt this was unrealistic of Thoreau, and he is not as explicit as one could wish in developing this argument. Still, the germ of what is now sometimes called "moral jujitsu"—the exemplary force of going to jail for one's convictions—is at work in his thoughts.

Was Thoreau's Purpose Educative or Revolutionary? The "primary function" of civil disobedience, it has been said recently, is "always an educative one."[12] Thoreau, too, declares that by not paying taxes, "I am doing my part to educate my fellow countrymen." Quite apart from whatever educative effect his civil disobedience may have had, there is no reason to doubt the educative intention of his act. However, this cannot have been his sole or even primary purpose. Part of his purpose was surely to exculpate himself from complicity in perpetrating injustice; I shall return to this theme below.

Yet even these two ambitions—the educative and the exculpatory—fall short of describing Thoreau's full intention. He declares that "all men recognize the right of revolution," and that now "is not too soon for honest men to rebel and revolutionize." This language he soon modifies into talk about "peaceable revolution," of taking steps beyond "democracy [and] . . . toward a true respect for the individual," toward "a State . . . which can afford to be just to all men, and to treat the individual with respect as a neighbor . . ." Nevertheless, these sentiments if taken as glosses on his famous opening motto and its corollary ("which I also believe . . . 'That government is best which governs not at all' ") have understandably led many interpreters to see Thoreau as a wild-eyed radical. No wonder he has been described as "the greatest American Anarchist."[13] Actually, however, Thoreau is not so much an anarchist or revolutionary as he is a utopian. His vision is not of men ruled by no law at all, or only by a law of each man's own devising, but of a life in which the claims of government have little significance in the day-to-day activities of the individual. Thoreau is not so much opposed to government as he is unimpressed by and uninterested in it. The true revolutionary spirit of the barricades is wholly absent in him.

There are, undeniably, anarchistic strains in his essay, but as often as not their result is curiously irresponsible and free of political ideology. He is at his most vexing when he remarks, for instance, "I quietly declare war with the State, after my fashion, though I will still make what use and get what advantage of her I can, as is usual in such cases." Is this the flippant aside of one who judges the State so corrupt that there is no moral taint in gaining selfish advantage from it where and when he can? Or is it the somewhat embarrassed confession of a cheat, of one who cannot deny (but refuses to acknowledge) the indispensable benefits provided even by a government which tolerates slave-holding and sporadic outbursts of expansionist warfare? One cannot be certain. But one can be sure that insofar as Thoreau's purpose in civil disobedience was revolutionary and anarchic (yes, and even utopian), it is not typical of the purposes of his successors, as the selections in Parts II and III will show.

One's motives and intention in committing civil disobedience are one thing; the actual consequences may be quite different, and in theory at least, the two must be separately appraised. Recently, a former president of the American Bar Association asserted that "The logical and inescapable end of civil disobedience is the destruction of public order."[14] A retired Justice of the United States Supreme Court has declared that "mass civil disobedience," no matter what the "provocation . . . is anarchy, which always results in chaos."[15] From Thoreau's act there seem to have been few social or political consequences whatever, and certainly none in the direction of revolutionary chaos and anarchy. This should not blind us to an important fact about his particular act. Its logic was, after all, as revolutionary as one could wish. Nonpayment of taxes is a revolutionary act in the sense that, if it is widely practiced, it will bring any government to its knees. This is why Gandhi warned, "Civil nonpayment of taxes is indeed the last stage in non-cooperation. We must not resort to it till we have tried the other forms of civil disobedience."[16] Refusing to pay one's taxes is not, therefore, merely another case of disobeying the law. It is performing an act the nature of which is to deny to government its capacity to govern, to administer and enforce *any* of its laws. Contrast this with trespassing and sit-ins: any government can accommodate this sort of civil disobedience and still survive, no matter how widespread it becomes. Such acts are inevitably symbolic, at worst a regrettable nuisance and inconvenience, but never revolutionary. The same is true even of draft resistance: no man is prohibited from volunteering for military service because other men refuse to be conscripted. No government totters simply because its jails are filled with men who won't go. But tax resistance undercuts the possibility of any government; Hobbes did not exaggerate when he spoke of revenues as "the sanguinification of the commonwealth." Thoreau's act, then (whatever may have been its avowed aims or actual consequences), was in its logic—that is, when thought of in terms of universalizing the principle on which he has acted—a revolutionary act, and any adequate appraisal of it must ultimately take this into account. This revolutionary quality, however, is not present in most acts of civil disobedience committed in recent years on behalf of civil rights and peace.

Why Does Thoreau Think His Act is Justified? There are typically two steps to be taken in justifying civil disobedience: (a) showing that the object of protest is an injustice perpetrated by government (and not merely a hardship, or an inevitable natural affliction), and (b) showing that some form of civil disobedience (rather than purely legal redress or violent resistance) is the proper response. Thoreau actually expends little effort on either point. As to the first, he finds it sufficient to mention in passing the one out of six Americans who are "slaves," Mexico—"a whole country—unjustly overrun and conquered by a foreign army," and "the Indian come to plead the wrongs of his race." Those who heard his lecture in 1848 knew well the crimes to which he referred. It is, therefore, misleading to say, as one commentator has, that Thoreau's "whole political philosophy was based on the theoretical premise of individual conscience as the only true criterion of what is politically right and just."[17] True, Thoreau declares, "The only obligation which I have a right to assume, is to do at any time what I think right." But he is led to tax refusal as the right thing to do because, as he later explains, he respects "human rights" . . . "the rights of man." However, in the Mexican War, southern slavery, and the treatment of the Indians, his government has systematically violated these "rights." His sympathies are aroused by the plight of these unfortunate victims; his judgment and his principles assure him that their sufferings are not merely regrettable hardships but inexcusable injustices. Since he also views himself as a free man, he knows he must answer for his compliance with the laws of such a government, including its tax laws. The "appeal to conscience," for Thoreau and others who would justify civil disobedience, does not exist in isolation as their sole "criterion" of political conduct. It is inseparable from an appeal to common moral standards, humane sensibilities, and individual responsibility.

When we turn from the first of the points above to the second, we find Thoreau somewhat more exact and explicit. He pointedly says that if "the injustice . . . is of such a nature that it requires you to be the agent of injustice to another, then I say, break the law . . . What I have to do is to see . . . that I do not lend myself to the wrong I condemn." In taking this position, Thoreau suggests two important aspects of his own understanding of civil disobedience which are also of general relevance: (i) He has no complaint as such, he implies, against taxation. "I have never declined paying the highway tax." The trouble with paying the state poll tax is that it expresses "allegiance" to an unjust government, and it helps to support however slightly and indirectly the distant practices of slavery and warfare, both of which were tolerated by the Commonwealth of Massachusetts. County highway taxes, on the other hand, were presumably merely a neighborly way of paying one's share of road upkeep, and as such were morally unobjectionable. Thus, in violating laws, Thoreau did not act like Antigone, who accorded her brother proper burial in the face of Creon's edict to the contrary, and thereby violated the specific law which she regarded as unjust. Thoreau's act and his reasoning behind it imply that civil disobedience which assaults injustice indirectly is not less justified than that which assaults it directly. This proposition is one of the most controversial in the entire theory of civil disobedience. Justice Abe Fortas of the Supreme Court has recently written that "civil disobedience . . . is never justified in our nation where the law being violated is not, itself, the focus or target of the protest."[18] This is hard to reconcile with the fact, which Thoreau plainly grasped, that it is only acts of indirect resistance which make it possible for the ordinary citizen to commit civil disobedience because of the injustice of any of his government's laws or policies; if such recourse is "never justified," then most of the decisions of his government will remain totally inaccessible to his active resistance. (ii) Thoreau implies that by providing tax support to Massachusetts, when it tolerates injustices imposed by governments federated with it, he will become implicated in the guilt stemming from these injustices he "condemns." Thoreau's position is thus quite different from that of those engaged in the great campaigns of mass civil disobedience in South Africa, India, Occupied Europe, and in our own civil rights movement. In these instances, it was the self-judged victims who refused to cooperate with the authorities in imposing upon themselves the yoke of injustice. Thoreau, we must notice, is silent on the question of disobedience as it is confronted by those who are the victims of injustice. (Perhaps he would consider violent and armed resistance their proper and sole recourse.) Today's draft resisters present an interesting example of civil disobedients who straddle this distinction. They would agree with Thoreau that their "duty" is "the more urgent [because] . . . the country . . . overrun is not our own, but ours is the invading army." But many of them also see the current draft, unlike taxation in Thoreau's eyes, as undemocratic and inherently wrong. Perhaps they would wish to be, in Camus's memorable phrase, "neither victims nor executioners."

What remains doubtful is Thoreau's claim that "the only mode in which a man situated as I am" necessarily meets his government or its representatives is "in the person of its tax-gatherer." Is this really true, or only a testimony to his culpable lack of imagination in seeking other ways to confront his government? He would have us believe that he has no time to pursue "the ways in which the State has provided for remedying the evil" he wishes to protest. "I have other affairs to attend to . . . It is not my business to be petitioning the Government or the Legislature." One wonders why this is not, indeed, the first order of "business" of anyone who disagrees with the majority. As for electoral politics, he dismisses it in a phrase. "All voting is a sort of gaming . . . a playing with right and wrong . . ." Thoreau, it is plain, shows no concern to explore any alternative ways within the law to protest the injustices he perceives before resorting to civil disobedience, and he considers no modes of civil disobedience except tax refusal. Exhaustive pursuit of all legal alternatives short of civil disobedience is not Thoreau's predicament. Conventional criticism in our own time, as several essays below will show, would seize on this point as perhaps the most important defect of Thoreau's theory and practice. Only a person uncommitted to constitutional democracy (or blind to the nature of his own acts) could so flout its principles—such is the verdict of many who would regard Thoreau's civil disobedience as unjustified.

Despite the signal merits and deserved influence of Thoreau's essay, I confess that if I am to believe his own account, I cannot regard his act as a paradigm of justifiable and effective civil disobedience. As we shall see amply displayed by the subsequent essays, few of the features of Thoreau's civil disobedience are preserved in the acts of his successors in contemporary America. True, he is like many in the civil rights and peace movements who are not and do not think of themselves as true pacifists in the Quaker or Gandhian mold and who flirt with the rhetoric of anarchism. But he is also unlike them in so many ways. His act is not a tactic in a campaign of mass disobedience and other (often legal) efforts to effect change in the law; he is wholly unconcerned whether the Constitution of the United States in any way protects his disobedience as a form of justifiable protest; he scorns any appeal to the utility of his act, and he is wholly unmoved by its possible inexpediency (as his dismissal of Paley shows); he shows no great imagination in seeking ways to confront and challenge the government he accuses of injustice; he acknowledges no value in a system of law, much less emphasizes his respect for it; he allows nearly two years to pass before he publicizes his act. In these and other ways, Thoreau remains somewhat unconvincing and alien. Yet one also senses an enviable integrity in his statement and his conduct; it is hard to deny him at least a grudging approval. Perhaps, in the end, he eludes any final judgment.

CIVIL DISOBEDIENCE

Henry D. Thoreau

I heartily accept the motto—"That government is best which governs least"; and I should like to see it acted up to more rapidly and systematically. Carried out, it finally amounts to this, which also I believe—"That government is best which governs not at all"; and when men are prepared for it, that will be the kind of government which they will have. Government is at best but an expedient; but most governments are usually, and all governments are sometimes, inexpedient. The objections which have been brought against a standing army, and they are many and weighty, and deserve to prevail, may also at last be brought against a standing government. The standing army is only an arm of the standing government. The government itself, which is only the mode which the people have chosen to execute their will, is equally liable to be abused and perverted before the people can act through it. Witness the present Mexican war, the work of comparatively a few individuals using the standing government as their tool; for, in the outset, the people would not have consented to this measure.

This American government—what is it but a tradition, though a recent one, endeavoring to transmit itself unimpaired to posterity, but each instant losing some of its integrity? It has not the vitality and force of a single living man; for a single man can bend it to his will. It is a sort of wooden gun to the people themselves. But it is not the less necessary for this; for the people must have some complicated machinery or other, and hear its din, to satisfy that idea of government which they have. Governments show thus how successfully men can be imposed on, even impose on themselves, for their own advantage. It is excellent, we must all allow. Yet this government never of itself furthered any enterprise, but by the alacrity with which it got out of its way. *It* does not keep the country free. *It* does not settle the West. *It* does not educate.

The character inherent in the American people has done all that has been accomplished; and it would have done somewhat more, if the government had not sometimes got in its way. For government is an expedient by which men would fain succeed in letting one another alone; and, as has been said, when it is most expedient, the governed are most let alone by it. Trade and commerce, if they were not made of India-rubber, would never manage to bounce over the obstacles which legislators are continually putting in their way; and, if one were to judge these men wholly by the effects of their actions and not partly by their intentions, they would deserve to be classed and punished with those mischievous persons who put obstructions on the railroads.

But, to speak practically and as a citizen, unlike those who call themselves no-government men, I ask for, not at once no government, but *at once* a better government. Let every man make known what kind of government would command his respect, and that will be one step toward obtaining it.

After all, the practical reason why, when the power is once in the hands of the people, a majority are permitted, and for a long period continue, to rule, is not because they are most likely to be in the right, nor because this seems fairest to the minority, but because they are physically the strongest. But a government in which the majority rule in all cases cannot be based on justice, even as far as men understand it. Can there not be a government in which majorities do not virtually decide right and wrong, but conscience?—in which majorities decide only those questions to which the rule of expediency is applicable? Must the citizen ever for a moment, or in the least degree, resign his conscience to the legislator? Why has every man a conscience, then? I think that we should be men first, and subjects afterward. It is not desirable to cultivate a respect for the law, so much as for the right. The only obligation which I have a right to assume, is to do at any time what I think right. It is truly enough said, that a corporation has no conscience; but a corporation of conscientious men is a corporation *with* a conscience. Law never made men a whit more just; and, by means of their respect for it, even the well-disposed are daily made the agents of injustice. A common and natural result of an undue respect for law is, that you may see a file of soldiers, colonel, captain, corporal, privates, powder-monkeys, and all, marching in admirable order over hill and dale to the wars, against their wills, ay, against their common sense and consciences, which makes it very steep marching indeed, and produces a palpitation of the heart. They have no doubt that it is a damnable business in which they are concerned; they are all peaceably inclined. Now, what are they? Men at all? or small movable forts and magazines, at the service of some unscrupulous man in power? Visit the Navy-Yard, and behold a marine, such a man as an American government can make, or such as it can make a man with its black arts—a mere shadow and reminiscence of humanity, a man laid out alive and standing, and already, as one may say, buried under arms with funeral accompaniments, though it may be—

> "Not a drum was heard, not a funeral note,
> As his corpse to the rampart we hurried;
> Not a soldier discharged his farewell shot
> O'er the grave where our hero we buried."

The mass of men serve the state thus, not as men mainly, but as machines, with their bodies. They are the standing army, and the militia, jailers, constables, posse comitatus, &c. In most cases there is no free exercise whatever of the judgment or of the moral sense; but they put themselves on a level with wood and earth and stones; and wooden men can perhaps be manufactured that will serve the purpose as well. Such command no more respect than men of straw or a lump of dirt. They have the same sort of worth only as horses and dogs. Yet such as these even are commonly esteemed good citizens. Others—as most legislators, politicians, lawyers, ministers, and officeholders—serve the state chiefly with their heads; and, as they rarely make any moral distinctions, they are as likely to serve the Devil, without *intending* it, as God. A very few, as heroes, patriots, martyrs, reformers in the great sense, and *men*, serve the state with the consciences also, and so necessarily resist it for the most part; and they are commonly treated as enemies by it. A wise man will only be useful as a man, and will not submit to be "clay," and "stop a hole to keep the wind away," but leave that office to his dust at least:

> "I am too high-born to be propertied,
> To be a secondary at control,

> Or useful serving-man and instrument
> To any sovereign state throughout the world."

He who gives himself entirely to his fellow-men appears to them useless and selfish; but he who gives himself partially to them is pronounced a benefactor and philanthropist.

How does it become a man to behave toward this American government to-day? I answer, that he cannot without disgrace be associated with it. I cannot for an instant recognize the political organization as *my* government which is the *slave's* government also.

All men recognize the right of revolution; that is, the right to refuse allegiance to, and to resist, the government, when its tyranny or its inefficiency are great and unendurable. But almost all say that such is not the case now. But such was the case, they think, in the Revolution of '75. If one were to tell me that this was a bad government because it taxed certain foreign commodities brought to its ports, it is most probable that I should not make an ado about it, for I can do without them. All machines have their friction; and possibly this does enough good to counterbalance the evil. At any rate, it is a great evil to make a stir about it. But when the friction comes to have its machine, and oppression and rob-bery are organized, I say, let us not have such a machine any longer. In other words, when a sixth of the population of a na-tion which has undertaken to be the refuge of liberty are slaves, and a whole country is unjustly overrun and conquered by a foreign army, and subjected to military law, I think that it is not too soon for honest men to rebel and revolutionize. What makes this duty the more urgent is the fact, that the country so overrun is not our own, but ours is the invading army.

Paley, a common authority with many on moral questions, in his chapter on the "Duty of Submission to Civil Government,"* resolves all civil obligation into expediency; and he proceeds to say, "that so long as the interest of the whole society requires it,

---

*[Ed. note. Thoreau's reference is to Bk. VI, Ch. III, of *The Principles of Moral and Political Philosophy,* by William Paley (1743–1805). The next chapter Paley titles, "Of the Duty of Civil Obedience, as Stated in the Christian Scriptures." This very likely inspired the title Thoreau eventually gave to his own essay.]

that is, so long as the established government cannot be resisted or changed without public inconveniency, it is the will of God that the established government be obeyed, and no longer. . . . This principle being admitted, the justice of every particular case of resistance is reduced to a computation of the quantity of the danger and grievance on the one side, and of the probability and expense of redressing it on the other." Of this, he says, every man shall judge for himself. But Paley appears never to have contemplated those cases to which the rule of expediency does not apply, in which a people, as well as an individual, must do justice, cost what it may. If I have unjustly wrested a plank from a drowning man, I must restore it to him though I drown myself. This, according to Paley, would be inconvenient. But he that would save his life, in such a case, shall lose it. This people must cease to hold slaves, and to make war on Mexico, though it cost them their existence as a people.

In their practice, nations agree with Paley; but does any one think that Massachusetts does exactly what is right at the present crisis?

"A drab of state, a cloth-o'-silver slut,
To have her train borne up, and her soul trail in the dirt."

Practically speaking, the opponents to a reform in Massachusetts are not a hundred thousand politicians at the South, but a hundred thousand merchants and farmers here, who are more interested in commerce and agriculture than they are in humanity, and are not prepared to do justice to the slave and to Mexico, *cost what it may.* I quarrel not with far-off foes, but with those who, near at home, co-operate with, and do the bidding of, those far away, and without whom the latter would be harmless. We are accustomed to say, that the mass of men are unprepared; but improvement is slow, because the few are not materially wiser or better than the many. It is not so important that many should be as good as you, as that there be some absolute goodness somewhere; for that will leaven the whole lump. There are thousands who are *in opinion* opposed to slavery and to the war, who yet in effect do nothing to put an end to them; who, esteeming themselves children of Washington and Franklin, sit down with their hands in their pockets, and say that they know not what to do, and do nothing;

who even postpone the question of freedom to the question of free-trade, and quietly read the prices-current along with the latest advices from Mexico, after dinner, and, it may be, fall asleep over them both. What is the price-current of an honest man and patriot to-day? They hesitate, and they regret, and sometimes they petition; but they do nothing in earnest and with effect. They will wait, well disposed, for others to remedy the evil, that they may no longer have it to regret. At most, they give only a cheap vote, and a feeble countenance and God-speed, to the right, as it goes by them. There are nine hundred and ninety-nine patrons of virtue to one virtuous man. But it is easier to deal with the real possessor of a thing than with the temporary guardian of it.

All voting is a sort of gaming, like checkers or backgammon, with a slight moral tinge to it, a playing with right and wrong, with moral questions; and betting naturally accompanies it. The character of the voters is not staked. I cast my vote, perchance, as I think right; but I am not vitally concerned that that right should prevail. I am willing to leave it to the majority. Its obligation, therefore, never exceeds that of expediency. Even voting *for the right* is *doing* nothing for it. It is only expressing to men feebly your desire that it should prevail. A wise man will not leave the right to the mercy of chance, nor wish it to prevail through the power of the majority. There is but little virtue in the action of masses of men. When the majority shall at length vote for the abolition of slavery, it will be because they are indifferent to slavery, or because there is but little slavery left to be abolished by their vote. *They* will then be the only slaves. Only *his* vote can hasten the abolition of slavery who asserts his own freedom by his vote.

I hear of a convention to be held at Baltimore, or elsewhere, for the selection of a candidate for the Presidency, made up chiefly of editors, and men who are politicians by profession; but I think, what is it to any independent, intelligent, and respectable man what decision they may come to? Shall we not have the advantage of his wisdom and honesty, nevertheless? Can we not count upon some independent votes? Are there not many individuals in the country who do not attend conventions? But no: I find that the respectable man, so called, has immediately drifted from his position, and despairs of his country, when his country has more reason to despair of him. He forthwith adopts one of the candidates thus selected as the only *available* one, thus proving that he is himself *available* for any purposes of the demagogue. His vote is of no more worth than that of any unprincipled foreigner or hireling native, who may have been bought. O for a man who is a *man*, and, as my neighbor says, has a bone in his back which you cannot pass your hand through! Our statistics are at fault: the population has been returned too large. How many *men* are there to a square thousand miles in this country? Hardly one. Does not America offer any inducement for men to settle here? The American has dwindled into an Odd Fellow—one who may be known by the development of his organ of gregariousness, and a manifest lack of intellect and cheerful self-reliance; whose first and chief concern, on coming into the world, is to see that the Almshouses are in good repair; and, before yet he has lawfully donned the virile garb, to collect a fund for the support of the widows and orphans that may be; who, in short, ventures to live only by the aid of the Mutual Insurance Company, which has promised to bury him decently.

It is not a man's duty, as a matter of course, to devote himself to the eradication of any, even the most enormous wrong; he may still properly have other concerns to engage him; but it is his duty, at least, to wash his hands of it, and, if he gives it no thought longer, not to give it practically his support. If I devote myself to other pursuits and contemplations, I must first see, at least, that I do not pursue them sitting upon another man's shoulders. I must get off him first, that he may pursue his contemplations too. See what gross inconsistency is tolerated. I have heard some of my townsmen say, "I should like to have them order me out to help put down an insurrection of the slaves, or to march to Mexico— see if I would go"; and yet these very men have each, directly by their allegiance, and so indirectly, at least, by their money, furnished a substitute. The soldier is applauded who refuses to serve in an unjust war by those who do not refuse to sustain the unjust government which makes the war; is applauded by those whose own act and authority he disregards and sets at naught; as if the State were penitent to that degree that it hired one to scourge it while it sinned, but not to that degree that it left off sinning for a moment. Thus, under the name of Order and Civil Government, we

are all made at last to pay homage to and support our own mean-
ness. After the first blush of sin comes its indifference; and from
immoral it becomes, as it were, *un*moral, and not quite unnecessary
to that life which we have made.

The broadest and most prevalent error requires the most dis-
interested virtue to sustain it. The slight reproach to which the
virtue of patriotism is commonly liable, the noble are most likely
to incur. Those who, while they disapprove of the character and
measures of a government, yield to it their allegiance and support,
are undoubtedly its most conscientious supporters, and so frequently
the most serious obstacles to reform. Some are petitioning the State
to dissolve the Union, to disregard the requisitions of the President.
Why do they not dissolve it themselves—the union between themselves and the State—and refuse to pay their quota into its treasury?
Do not they stand in the same relation to the State, that the State
does to the Union? And have not the same reasons prevented the
State from resisting the Union, which have prevented them from
resisting the State?

How can a man be satisfied to entertain an opinion merely, and
enjoy *it?* Is there any enjoyment in it, if his opinion is that he
is aggrieved? If you are cheated out of a single dollar by your
neighbor, you do not rest satisfied with knowing that you are
cheated, or with saying that you are cheated, or even with petitioning him to pay you your due; but you take effectual steps at once
to obtain the full amount, and see that you are never cheated
again. Action from principle, the perception and the performance
of right, changes things and relations; it is essentially revolutionary,
and does not consist wholly with anything which was. It not only
divides states and churches, it divides families; ay, it divides the
individual, separating the diabolical in him from the divine.

Unjust laws exist: shall we be content to obey them, or shall
we endeavor to amend them, and obey them until we have succeeded, or shall we transgress them at once? Men generally, under
such a government as this, think that they ought to wait until
they have persuaded the majority to alter them. They think that,
if they should resist, the remedy would be worse than the evil. But
it is the fault of the government itself that the remedy *is* worse
than the evil. *It* makes it worse. Why is it not more apt to antici-
pate and provide for reform? Why does it not cherish its wise

minority? Why does it cry and resist before it is hurt? Why does it not encourage its citizens to be on the alert to point out its faults, and *do* better than it would have them? Why does it always crucify Christ, and excommunicate Copernicus and Luther, and pronounce Washington and Franklin rebels?

One would think, that a deliberate and practical denial of its authority was the only offence never contemplated by government; else, why has it not assigned its definite, its suitable and proportionate penalty? If a man who has no property refuses but once to earn nine shillings for the State, he is put in prison for a period unlimited by any law that I know, and determined only by the discretion of those who placed him there; but if he should steal ninety times nine shillings from the State, he is soon permitted to go at large again.

If the injustice is part of the necessary friction of the machine of government, let it go, let it go: perchance it will wear smooth —certainly the machine will wear out. If the injustice has a spring, or a pulley, or a rope, or a crank, exclusively for itself, then perhaps you may consider whether the remedy will not be worse than the evil; but if it is of such a nature that it requires you to be the agent of injustice to another, then, I say, break the law. Let your life be a counter friction to stop the machine. What I have to do is to see, at any rate, that I do not lend myself to the wrong which I condemn.

As for adopting the ways which the State has provided for remedying the evil, I know not of such ways. They take too much time, and a man's life will be gone. I have other affairs to attend to. I came into this world, not chiefly to make this a good place to live in, but to live in it, be it good or bad. A man has not everything to do, but something; and because he cannot do *everything,* it is not necessary that he should do *something* wrong. It is not my business to be petitioning the Governor or the Legislature any more than it is theirs to petition me; and, if they should not hear my petition, what should I do then? But in this case the state has provided no way: its very Constitution is the evil. This may seem to be harsh and stubborn and unconciliatory; but it is to treat with the utmost kindness and consideration the only spirit that can appreciate or deserves it. So is all change for the better, like birth and death, which convulse the body.

I do not hesitate to say, that those who call themselves Abolitionists should at once effectually withdraw their support, both in person and property, from the government of Massachusetts, and not wait till they constitute a majority of one, before they suffer the right to prevail through them. I think that it is enough if they have God on their side, without waiting for that other one. Moreover, any man more right than his neighbors constitutes a majority of one already.

I meet this American government, or its representative, the State government, directly, and face to face, once a year—no more—in the person of its tax-gatherer; this is the only mode in which a man situated as I am necessarily meets it; and it then says distinctly, Recognize me; and the simplest, the most effectual, and, in the present posture of affairs, the indispensablest mode of treating with it on this head, of expressing your little satisfaction with and love for it, is to deny it then. My civil neighbor, the tax-gatherer, is the very man I have to deal with—for it is, after all, with men and not with parchment that I quarrel—and he has voluntarily chosen to be an agent of the government. How shall he ever know well what he is and does as an officer of the government, or as a man, until he is obliged to consider whether he shall treat me, his neighbor, for whom he has respect, as a neighbor and well-disposed man, or as a maniac and disturber of the peace, and see if he can get over this obstruction to his neighborliness without a ruder and more impetuous thought or speech corresponding with his action. I know this well, that if one thousand, if one hundred, if ten men whom I could name—if ten *honest* men only—ay, if *one* HONEST man, in this State of Massachusetts, *ceasing to hold slaves,* were actually to withdraw from this copartnership, and be locked up in the county jail therefor, it would be the abolition of slavery in America. For it matters not how small the beginning may seem to be: what is once well done is done forever. But we love better to talk about it: that we say is our mission. Reform keeps many scores of newspapers in its service, but not one man. If my esteemed neighbor, the State's ambassador, who will devote his days to the settlement of the question of human rights in the Council Chamber, instead of being threatened with the prisons of Carolina, were to sit down the prisoner of Massachusetts, that State which is so anxious to foist the sin of slavery upon her sister—though at present she can discover only an act of inhospitality to be the ground of a quarrel with her—the Legislature would not wholly waive the subject the following winter.

Under a government which imprisons any unjustly, the true place for a just man is also a prison. The proper place to-day, the only place which Massachusetts has provided for her freer and less desponding spirits, is in her prisons, to be put out and locked out of the State by her own act, as they have already put themselves out by their principles. It is there that the fugitive slave, and the Mexican prisoner on parole, and the Indian come to plead the wrongs of his race, should find them; on that separate, but more free and honorable ground, where the State places those who are not *with* her, but *against* her—the only house in a slave State in which a free man can abide with honor. If any think that their influence would be lost there, and their voices no longer afflict the ear of the State, that they would not be as an enemy within its walls, they do not know by how much truth is stronger than error, nor how much more eloquently and effectively he can combat injustice who has experienced a little in his own person. Cast your whole vote, not a strip of paper merely, but your whole influence. A minority is powerless while it conforms to the majority; it is not even a minority then; but it is irresistible when it clogs by its whole weight. If the alternative is to keep all just men in prison, or give up war and slavery, the State will not hesitate which to choose. If a thousand men were not to pay their tax-bills this year, that would not be a violent and bloody measure, as it would be to pay them, and enable the State to commit violence and shed innocent blood. This is, in fact, the definition of a peaceable revolution, if any such is possible. If the tax-gatherer, or any other public officer, asks me, as one has done, "But what shall I do?" my answer is, "If you really wish to do anything, resign your office." When the subject has refused allegiance, and the officer has resigned his office, then the revolution is accomplished. But even suppose blood should flow. Is there not a sort of blood shed when the conscience is wounded? Through this wound a man's real manhood and immortality flow out, and he bleeds to an everlasting death. I see this blood flowing now.

I have contemplated the imprisonment of the offender, rather than the seizure of his goods—though both will serve the same purpose—because they who assert the purest right, and consequently are most dangerous to a corrupt State, commonly have not spent much time in accumulating property. To such the State renders comparatively small service, and a slight tax is wont to appear exorbitant, particularly if they are obliged to earn it by special labor with their hands. If there were one who lived wholly without the use of money, the State itself would hesitate to demand it of him. But the rich man—not to make any invidious comparison—is always sold to the institution which makes him rich. Absolutely speaking, the more money, the less virtue; for money comes between a man and his objects, and obtains them for him; and it was certainly no great virtue to obtain it. It puts to rest many questions which he would otherwise be taxed to answer; while the only new question which it puts is the hard but superfluous one, how to spend it. Thus his moral ground is taken from under his feet. The opportunities of living are diminished in proportion as what are called the "means" are increased. The best thing a man can do for his culture when he is rich is to endeavor to carry out those schemes which he entertained when he was poor. Christ answered the Herodians according to their condition. "Show me the tribute-money," said he—and one took a penny out of his pocket; if you use money which has the image of Caesar on it, and which he has made current and valuable, that is, *if you are men of the State,* and gladly enjoy the advantages of Caesar's government, then pay him back some of his own when he demands it; "Render therefore to Caesar that which is Caesar's, and to God those things which are God's"—leaving them no wiser than before as to which was which; for they did not wish to know.

When I converse with the freest of my neighbors, I perceive that, whatever they may say about the magnitude and seriousness of the question, and their regard for the public tranquillity, the long and the short of the matter is, that they cannot spare the protection of the existing government, and they dread the consequences to their property and families of disobedience to it. For my own part, I should not like to think that I ever rely on the protection of the State. But, if I deny the authority of the State when it presents its tax-bill, it will soon take and waste all my property, and so harass me and my children without end. This is hard. This makes it impossible for a man to live honestly, and at the same time comfortably, in outward respects. It will not be worth the while to accumulate property; that would be sure to go again. You must hire or squat somewhere, and raise but a small crop, and eat that soon. You must live within yourself, and depend upon yourself always tucked up and ready for a start, and not have many affairs. A man may grow rich in Turkey even, if he will be in all respects a good subject of the Turkish government. Confucius said: "If a state is governed by the principles of reason, poverty and misery are subjects of shame; if a state is not governed by the principles of reason, riches and honors are the subjects of shame." No: until I want the protection of Massachusetts to be extended to me in some distant Southern port, where my liberty is endangered, or until I am bent solely on building up an estate at home by peaceful enterprise, I can afford to refuse allegiance to Massachusetts, and her right to my property and life. It costs me less in every sense to incur the penalty of disobedience to the State, than it would to obey. I should feel as if I were worth less in that case.

Some years ago, the State met me in behalf of the Church, and commanded me to pay a certain sum toward the support of a clergyman whose preaching my father attended, but never I myself. "Pay," it said, "or be locked up in the jail." I declined to pay. But, unfortunately, another man saw fit to pay it. I did not see why the schoolmaster should be taxed to support the priest, and not the priest the schoolmaster; for I was not the State's schoolmaster, but I supported myself by voluntary subscription. I did not see why the lyceum should not present its tax-bill, and have the State to back its demand, as well as the Church. However, at the request of the selectmen, I condescended to make some such statement as this in writing: "Know all men by these presents, that I, Henry Thoreau, do not wish to be regarded as a member of any incorporated society which I have not joined." This I gave to the town clerk; and he has it. The State, having thus learned that I did not wish to be regarded as a member of that church, has never made a like demand on me since; though it said that it must adhere to its original presumption that time. If I had known how to name them, I should then have signed off in detail from all the societies which I never signed on to; but I did not know where to find a complete list.

I have paid no poll-tax for six years. I was put into a jail once on this account, for one night; and, as I stood considering the walls of solid stone, two or three feet thick, the door of wood and iron, a foot thick, and the iron grating which strained the light, I could not help being struck with the foolishness of that institution which treated me as if I were mere flesh and blood and bones, to be locked up. I wondered that it should have concluded at length that this was the best use it could put me to, and had never thought to avail itself of my services in some way. I saw that, if there was a wall of stone between me and my townsmen, there was a still more difficult one to climb or break through, before they could get to be as free as I was. I did not for a moment feel confined, and the walls seemed a great waste of stone and mortar. I felt as if I alone of all my townsmen had paid my tax. They plainly did not know how to treat me, but behaved like persons who are underbred. In every threat and in every compliment there was a blunder; for they thought that my chief desire was to stand the other side of that stone wall. I could not but smile to see how industriously they locked the door on my meditations, which followed them out again without let or hindrance, and *they* were really all that was dangerous. As they could not reach me, they had resolved to punish my body; just as boys, if they cannot come at some person against whom they have a spite, will abuse his dog. I saw that the State was half-witted, that it was timid as a lone woman with her silver spoons, and that it did not know its friends from its foes, and I lost all my remaining respect for it, and pitied it.

Thus the State never intentionally confronts a man's sense, intellectual or moral, but only his body, his senses. It is not armed with superior wit or honesty, but with superior physical strength. I was not born to be forced. I will breathe after my own fashion. Let us see who is the strongest. What force has a multitude? They can only force me who obey a higher law than I. They force me to become like themselves. I do not hear of *men* being *forced* to live this way or that by masses of men. What sort of life were that to live? When I meet a government which says to me, "Your money or your life," why should I be in haste to give it my money? It may be in a great strait, and not know what to do: I cannot help that. It must help itself; do as I do. It is not worth the while to snivel about it. I am not responsible for the successful working of the machinery of society. I am not the son of the engineer. I perceive that, when an acorn and a chestnut fall side by side, the one does not remain inert to make way for the other, but both obey their own laws, and spring and grow and flourish as best they can, till one, perchance, overshadows and destroys the other. If a plant cannot live according to its nature, it dies; and so a man.

The night in prison was novel and interesting enough. The prisoners in their shirtsleeves were enjoying a chat and the evening air in the doorway, when I entered. But the jailer said, "Come, boys, it is time to lock up"; and so they dispersed, and I heard the sound of their steps returning into the hollow apartments. My roommate was introduced to me by the jailer, as "a first-rate fellow and a clever man." When the door was locked, he showed me where to hang my hat, and how he managed matters there. The rooms were whitewashed once a month; and this one, at least, was the whitest, most simply furnished, and probably the neatest apartment in the town. He naturally wanted to know where I came from, and what brought me there; and, when I had told him, I asked him in my turn how he came there, presuming him to be an honest man, of course; and, as the world goes, I believe he was. "Why," said he, "they accuse me of burning a barn; but I never did it." As near as I could discover, he had probably gone to bed in a barn when drunk, and smoked his pipe there; and so a barn was burnt. He had the reputation of being a clever man, had been there some three months waiting for his trial to come on, and would have to wait as much longer; but he was quite domesticated and contented, since he got his board for nothing, and thought that he was well treated.

He occupied one window, and I the other; and I saw, that, if one stayed there long, his principal business would be to look out the window. I had soon read all the tracts that were left there, and examined where former prisoners had broken out, and where a grate had been sawed off, and heard the history of the various occupants of that room; for I found that even here there was a history and a gossip which never circulated beyond the walls of the jail. Probably this is the only house in the town where verses are composed, which are afterward printed in a circular form, but not published. I was shown quite a long list of verses which were composed by some young men who had been detected in an attempt to escape, who avenged themselves by singing them.

I pumped my fellow-prisoner as dry as I could, for fear I should never see him again; but at length he showed me which was my bed, and left me to blow out the lamp.

It was like traveling into a far country, such as I had never expected to behold, to lie there for one night. It seemed to me that I never had heard the town-clock strike before, nor the evening sounds of the village; for we slept with the windows open, which were inside the grating. It was to see my native village in the light of the Middle Ages, and our Concord was turned into a Rhine stream, and visions of knights and castles passed before me. They were the voices of old burghers that I heard in the streets. I was an involuntary spectator and auditor of whatever was done and said in the kitchen of the adjacent village-inn—a wholly new and rare experience to me. It was a closer view of my native town. I was fairly inside of it. I never had seen its institutions before. This is one of its peculiar institutions; for it is a shire town. I began to comprehend what its inhabitants were about.

In the morning, our breakfasts were put through the hole in the door, in small oblong-square tin pans, made to fit, and holding a pint of chocolate, with brown bread, and an iron spoon. When they called for the vessels again, I was green enough to return what bread I had left; but my comrade seized it, and said that I should lay that up for lunch or dinner. Soon after he was let out to work at haying in a neighboring field, whither he went every day, and would not be back till noon; so he bade me good-day, saying that he doubted if he should see me again.

When I came out of prison—for some one interfered, and paid that tax—I did not perceive that great changes had taken place on the common, such as he observed who went in a youth, and emerged a tottering and gray-headed man; and yet a change had to my eyes come over the scene—the town, and State, and country —greater than any that mere time could effect. I saw yet more distinctly the State in which I lived. I saw to what extent the people among whom I lived could be trusted as good neighbors and friends; that their friendship was for summer weather only; that they did not greatly propose to do right; that they were a distinct race from me by their prejudices and superstitions, as the Chinamen and Malays are; that, in their sacrifices to humanity, they ran no risks, not even to their property; that, after all, they were not so noble but they treated the thief as he had treated them, and hoped, by a certain outward observance and a few prayers, and by walking in a particular straight though ueseless path from time to time, to save their souls. This may be to judge my neighbors harshly; for I believe that many of them are not aware that they have such an institution as the jail in their village.

It was formerly the custom in our village, when a poor debtor came out of jail, for his acquaintances to salute him, looking through their fingers, which were crossed to represent the grating of a jail window, "How do ye do?" My neighbors did not thus salute me, but first looked at me, and then at one another, as if I had returned from a long journey. I was put into jail as I was going to the shoemaker's to get a shoe which was mended. When I was let out the next morning, I proceeded to finish my errand, and having put on my mended shoe, joined a huckleberry party, who were impatient to put themselves under my conduct; and in half an hour—for the horse was soon tackled—was in the midst of a huckleberry field, on one of our highest hills, two miles off, and then the State was nowhere to be seen.

This is the whole history of "My Prisons."

I have never declined paying the highway tax, because I am as desirous of being a good neighbor as I am of being a bad subject; and, as for supporting schools, I am doing my part to educate my fellow-countrymen now. It is for no particular item in the tax-bill that I refuse to pay it. I simply wish to refuse allegiance to the State, to withdraw and stand aloof from it effectually. I do not care to trace the course of my dollar, if I could, till it buys a man or a musket to shoot one with—the dollar is innocent—but I am concerned to trace the effects of my allegiance. In fact, I quietly declare war with the State, after my fashion, though I will still make what use and get what advantage of her I can, as is usual in such cases.

If others pay the tax which is demanded of me, from a sympathy with the State, they do but what they have already done in their own case, or rather they abet injustice to a greater extent than the State requires. If they pay the tax from a mistaken interest in the individual taxed, to save his property, or prevent his going to jail, it is because they have not considered wisely how far they let their private feelings interfere with the public good.

This, then, is my position at present. But one cannot be too much on his guard in such a case, lest his action be biased by obstinacy, or an undue regard for the opinions of men. Let him see that he does only what belongs to himself and to the hour.

I think sometimes, Why, this people mean well; they are only ignorant; they would do better if they knew how: why give your neighbors this pain to treat you as they are not inclined to? But I think again, this is no reason why I should do as they do, or permit others to suffer much greater pain of a different kind. Again, I sometimes say to myself, When many millions of men, without heat, without ill will, without personal feeling of any kind, demand of you a few shillings only, without the possibility, such is their constitution, of retracting or altering their present demand, and without the possibility, on your side, of appeal to any other millions, why expose yourself to this overwhelming brute force? You do not resist cold and hunger, the winds and the waves, thus obstinately; you quietly submit to a thousand similar necessities. You do not put your head into the fire. But just in proportion as I regard this as not wholly a brute force, but partly a human force, and consider that I have relations to those millions as to so many millions of men, and not of mere brute or inanimate things, I see that appeal is possible, first and instantaneously, from them to the Maker of them, and secondly, from them to themselves. But, if I put my head deliberately into the fire, there is no appeal to fire or to the Maker of fire, and I have only myself to blame. If I could convince myself that I have any right to be satisfied with men as they are, and to treat them accordingly, and not according, in some respects, to my requisitions and expectations of what they and I ought to be, then, like a good Mussulman and fatalist, I should endeavor to be satisfied with things as they are, and say it is the will of God. And, above all, there is this difference between resisting this and a purely brute or natural force, that I can resist this with some effect; but I cannot expect, like Orpheus, to change the nature of the rocks and trees and beasts.

I do not wish to quarrel with any man or nation. I do not wish to split hairs, to make fine distinctions, or set myself up as better than my neighbors. I seek rather, I may say, even an excuse for conforming to the laws of the land. I am but too ready to conform to them. Indeed, I have reason to suspect myself on this head; and each year, as the tax-gatherer comes round, I find myself disposed to review the acts and position of the general and State governments, and the spirit of the people, to discover a pretext for conformity.

"We must affect our country as our parents;
And if at any time we alienate
Our love or industry from doing it honor,
We must respect effects and teach the soul
Matter of conscience and religion,
And not desire of rule or benefit."

I believe that the State will soon be able to take all my work of this sort out of my hands, and than I shall be no better a patriot than my fellow-countrymen. Seen from a lower point of view, the Constitution, with all its faults, is very good; the law and the courts are very respectable; even this State and this American government are, in many respects, very admirable and rare things, to be thankful for, such as a great many have described them; but seen from a point of view a little higher, they are what I have described them; seen from a higher still, and the highest, who shall say what they are, or that they are worth looking at or thinking of at all?

However, the government does not concern me much, and I shall bestow the fewest possible thoughts on it. It is not many moments that I live under a government, even in this world. If a man is thought-free, fancy-free, imagination-free, that which *is not* never for a long time appearing *to be* to him, unwise rulers or reformers cannot fatally interrupt him.

I know that most men think differently from myself; but those whose lives are by profession devoted to the study of these or kindred subjects, content me as little as any. Statesmen and legislators, standing so completely within the institution, never distinctly and nakedly behold it. They speak of moving society, but have no resting-place without it. They may be men of a certain experience and discrimination, and have no doubt invented ingenious and even useful systems, for which we sincerely thank them; but all their wit and usefulness lie within certain not very wide limits. They are wont to forget that the world is not governed by policy and expediency. Webster never goes behind government, and so cannot speak with authority about it. His words are wisdom to those legislators who contemplate no essential reform in the existing government; but for thinkers, and those who legislate for all time, he never once glances at the subject. I know of those whose serene and wise speculations on this theme would soon reveal the limits of his mind's range and hospitality. Yet, compared with the cheap professions of most reformers, and the still cheaper wisdom and eloquence of politicians in general, his are almost the only sensible and valuable words, and we thank Heaven for him. Comparatively, he is always strong, original, and, above all, practical. Still his quality is not wisdom, but prudence. The lawyer's truth is not Truth, but consistency, or a consistent expediency. Truth is always in harmony with herself, and is not concerned chiefly to reveal the justice that may consist with wrong-doing. He well deserves to be called, as he has been called, the Defender of the Constitution. There are really no blows to be given by him but defensive ones. He is not a leader, but a follower. His leaders are the men of '87. "I have never made an effort," he says, "and never propose to make an effort; I have never countenanced an effort, and never mean to countenance an effort, to disturb the arrangement as originally made, by which the various States came into the Union." Still thinking of the sanction which the Constitution gives to slavery, he says, "Because it was a part of the original compact—let it stand." Notwithstanding his special acuteness and ability, he is unable to take a fact out of its merely political relations, and behold it as it lies absolutely to be disposed of by the intellect—what, for instance, it behooves a man to do here in America today with regard to slavery, but ventures, or is driven, to make some such desperate answer as the following, while professing to speak absolutely, and as a private man—from which what new and singular code of social duties might be inferred? "The manner," says he, "in which the governments of those States where slavery exists are to regulate it, is for their own consideration, under their responsibility to their constituents, to the general laws of propriety, humanity, and justice, and to God. Associations formed elsewhere, springing from a feeling of humanity, or any other cause, have nothing whatever to do with it. They have never received any encouragement from me, and they never will."

They who know of no purer sources of truth, who have traced

up its stream no higher, stand, and wisely stand, by the Bible and the Constitution, and drink at it there with reverence and humility; But they who behold where it comes trickling into this lake or that pool, gird up their loins once more, and continue their pilgrimage towards its fountain-head.

No man with a genius for legislation has appeared in America. They are rare in the history of the world. There are orators, politicians, and eloquent men, by the thousand; but the speaker has not yet opened his mouth to speak, who is capable of settling the much-vexed questions of the day. We love eloquence for its own sake, and not for any truth which it may utter, or any heroism it may inspire. Our legislators have not yet learned the comparative value of free-trade and of freedom, of union, and of rectitude, to a nation. They have no genius or talent for comparatively humble questions of taxation and finance, commerce and manufactures and agriculture. If we were left solely to the wordy wit of legislators in Congress for our guidance, uncorrected by the seasonable experience and the effectual complaints of the people, America would not long retain her rank among the nations. For eighteen hundred years, though perchance I have no right to say it, the New Testament has been written, yet where is the legislator who has wisdom and practical talent enough to avail himself of the light which it sheds on the science of legislation?

The authority of government, even such as I am willing to submit to—for I will cheerfully obey those who know and can do better than I, and in many things even those who neither know nor can do so well—is still an impure one: to be strictly just, it must have the sanction and consent of the governed. It can have no pure right over my person and property but what I concede to it. The progress from an absolute to a limited monarchy, from a limited monarchy to a democracy, is a progress toward a true respect for the individual. Even the Chinese philosopher was wise enough to regard the individual as the basis of the empire. Is a democracy, such as we know it, the last improvement possible in government? Is it not possible to take a step further toward recognizing and organizing the rights of man? There will never be a really free and enlightened State, until the State comes to recognize the individual as a higher and independent power, from which all its own power and authority are derived, and treats him accordingly.

I please myself with imagining a State at last which can afford to be just to all men, and to treat the individual with respect as a neighbor; which even would not think it inconsistent with its own repose, if a few were to live aloof from it, not meddling with it, nor embraced by it, who fulfilled all the duties of neighbors and fellow-men. A State which bore this kind of fruit, and suffered it to drop off as fast as it ripened, would prepare the way for a still more perfect and glorious State, which also I have imagined, but not yet anywhere seen.

Part Two:

———

AGAINST RACISM

———

INTRODUCTION

On December 1, 1955, Mrs. Rosa Parks refused to give up her seat in the back of the bus to a white man, and was promptly arrested for refusing to obey the driver's request. Out of this incident grew the epochal Montgomery Bus Boycott.[1] However, civil disobedience did not become a deliberate and influential feature of civil rights activity until the lunch counter "sit-ins" began on February 1, 1960, in Greensboro, N.C. They were soon followed by campaigns waged all over the south, under the direction of the Congress of Racial Equality (CORE), the Southern Christian Leadership Conference (SCLC), and the Student Nonviolent Coordinating Committee (SNCC).[2] These two dates in 1955 and 1960 mark the origins of the nationwide effort to transform the century-old struggle for racial equality by what Arthur Waskow has called "the politics of creative disorder." Central to the movement has been the use of civil disobedience by persons not fundamentally pacifist in religious or moral commitment, but who recognized civil disobedience as an effective tactical weapon for the weak in their struggle against an armed, self-righteous majority in full command of all the instruments of social control. It is difficult and perhaps impossible to isolate the specific accomplishments in the decade of struggle that are attributable solely to civil disobedience, but even the most grudging observers have granted that "civil disobedience tactics undoubtedly accelerated the pace of legislative reform."[3] Nor is there doubt that it has also played an important role in channeling explosive emotions impossible to stifle and otherwise difficult to vent. As Martin Luther King, Jr., noted, "there was less loss of life in ten years of Southern protest than in ten days of Northern riots."[4] Admittedly, the current civil rights movement is not the first time in our national life when mass nonviolence has helped to save lives and property and to prod a reluctant majority down the path of social justice. Earlier in this century both the suffragette and labor union movements employed civil disobedience as part of their campaigns. Still, the present generation owes most of its knowledge of the practice and theory of civil disobedience to the continuing struggle for racial equality, and for this reason the basic texts and interpretations of this phase of the civil rights movement warrant the closest scrutiny.

Harris Wofford, Jr.'s address (reprinted below), given in October 1957 at Howard University, has been said to be "the first published articulated suggestion . . . that Gandhian techniques should be applied by American Negroes" in their efforts to secure equal rights and the full protection of the federal constitution.[5] Wofford's essay is not only a historic document; it also provides ample background on the civil rights movement, and develops the similarity of the predicament faced by American blacks and the Indian masses under British rule. More importantly, Wofford helped to popularize two of the ideas basic to the whole moral perspective of the current theory of civil disobedience. One is that "We accept personal responsibility for injustice." This is the conviction which transforms civil disobedience of the classic Thoreauvian sort into a tactic for social change. Thoreau did not, after all, have any hopes that his refusal to pay taxes would end the injustices of the Mexican War and of slave-holding; he did not speak of himself as attempting by his act to *force* the government to reconsider its course; he made no attempt whatever to *organize* tax withholding. His act was, in short, the solitary act of an individual concerned about his own moral health, not the undertaking of a social revolutionary, intent upon bringing mass nonviolent direct action against unjust practices.

The other important notion Wofford's essay helped bring into prominence is expressed in the dictum he attributes to Justice Holmes: "A free man should look on each law not as a command, but as a question," as though the Law, if it could speak, would say: Do you choose to follow the rule laid down, or do you prefer to take the consequences specified for disobedience?[6] Surely this Holmesian notion is a gross oversimplification (how, for instance, is one to explain on this view the moral obloquy which is typically incurred when one commits a crime of personal violence?); it has never found much favor with philosophers of law since Holmes first propounded it before the turn of this century. But it has proved significant in the thinking of some civil rights leaders, and for that reason deserves special notice in the present context.

In the early 1960's, it was often said of Birmingham, Alabama, that it was the most segregated city in the nation and had the most disgraceful record on race relations of any major urban area. In April 1963, the Alabama Christian Movement for Human Rights opened its "Birmingham Manifesto" with the ominous words,

> The patience of an oppressed people cannot endure forever. The Negro citizens of Birmingham for the last several years have hoped in vain for some evidence of good faith resolution of our just grievances.[7]

A few days later, as the announced mass protest began to unfold, a public statement was directed to Martin Luther King, Jr., by a group of leading clergymen in the Birmingham area urging "our own Negro community to withdraw support from these demonstrations." The statement ended with these words:

> When rights are consistently denied, a cause should be pressed in the courts and in negotiations among local leaders, and not in the streets. We appeal to both our white and Negro citizenry to observe the principles of law and order and common sense.[8]

To the clash of sentiments expressed in these two statements King addressed his now famous "Letter from Birmingham City Jail," probably the most widely read and discussed manifesto on civil disobedience since Thoreau's own essay.

In his book on the Montgomery Bus Boycott, King has stated how he first became acquainted with the theory of civil disobedience.

> When I went to Atlanta's Morehouse College as a freshman in 1944, my concern for racial and economic justice was already substantial. During my student days at Morehouse, I read Thoreau's *Essay on Civil Disobedience* for the first time. Fascinated by the idea of refusing to cooperate with an evil system, I was so deeply moved that I reread the work several times. This was my first intellectual contact with the theory of nonviolent resistance.[9]

King added that, on the threshold of the Bus Boycott, ". . . I began to think about Thoreau's *Essay on Civil Disobedience* . . . I became convinced that what we were preparing to do in Montgomery was related to what Thoreau had expressed. We were simply saying to the white community, 'We can no longer lend our cooperation to an evil system.' "[10] Seven years later, the Birmingham demonstration involved orderly files of marchers, lunch-counter sit-ins, economic boycott of segregationist merchants, kneel-ins at churches, sit-ins at libraries, as well as a voter registration drive. All the time, the jails were being filled with blacks arrested for "parading without a permit" and other such offenses. After ten days of mass protest of this sort, the city attorneys obtained a court injunction directing cessation of the demonstration until the right to continue had been affirmed by judicial review. Two days later, King and his associates disobeyed this injunction, on the grounds that "the courts of Alabama had misused the judicial process in order to perpetuate injustice and segregation. Consequently, we could not, in good conscience, obey their findings."[11]

In his "Letter," King follows the path of Thoreau (and, indeed, of Jefferson) in distinguishing between "just" and "unjust" laws, and argues that the law which men enact and administer may be wholly "out of harmony" with "the moral law," the "eternal and natural law." As he states it,

> An unjust law is a code inflicted upon a minority which that minority had no part in enacting or creating because they did not have the unhampered right to vote.

Segregation laws, or other laws which have the effect of discriminating against a voteless minority, are by this test obviously unjust. Although King does not himself develop a theory of justice or of the natural law, his entire case for breaking the law as he did rests upon the appeal to these notions. They are, accordingly, among the central issues investigated in Part IV.

The remaining three essays in this Part are a series of reflections by the legal establishment on civil rights demonstrations where civil disobedience was involved. The article by

Harrison Tweed, Bernard Segal, and Herbert Packer has been praised by Vice-President Hubert Humphrey as "one of the best-informed and most thoughtful discussions I have read on this troublesome problem."[12] Its value in the present context consists in its attempt to distinguish between the disobedience of a Governor George Wallace, barring the school doorway to qualified Negro students in defiance of a federal court order, and of a Martin Luther King defying a state court order prohibiting him from continuing a mass demonstration. The distinction, they argue, rests upon the ultimate legality under the federal law and constitution and thus the finality of the court order in the first instance but not in the second, and therefore of the reasonable belief that disobedience will be vindicated by a higher tribunal in the second case but not in the first. (The same argument, of course, would seem to entail that the many Abolitionists who broke the Fugitive Slave Law during the years after the Dred Scott decision but before the Emancipation Proclamation had no legal, and therefore no justifiable, ground on which to stand.) Tweed, Packer, and Segal do not argue that antisegregationist civil disobedience is not genuine civil disobedience; they argue, rather, that such civil disobedience is likely to be justified and is legally justified if the highest courts say it is. They do agree that "Disobedience to the law is always prima facie unjustifiable," that is, that the burden of justification for disobeying the law is always upon the lawbreaker, and that in the absence of specific argument on his behalf, he stands condemned for his disobedience. But they point out that the structure of our complex legal system provides many avenues whereby such justification can be found within the law, through appeal to a higher tribunal based on some superseding or preempting consideration. In this way, particular acts of civil disobedience can in fact receive a legal vindication as justifiable acts to seek redress and remedy under the law of the land.

The essay by William Taylor is a detailed development of exactly this argument; it is one which has gained increasing popularity among lawyers sympathetic to the civil rights movement.[13] It does lead to the somewhat paradoxical conclusion that all (or almost all—there are a few interesting exceptions) of the so-called "civil disobedience" in the civil rights movement was, in fact, not really disobedience at all! As with the "freedom rides," they were, argues Taylor, "appeals to law, rather than acts of civil disobedience." By this conclusion, he does not mean merely that these acts were held to be justified subsequently by the highest courts. He means that, strictly, they "violated no valid law" in the first instance and thus, no matter what these acts may have seemed like to those who committed them or to those who enforced local ordinances against the civil rights workers, no genuine "civil disobedience" had been committed. What this line of argument suggests is that, under our system, anyone with a profound grievance who can both appeal to principles of justice and persuade the courts of his cause, and who breaks the unjust law or some other law to protest an unjust law, really has not committed true civil disobedience. He will only have exercised his rights of free speech and quest for redress of grievances, both of which are amply protected by our constitution! At least, this will be true if he willingly accepts the penalty for his (apparent) lawbreaking.

The final selection by Louis Waldman is a strident attack on Martin Luther King, Jr.'s address in 1965 before the Association of the Bar of New York City, delivered exactly two years after his "Letter." Waldman's criticism is typical of the kind of attack many leaders of the bar have directed against civil disobedience in the civil rights movement.[14] King's address, much of which Waldman quotes, and Waldman's rebuttal not only foreshadow the demise of "civil rights" and the birth of "Black Power" and "civil disorder," but it also shows how much confusion and disagreement remain over the precise nature and justification of civil disobedience in the past ten years' struggle for racial equality under law.

The one great question unanswered by the selections reprinted below is whether and to what degree mass civil disobedience depends upon the implicit threat of violence to achieve its goals and, irrespective of this, to what degree it has in fact resulted in otherwise avoidable violence. Critics of civil disobedience in the civil rights movement have uniformly insisted that whatever the intentions of the leaders may have been, civil disobedience has provoked violence in the white majority and has planted the seeds of later violence in the demonstrators themselves. There is no doubt that, in the south, overtly peaceful demonstrations (with and without civil disobedience) have often been violently repressed by white bystanders, white police forces, and the white Ku Klux Klan. But it is hard to see how those advocating equal rights through direct nonviolent action should be blamed for the brutality and intransigence of their oppressors. Violence unleashed by the oppressors cannot be so easily laid at the door of their victims. For the system of racial segregation enforced by tacit consent is at best only a superficially decent equivalent for the institutions of slavery with their unbridled assault on human dignity. If violent resistance by slaves does not seem unjustifiable, how can nonviolent resistance against those who are attempting to preserve the effects of slavery be regarded as unjustified, even though it may provoke the oppressor to violence in defense of the status quo? As for the violence of northern ghetto dwellers since 1965, it is attributable not to irresponsible black demagoguery or to miscalculations, but to excusable resentment at justice long delayed and the hopelessness of a better future. Or so any unbiased reader of the *Report* of the President's Advisory Commission on Civil Disorder is bound to conclude.

It is beyond the purpose of this book to try to tell the story of the decade from Mrs. Parks's arrest in Montgomery to the open warfare of recent summers in the ghettos of Los Angeles, Detroit, and Newark; a whole shelf of books would be required for this task. It is saddening and even terrifying that the basic volumes of this period begin with *Stride Toward Freedom* (1958) and culminate in the *Report of the National Advisory Commission on Civil Disorder* (1968). Yet it might have been foreseen. That nonviolent civil disobedience should have given way to violent "civil disorder"—that the politics of creative disorder, culminating in the great March on Washington in August 1963 should have been all but swallowed up in the politics of destructive violence—can surprise no one who has studied the history of race relations in this country.

It is filled with violence and bloodshed, almost all of it inflicted by whites and suffered by blacks. Taken against this background, the following selections are unrepresentative indeed.

Whether civil disobedience can soon be restored to the dominant role it so recently occupied in the civil rights struggle is doubtful. To believe that the struggle itself will soon cease, either because true economic and political democracy has prevailed or because the non-white minority will abandon its causes, is all but impossible. Writing in the spring of 1968, only a week before he was killed, Martin Luther King, Jr., announced a major national effort at nonviolent direct action, charging "Nonviolence was never more relevant as an effective tactic than today for the North. It also may be the instrument of our national salvation. . . . We have, through massive nonviolent action, an opportunity to avoid a national disaster and create a new spirit of class and racial harmony."[15] Only time will tell whether civil disobedience in race relations can be saved from becoming a museum specimen of the power and the limits of mass nonviolent action as an instrument of rapid social change.

NON-VIOLENCE AND THE
LAW: THE LAW NEEDS HELP

Harris Wofford, Jr.

Today is the fortieth anniversary of the Communist Revolution in
Russia. This forty-first annual convocation of the Howard University School of Religion may not seem like much competition
to the massive parade of troops and tanks moving this day through
Red Square. But your subject, "Non-Violence and Social Change,"
ought to be bothering the men, whoever they may today be, who
are now reviewing the physical marks of Soviet power from the
Kremlin stand. For let me venture a prediction: it will be through
the non-violent resistance of the people suffering under communism,
not through any Western policy of massive retaliation, that communism will be finally transformed. Hungary demonstrated that
the Red Army can crush even the bravest armed rebellion, but
events in Eastern Europe and the Soviet Union itself suggest that
beneath the surface non-violent resistance to Stalinism has already
been of some effect in changing Communism. Poland is already
a long way toward freedom, thanks in large part to the courageous
and peaceful resistance, and jail-going, of two very different men,
Cardinal Wyszinski of the Church and Wladaslav Gomulka of
the Party. "Non-violence," Gandhi said, "means the putting of
one's whole soul against the will of the tyrant." "Working under

Reprinted by permission from *The Journal of Religious Thought,* XV (Autumn-Winter,
1957–58), pp. 25–36.

this law of our being," he said, "it is possible for a single individual to defy the whole might of an unjust empire to save his honor, his religion, his soul, and lay the foundation for that empire's fall or its regeneration." Djilas is trying to do this in Yugoslavia, from his jail cell, and Dudintsev, the author of *Not By Bread Alone,* is doing it by his civil defiance in Moscow.

So "non-violence" is a world wide question, just as is integration of different racial or cultural or national groups. Any light which we in this country can throw on the problem of democratic and peaceful integration will be valuable in other lands plagued by the same stubborn problem—in India, where untouchability and caste is as ingrained as are any prejudices in this country; in Israel, the pressure-cooker of a hundred cultures; in all of Africa. And any new demonstration here that non-violent change is possible will encourage and strengthen the forces of peaceful change everywhere.

I

But I have been asked to talk as a lawyer about how the law comes into this big question you are considering. Let me start by saying that a school of religion is a good place for this question to be asked. As a lawyer I am convinced that the leadership in social change, particularly in bringing about the change in racial relationships now underway in this country, must not be left to lawyers.

We lawyers have our function. We can draft laws and interpret them; we can try cases in court and win legal decisions; we can advise clients about their rights and defend their rights with every clause of the Constitution and every legal trick at our command. But social change is not ordinarily one of our skills. For the most part we are trained to win cases or at least to keep our clients out of jail, not to reconstruct the relationships of a community, not to change the minds and hearts of people.

Yet unless people's minds and hearts are changed, what can the law do? "In this and like communities," Lincoln said, "public sentiment is everything. With public sentiment, nothing can fail; without it nothing can succeed. Consequently he who moulds public sentiment goes deeper than he who enacts statutes or pronounces decisions. He makes statutes and decisions possible or impossible to be executed." Lincoln was not one to sell his profession short. The law has a big role to play, and not the least of that role is its own part in moulding public sentiment. The Constitution must be enforced, said Lincoln, knowing that enforcement of the law is itself a form of persuasion. The law is a teacher. People learn to drive on the right side of the street by obeying the law requiring them to drive on that side. Citizens of the thirteen original states came to consider themselves citizens of the United States because the Constitution of the United States was ratified, established, and enforced. Without the working of the Constitution, no amount of talk would have convinced Americans to abandon their parochial loyalties for a higher allegiance.

Today compliance with the Constitution is still the best instruction in our constitutional duties. Negroes voting will do more to change the habits and opinions of those who oppose such voting than any amount of talk. Children of all races going to school with each other will do more than anything else to persuade young people and their parents that integration can work. Thus the decisions of the Supreme Court fulfilling the Constitution's promise of equal protection of the laws are great and necessary milestones. But they do not mark the end of the road. They only point the way. And in fact, despite the impressive unanimity of the Court and the determination of the President to enforce the law, they seem to leave us at an impasse. For racial segregation in the public schools is unconstitutional and must be ended with all deliberate speed. But a substantial and dominant part of the public in a number of states is opposed to compliance with this and other applications of the constitutional guarantee of equal rights. It will not be enough to get more court orders. Nor can bayonets be relied upon to do the trick. The law needs help. The courts and the Department of Justice and federal policing powers cannot by themselves overcome the popular, emotional, psychological obstacles to integration in some of the states. The law cannot act as teacher where the conditions necessary for the educational process do not exist. Where opposition to the law is violent and widespread the law may not be obeyed at all, or may be obeyed only in form while the spirit is submerged in a wave of irrationality.

This does not mean that the situation in Little Rock or elsewhere is hopeless. In fact, Little Rock may be a case where straight enforcement will suffice. The local school board had decided to comply with the Supreme Court, it had devised a gradual plan for integration that had substantial support in the community, and the city authorities were themselves willing to enforce it. A spark of demagoguery inflamed the situation, but there is reason to hope that federal authority plus local common sense will put out the fire and give the plan for integration a chance to succeed. The example of Little Rock may help prevent other such outbreaks in areas where the Negro population is small and integration not in reality a very big problem.

But in the deep South, particularly in the Black Belt counties containing a majority of disfranchised Negroes, no simple solution is open. Local school boards in many cases will refuse to adopt even the most gradual integration plan, and if pressed by litigation, the public school system may itself be abandoned. Or the public schools in these Black Belt counties may be preserved for Negro children, with the whites establishing private schools. How can the courts compel state legislatures to appropriate funds for integrated schools?

The question then is what else can be done to mould public sentiment. How can we help the law? What can we do to break up the concentration of emotions on this issue, to disperse the hatred, violence, and irrationality gathered around public school integration, to take the initiative out of the hands of racial demagogues, to release the forces of moderation, of ethics and sanity and Christianity, of respect for law?

II

This is where non-violence and Gandhi and Martin Luther King and Ralph Abernathy and the Montgomery Improvement Association come in. It is time for Thurgood Marshall, a master craftsman whose legal victories have contributed greatly to the reconstruction of racial relationships in this country, to reconsider Thoreau's *Essay on Civil Disobedience*. For there must be further actions, in and out of court, that go deeper in moulding public sentiment. And for this the ministers of the gospel of the new law, the law of Love, should step forward. It is time for you to light new paths for your legal brethren who too often take a too narrow, litigious view of the law.

The Supreme Court, thanks to the civil rights lawyers in our midst, has ordained justice. But human nature is recalcitrant stuff, and once again, albeit in pale and distant imitation, it seems that in the agonizing way of the New Testament it is necessary for the word to become flesh. You will call this the way of Love. Gandhi called it non-violence, or as he put it, living the Sermon on the Mount. As a lawyer I see it as a form of persuasion. And as a lawyer I would rather define what I mean by citing cases.

In 1935 Dr. and Mrs. Thurman, while visiting Gandhi, asked him to come to America, not for White America but to help the Negro in his fight for civil rights. Gandhi said he had to make good the message of non-violence in India first, but added that "it may be through the Negroes that the unadulterated message of non-violence will be delivered to the world."

In 1951 a former associate of Gandhi, Rammanohar Lohia, visited this country and to American Negroes and whites who wanted to advance civil rights he prescribed jail-going and non-violent struggle against unjust racial laws and practices. No, said President Johnson of Fisk, we are too weak a minority and here we have the law and Constitution on our side, unlike the situation you faced in India. There are only a handful of Negroes in Montgomery who would stand together in any Gandhian struggle, sadly said that courageous Alabama NAACP leader, Mr. E. D. Nixon, himself a veteran of many struggles. When, at Hampton Institute in November 1955, I happened to propose that the Negro and white of the South try the Gandhian way, a respected Negro leader who had known and loved Gandhi and who had tried to spread his message in America told me that he had about given up hope. The American Negro, everyone seemed to say, does not have the Gandhian dimension in him. Then came the Montgomery bus boycott. And by Christmas 1955 the world knew that the Negroes of Montgomery, Alabama, were walking with God, praying for those that oppose them, and regularly rededicating themselves to the methods of non-violence. Mrs. Rosa Parks says that she had been forced to move many times before but that for some reason "this time I just didn't move." When the driver threatened to call the police she said: "Then just call them." With her arrest, the spark was struck that started the first great Gandhian fire in our midst. A year later the world knew that the Negro of Montgomery had it in him. Under the inspired leadership of Martin Luther

King and his brother ministers the Gandhian alchemy, as in India and South Africa, made heroes out of common clay. In passing I note that the ratio of ministers to lawyers in the Montgomery struggle, judging from those arrested, was twenty-four to one. A year later the Supreme Court struck down bus segregation in Montgomery as unconstitutional. "All that walking for nothing," said a lawyer friend of mine. "They could just as well have waited while the bus case went up through the courts, without all the work and worry of the boycott."

Would that have been better? Would it have been better if forty thousand Negroes had not spoken up against segregation with their prayers and their feet? Would it have been better if the ministers had never been arrested, if the bombs had not been exploded, if there had been a court victory without a popular struggle? That is a rhetorical question because you know and I know that the Montgomery bus boycott was the most exciting and most significant thing that has happened in this country for a long time. Of course we are glad it happened. A new element came into our national life. New dignity was added to the fight for civil rights. The words of the court took on substance and life; they had no hollow ring from on high because they were part of a human dialogue, because in Montgomery there was a deep human response, because through the boycott public sentiment was moulded so that it became possible to establish the law.

III

We know this instinctively, but we would do well to examine the nature of this new element and understand its implications. What Martin Luther King has given us is the unadulterated message of non-violence which Gandhi wanted the Negroes finally to deliver to the world. That message can be summarized in these terms: We accept personal responsibility for injustice. We will take direct action against injustice without waiting for the government to act or a majority to agree with us or a court to rule in our favor. We will not obey unjust laws or submit to unjust practices. We will do this peacefully, openly, cheerfully, because our aim is to persuade. We adopt the means of non-violence because our end is a community at peace with itself. We will try to persuade with our words, but if our words fail we will try to persuade with our acts. We will always be ready to talk and to seek fair compromise, but we are also ready to suffer when necessary, to go to jail or risk our lives, to become witnesses to the truth as we see it.

At first this may sound un-American, for lately we have been committed to wait upon Congress and the courts—or the next election—for the resolution of all our troubles. But Gandhi got his theory of civil disobedience from Thoreau, and at least once before in our history when the law was at another impasse, with the Dred Scott decision and the Fugitive Slave Law, there was a fruitful era of non-violent action. The abolitionists awakened the conscience of the nation and set the stage for Lincoln by refusing to acquiesce in slavery. When Emerson came to ask Thoreau why he was in jail, the Concord prisoner asked, "Why are you outside?" Prison, he said, was apparently the place for fugitive slaves, Mexican prisoners, Indians, and honest men. "Under a government which imprisons any unjustly," he wrote, "the true place for a just man is also a prison." Thoreau advised the abolitionists not to "wait till they constitute a majority of one." It is enough, he said, "if they have God on their side, without waiting for that other one." "Unjust laws exist: shall we be content to obey them, or shall we endeavor to amend them, and obey them until we have succeeded, or shall we transgress them at once?" Thoreau asked. His answer was this: "If this injustice is part of the necessary friction of the machine of government, let it go, let it go: perchance it will wear smooth . . . but if it is of such a nature that it requires you to be the agent of injustice to another, then, I say, break the law. Let your life be a counter friction to stop the machine. . . . Cast your whole vote, not a strip of paper merely, but your whole influence."

In Western law and philosophy there is ample theoretical justification for this approach. "An unjust law is not a law," argued Aristotle, quoting Antigone. Aquinas, quoting Augustine, agreed, and added that human laws unjust because contrary to Divine law or good ought nowise to be obeyed. St. Thomas was less sure of what to do about laws contrary to human good, such as laws imposing unequal burdens on the community. He held that such laws were not binding "in conscience" except perhaps to avoid "scandal or disturbance."

It is here that Gandhi, a British-trained lawyer, comes in, adding non-violence as the method of resisting injustice. *Civil* disobedience, he demonstrated, is not subversive of the law, does not lead to the kind of scandal and disturbance St. Thomas feared. On the contrary it involves the highest possible respect for the law. If we secretly violated the law, or tried to evade it, or violently tried to overthrow it, that would be undermining the idea of law, Gandhi argued. But by openly and peacefully disobeying an unjust law and asking for the penalty, we are saying that we so respect the law that when we think it is so unjust that in conscience we cannot obey, then we belong in jail until that law is changed.

It seems to me this is good legal theory. Justice Holmes once argued even that a party to a private contract has a right to refuse to comply with the contract if he is ready to pay the penalty. I am not going that far. I do not say we have a right to break the social contract which is our legal system, except through constitutional amendments. But I am arguing that under our social contract man is to be free, and that a free man should look on each law not as a command but as a question, for implicit in each law is the alternative of obedience or of respectful civil disobedience and full acceptance of the consequences. Once men no longer believe that they as good citizens must obey any law passed by the legislature, no matter how bad, then they must ask themselves of each law, Is this a law that I should obey? Is it a just law? Is it so unjust that it needs to be resisted from the very inception, and cannot wait the slow process of parliamentary reform? This choice we always have to make. It is the choice which makes us free. I am talking about the freedom which Socrates felt on that morning when, having refused to obey the law abridging his freedom of speech but also refusing to evade the law by escaping from Athens, he peacefully drank the hemlock.

Perhaps I have reached a realm beyond the law. But this I think is the spirit of our laws. The principle of an aristocracy is honor, says Montesquieu; of a tyranny, it is fear; of a democracy, it is learning. The law will play its full role as a teacher only when we look upon it as a question. The law is not some final arbiter. It is the voice of our body politic with which we must remain in dialogue. For the proposition to which we are dedicated is self-government. We must respond to the law, resist it, change it, and fulfill it, even as it challenges, changes, and educates us.

IV

Now there is at least one other vital argument which Gandhi and Martin Luther King would make, which is beyond the legal pale, but I will try to make it. "Non-violence in its dynamic condition means conscious suffering," said Gandhi. "Rivers of blood may have to flow before we gain our freedom but it must be our blood," he said to his countrymen. And hundreds of thousands of Indians did withstand the blows of British clubs, about half a million courted jail, and not a few gave their lives without striking back. What was Gandhi's justification for this ordeal to which he invited his countrymen, for this mass political application of the ancient doctrine of turning the other cheek? As ministers of a church nourished by the blood of martyrs, dedicated to the imitation of Him who chose the Cross, there should be little that a lawyer need say to convince you of the educational potentialities of suffering. "Things of fundamental importance to people are not secured by reason alone but have to be purchased with their suffering," said Gandhi. "Suffering is infinitely more powerful than the law of the jungle for converting the opponent and opening his ears, which are otherwise shut, to the voice of reason." "The appeal of reason is more to the head," he said, "but the penetration of the heart comes from suffering. It opens up the inner understanding in man."

Does it? In practice does non-violent action change the minds and hearts of people? Is it practical in a democratic system of law where there is a Constitution with a Bill of Rights to which one can appeal through regular legal channels? Is it advisable, when the spirit of violent disobedience is afoot, to adopt any methods other than strict reliance on law and order? These questions answer themselves. For the very use of violence by the opponents of integration invites a non-violent response. At least it presents the alternative of acquiescence to intimidation or of the use of violence in return or of non-violent resistance. Gandhi often said he would prefer violence to cowardice, but he and you and I would prefer the courageous non-violence of Rosa Parks or of Elizabeth Eckford to the use of shotguns and switchblades. The old law of an eye-for-an-eye-for-an-eye leaves everyone blind.

Nor is violent, lawless intimidation the only kind of injustice facing the Negro. There are still many unconstitutional discriminatory laws on the books, and state and local governments can add new ones faster than the Supreme Court can strike them down.

Nor does the existence of the Constitution at the top of our federal system mean that the majority in Congress or in a state legislature or in a city council may not enact an unjust law that is, at least for some time, upheld by the Court. Let us not forget the Fugitive Slave Law. Civil disobedience of laws or local ordinances which we believe violate the Bill of Rights is the quickest and surest way of testing their constitutionality. In this sense, as Thoreau wrote, "They are the lovers of law and order who observe the law when the government breaks it."

Also in this age of great centralized nation-states and monster bureaucracies we need some practical new Socratic technique to register popular dissent and to stir society from its dogmatic slumbers. Civil disobedience is an antidote to the centralization and standardization of our life, to the sense of fatality of the multitude as well as to the tyranny of the majority. The leviathans, our governments, if they give a minimum of good government, need have no fear of being stung too often, for the gadflies who will willingly go to jail to make their point are normally not so numerous.

Thus civil disobedience is a new answer to the question of how to divide our duties to Caesar and God. As the claims of Caesar have grown louder, our answer too often has been: We render unto Caesar that which Caesar says is Caesar's and go to church on Sunday. With non-violence we can make real decisions—effective moral choices—in this apportionment between God and Caesar, between our conscience and the state. That is what happened in Montgomery when churches filled on days other than Sunday and people started walking with God on their work days.

Was the Montgomery bus boycott effective in registering the convictions of the Negroes and in stirring the white conscience from its complacency? How can we measure the effect of the boycott—or of the courageous suffering of the children who have gone through jeering mobs and faced a line of guns in order to establish the civil rights guaranteed by the Constitution? The heart has its reasons, and the doctors of the mind recognize the occasional need for shock treatment. I would guess that the boycott had the effect of an electric shock on both the white and Negro people of Montgomery, shaking and to some extent changing the racial thought patterns of that community. Montgomery whites could no longer be so sure they knew their Negroes, and the Negroes could begin to be sure that they were not the docile children that they had been pictured.

This is not to suggest that men are easily moved out of their mental ruts or that prejudice and irrationality can be cured by non-violent words or a year's walking. Nehru once remarked that the British were never so angry as when the Indians resisted them with "non-violence," that he never saw eyes so full of hate as those of the British troops to whom he turned the other cheek when they beat him with lathis. But non-violent resistance at least changed the minds and hearts of the Indians, however impervious the British may have been. We cast away our fear, says Nehru. And in the end the British not only granted India freedom but came to have a new respect for Indians. Today a mutual friendship based on complete equality exists between these two peoples within the Commonwealth.

I do not predict the same happy ending for Montgomery because integration is more complicated than independence. But I am sure that the Negro of Montgomery is already walking straighter because of the boycott. And I expect that this generation of Negro children will grow up stronger and better because of the courage, the dignity, and the suffering of the nine children of Little Rock and their counterparts in Nashville and Clinton and Sturgis. And I like to believe that the white people of this country are being affected too, that beneath the surface this nation's conscience is being stirred.

I hope that is the case not just because the Gandhian theory seems right to me but because it is becoming clear that we are in for a season of suffering. The Constitution stands and it is colorblind, but the Fourteenth Amendment will not become the living law of this land until it is understood as well as enforced. And we are a long way from that understanding. Angry passions and deep prejudices are being aroused, and even as victories for civil rights mount in the federal courts, the mountain of state and local laws and practices remains unmoved. Negro leaders continue to be arrested and persecuted under city ordinances; state laws continue to be enacted to circumvent integration; and powerful community pressures are organized to support the whole web of racial injustice. What I hope is that recognizing the necessity of struggle and suffering, we will make of it a virtue. If only to save itself from bitterness, this generation of Negroes needs the vision to see its ordeal as the opportunity to transfigure itself and American society. If the jails must be filled, let them be entered, as Gandhi urged his countrymen, "as a bridegroom enters the bride's chamber." That is, with some trepidation but with great expectation.

V

It is a privilege that history gives only occasionally for men to become the instruments of a great idea. And one thing more about the idea of integration through non-violent action. "Non-violence" is not a negative concept. Its corollary must always be growth. Gandhi always insisted that the other side of the coin of civil disobedience against injustice was constructive service to establish justice. And in the Indian struggle there was a rhythm of alternation between dramatic boycotts and jail-going campaigns and periods of steady, hard construction of a better India. In South Africa, where Gandhi first experimented with his methods with an Indian community that was outnumbered ten to one by the whites, he began by listing all the grievances against the Indians by the whites and by asking his fellow Indians to consider which of these grievances were justified and then to do something about remedying them. To the Indian merchants before him, known for slick dealings and sharp bargaining, he proposed more responsibility to the community. He thought all Indians could do something to improve the unsanitary conditions in the Indian sections of town. Why wait for legal victories against discrimination for the necessary drain-cleaning, he asked. He organized constructive institutions to teach the impoverished Indians to read and write, to erase caste discriminations among the Indians themselves, to help end the demoralization of much of the Indian community.

I gather that it was in this spirit that the Montgomery Improvement Association was formed on the occasion of the bus boycott. As Martin Luther King said, "We are seeking to improve not the Negro of Montgomery but the whole of Montgomery." It was not an association to improve bus service by ending segregation but an association to improve Montgomery. And, as could be said of every city in this country, that leaves a lot of improving to do.

This then is the rhythm beyond the law which I as a lawyer commend to your ears: Non-violent resistance to all forms of racial injustice, including state and local laws and practices, even when this means a term in jail; and imaginative, bold, constructive action to end the demoralization caused by the legacy of slavery and segregation, inferior schools, slums, and second-class citizenship. The non-violent struggle, if conducted with the dignity and courage already shown in Montgomery and Little Rock, will itself help end the demoralization, but a new frontal assault on the poverty, disease, and ignorance of people too long behind God's back will make victory in the struggle more certain. This is the way, it seems to me, for public sentiment to be moulded. In taking the leadership in this great educational venture you will be going, as Lincoln said, deeper than those who make and interpret the laws. "The law will never make men free," Thoreau said; "it is men who have got to make the law free." That is only half true, for the law can help. But through non-violent action men, by becoming free themselves, in turn help our law at last to be free.

LETTER FROM BIRMINGHAM CITY JAIL

Martin Luther King, Jr.

My dear Fellow Clergymen,

While confined here in the Birmingham City Jail, I came across your recent statement calling our present activities "unwise and untimely." Seldom, if ever, do I pause to answer criticism of my work and ideas. If I sought to answer all of the criticisms that cross my desk, my secretaries would be engaged in little else in the course of the day, and I would have no time for constructive work. But since I feel that you are men of genuine goodwill and your criticisms are sincerely set forth, I would like to answer your statement in what I hope will be patient and reasonable terms.

I think I should give the reason for my being in Birmingham, since you have been influenced by the argument of "outsiders coming in." I have the honor of serving as president of the Southern Christian Leadership Conference, an organization operating in every Southern state, with headquarters in Atlanta, Georgia. We have some eighty-five affiliate organizations all across the South—one being the Alabama Christian Movement for Human Rights. Whenever necessary and possible we share staff, educational and financial resources with our affiliates. Several months ago our local affiliate here in Birmingham invited us to be on call to engage

Reprinted by permission of the author and publisher from *Liberation*, June 1963, pp. 10–16.

in a nonviolent direct action program if such were deemed necessary. We readily consented and when the hour came we lived up to our promises. So I am here, along with several members of my staff, because we were invited here. I am here because I have basic organizational ties here.

Beyond this, I am in Birmingham because injustice is here. Just as the eighth century prophets left their little villages and carried their "thus saith the Lord" far beyond the boundaries of their home towns; and just as the Apostle Paul left his little village of Tarsus and carried the gospel of Jesus Christ to practically every hamlet and city of the Graeco-Roman world, I too am compelled to carry the gospel of freedom beyond my particular home town. Like Paul, I must constantly respond to the Macedonian call for aid.

Moreover, I am cognizant of the interrelatedness of all communities and states. I cannot sit idly by in Atlanta and not be concerned about what happens in Birmingham. Injustice anywhere is a threat to justice everywhere. We are caught in an inescapable network of mutuality, tied in a single garment of destiny. Whatever affects one directly affects all indirectly. Never again can we afford to live with the narrow, provincial "outside agitator" idea. Anyone who lives inside the United States can never be considered an outsider anywhere in this country.

You deplore the demonstrations that are presently taking place in Birmingham. But I am sorry that your statement did not express a similar concern for the conditions that brought the demonstrations into being. I am sure that each of you would want to go beyond the superficial social analyst who looks merely at effects, and does not grapple with underlying causes. I would not hesitate to say that it is unfortunate that so-called demonstrations are taking place in Birmingham at this time, but I would say in more emphatic terms that it is even more unfortunate that the white power structure of this city left the Negro community with no other alternative.

In any nonviolent campaign there are four basic steps: 1) Collection of the facts to determine whether injustices are alive. 2) Negotiation. 3) Self-purification and 4) Direct Action. We have gone through all of these steps in Birmingham. There can be no gainsaying of the fact that racial injustice engulfs this community.

Birmingham is probably the most thoroughly segregated city

in the United States. Its ugly record of police brutality is known in every section of this country. Its injust treatment of Negroes in the courts is a notorious reality. There have been more unsolved bombings of Negro homes and churches in Birmingham than any city in this nation. These are the hard, brutal and unbelievable facts. On the basis of these conditions Negro leaders sought to negotiate with the city fathers. But the political leaders consistently refused to engage in good faith negotiation.

Then came the opportunity last September to talk with some of the leaders of the economic community. In these negotiating sessions certain promises were made by the merchants—such as the promise to remove the humiliating racial signs from the stores. On the basis of these promises Rev. Shuttlesworth and the leaders of the Alabama Christian Movement for Human Rights agreed to call a moratorium on any type of demonstrations. As the weeks and months unfolded we realized that we were the victims of a broken promise. The signs remained. Like so many experiences of the past we were confronted with blasted hopes, and the dark shadow of a deep disappointment settled upon us. So we had no alternative except that of preparing for direct action, whereby we would present our very bodies as a means of laying our case before the conscience of the local and national community. We were not unmindful of the difficulties involved. So we decided to go through a process of self-purification. We started having workshops on non-violence and repeatedly asked ourselves the questions, "Are you able to accept blows without retaliating?" "Are you able to endure the ordeals of jail?" We decided to set our direct action program around the Easter season, realizing that with the exception of Christmas, this was the largest shopping period of the year. Knowing that a strong economic withdrawal program would be the by-product of direct action, we felt that this was the best time to bring pressure on the merchants for the needed changes. Then it occurred to us that the March election was ahead and so we speedily decided to postpone action until after election day. When we discovered that Mr. Connor was in the run-off, we decided again to postpone action so that the demonstrations could not be used to cloud the issues. At this time we agreed to begin our nonviolent witness the day after the run-off.

This reveals that we did not move irresponsibly into direct action. We too wanted to see Mr. Connor defeated; so we went through postponement after postponement to aid in this community need. After this we felt that direct action could be delayed no longer.

You may well ask, "Why direct action? Why sit-ins, marches, etc.? Isn't negotiation a better path?" You are exactly right in your call for negotiation. Indeed, this is the purpose of direct action. Nonviolent direct action seeks to create such a crisis and establish such creative tension that a community that has constantly refused to negotiate is forced to confront the issue. It seeks so to dramatize the issue that it can no longer be ignored. I just referred to the creation of tension as a part of the work of the nonviolent resister. This may sound rather shocking. But I must confess that I am not afraid of the word tension. I have earnestly worked and preached against violent tension, but there is a type of constructive nonviolent tension that is necessary for growth. Just as Socrates felt that it was necessary to create a tension in the mind so that individuals could rise from the bondage of myths and half-truths to the unfettered realm of creative analysis and objective appraisal, we must see the need of having nonviolent gadflies to create the kind of tension in society that will help men to rise from the dark depths of prejudice and racism to the majestic heights of understanding and brotherhood. So the purpose of the direct action is to create a situation so crisis-packed that it will inevitably open the door to negotiation. We, therefore, concur with you in your call for negotiation. Too long has our beloved Southland been bogged down in the tragic attempt to live in monologue rather than dialogue.

One of the basic points in your statement is that our acts are untimely. Some have asked, "Why didn't you give the new administration time to act?" The only answer that I can give to this inquiry is that the new administration must be prodded about as much as the outgoing one before it acts. We will be sadly mistaken if we feel that the election of Mr. Boutwell will bring the millennium to Birmingham. While Mr. Boutwell is much more articulate and gentle than Mr. Connor, they are both segregationists, dedicated to the task of maintaining the status quo. The hope I see in Mr. Boutwell is that he will be reasonable enough to see the futility of massive resistance to desegregation. But he will not see this without pressure from the devotees of civil rights. My friends, I must say to you that we have not made a single gain in civil rights without determined legal and nonviolent pressure. History is the long and tragic story of the fact that privileged groups seldom give up their privileges voluntarily. Individuals may see the moral light and voluntarily give up their unjust posture; but as Reinhold Niebuhr has reminded us, groups are more immoral than individuals.

We know through painful experience that freedom is never voluntarily given by the oppressor; it must be demanded by the oppressed. Frankly, I have never yet engaged in a direct action movement that was "well timed," according to the timetable of those who have not suffered unduly from the disease of segregation. For years now I have heard the words "Wait!" It rings in the ear of every Negro with a piercing familiarity. This "Wait" has almost always meant "Never." It has been a tranquilizing thalidomide, relieving the emotional stress for a moment, only to give birth to an ill-formed infant of frustration. We must come to see with the distinguished jurist of yesterday that "justice too long delayed is justice denied." We have waited for more than three hundred and forty years for our constitutional and God-given rights. The nations of Asia and Africa are moving with jet-like speed toward the goal of political independence, and we still creep at horse and buggy pace toward the gaining of a cup of coffee at a lunch counter. I guess it is easy for those who have never felt the stinging darts of segregation to say, "Wait." But when you have seen vicious mobs lynch your mothers and fathers at will and drown your sisters and brothers at whim; when you have seen hate-filled policemen curse, kick, brutalize and even kill your black brothers and sisters with impunity; when you see the vast majority of your twenty million Negro brothers smothering in an air-tight cage of poverty in the midst of an affluent society; when you suddenly find your tongue twisted and your speech stammering as you seek to explain to your six-year-old daughter why she can't go to the public amusement park that has just been advertised on television, and see tears welling up in her little eyes when she is told that Funtown is closed to colored children, and see the depressing clouds of inferiority begin to form in her little mental sky, and see her begin to distort her little personality by unconsciously developing a bitterness toward white people; when you have to concoct an answer for a five-year-old son asking in agonizing pathos: "Daddy, why do white people treat colored people so mean?"; when you take a cross country drive and find it necessary to sleep night after night in the uncomfortable corners of your automobile because no motel will accept you; when you are humiliated day in and day out by nagging signs reading "white" and "colored"; when your first name becomes "nigger" and your middle name becomes "boy" (however old you are) and your last name becomes "John," and when your wife and mother are never given the respected title "Mrs."; when you are harried by day and haunted at night by the fact that you are a Negro, living constantly at tip-toe stance never quite knowing what to expect next, and plagued with inner fears and outer resentments; when you are forever fighting a degenerating sense of "nobodiness"; then you will understand why we find it difficult to wait. There comes a time when the cup of endurance runs over, and men are no longer willing to be plunged into an abyss of injustice where they experience the blackness of corroding despair. I hope, sirs, you can understand our legitimate and unavoidable impatience.

You express a great deal of anxiety over our willingness to break laws. This is certainly a legitimate concern. Since we so diligently urge people to obey the Supreme Court's decision of 1954 outlawing segregation in the public schools, it is rather strange and paradoxical to find us consciously breaking laws. One may well ask, "How can you advocate breaking some laws and obeying others?" The answer is found in the fact that there are two types of laws: There are *just* and there are *unjust* laws. I would agree with Saint Augustine that "An unjust law is no law at all."

Now what is the difference between the two? How does one determine when a law is just or unjust? A just law is a man-made code that squares with the moral law or the law of God. An unjust law is a code that is out of harmony with the moral law. To put it in the terms of Saint Thomas Aquinas, an unjust law is a human law that is not rooted in eternal and natural law. Any law that uplifts human personality is just. Any law that degrades human personality is unjust. All segregation statutes are unjust because segregation distorts the soul and damages the personality. It gives the segregator a false sense of superiority, and the segregated a false sense of inferiority. To use the words of Martin Buber, the great Jewish philosopher, segregation substitutes an "I-it" relationship for the "I-thou" relationship, and ends up relegating persons to the status of things. So segregation is not only politically, economically and sociologically unsound, but it is morally wrong and sinful. Paul Tillich has said that sin is separation. Isn't segregation an existential expression of man's tragic separation, an expression of his awful estrangement, his terrible sinfulness? So I can urge men to disobey segregation ordinances because they are morally wrong.

Let us turn to a more concrete example of just and unjust laws. An unjust law is a code that a majority inflicts on a minority that is not binding on itself. This is difference made legal. On the other hand a just law is a code that a majority compels a minority to follow that it is willing to follow itself. This is sameness made legal.

Let me give another explanation. An unjust law is a code inflicted upon a minority which that minority had no part in enacting or creating because they did not have the unhampered right to vote. Who can say that the legislature of Alabama which set up the segregation laws was democratically elected? Throughout the state of Alabama all types of conniving methods are used to prevent Negroes from becoming registered voters and there are some counties without a single Negro registered to vote despite the fact that the Negro constitutes a majority of the population. Can any law set up in such a state be considered democratically structured?

These are just a few examples of unjust and just laws. There are some instances when a law is just on its face and unjust in its application. For instance, I was arrested Friday on a charge of parading without a permit. Now there is nothing wrong with an ordinance which requires a permit for a parade, but when the ordinance is used to preserve segregation and to deny citizens the First Amendment privilege of peaceful assembly and peaceful protest, then it becomes unjust.

I hope you can see the distinction I am trying to point out. In no sense do I advocate evading or defying the law as the rabid segregationist would do. This would lead to anarchy. One who breaks an unjust law must do it *openly, lovingly* (not hatefully as the white mothers did in New Orleans when they were seen on television screaming "nigger, nigger, nigger"), and with a willingness to accept the penalty. I submit that an individual who breaks a law that conscience tells him is unjust, and willingly accepts the penalty by staying in jail to arouse the conscience of the community over its injustice, is in reality expressing the very highest respect for law.

Of course, there is nothing new about this kind of civil disobedience. It was seen sublimely in the refusal of Shadrach, Meshach and Abednego to obey the laws of Nebuchadnezzar because a higher moral law was involved. It was practiced superbly by the early Christians who were willing to face hungry lions and the excruciating pain of chopping blocks, before submitting to certain unjust laws of the Roman empire. To a degree academic freedom is a reality today because Socrates practiced civil disobedience.

We can never forget that everything Hitler did in Germany was "legal" and everything the Hungarian freedom fighters did in Hungary was "illegal." It was "illegal" to aid and comfort a Jew in Hitler's Germany. But I am sure that if I had lived in Germany during that time I would have aided and comforted my Jewish brothers even though it was illegal. If I lived in a Communist country today where certain principles dear to the Christian faith are suppressed, I believe I would openly advocate disobeying these anti-religious laws. I must make two honest confessions to you, my Christian and Jewish brothers. First, I must confess that over the last few years I have been gravely disappointed with the white moderate. I have almost reached the regrettable conclusion that the Negro's great stumbling block in the stride toward freedom is not the White Citizen's Council-er or the Ku Klux Klanner, but the white moderate who is more devoted to "order" than to justice; who prefers a negative peace which is the absence of tension to a positive peace which is the presence of justice; who constantly says, "I agree with you in the goal you seek, but I can't agree with your methods of direct action"; who paternalistically feels that he can set the timetable for another man's freedom; who lives by the myth of time and who constantly advises the Negro to wait until a "more convenient season." Shallow understanding from people of goodwill is more frustrating than absolute misunderstanding from people of ill will. Lukewarm acceptance is much more bewildering than outright rejection.

I had hoped that the white moderate would understand that law and order exist for the purpose of establishing justice, and that when they fail to do this they become dangerously structured dams that block the flow of social progress. I had hoped that the white moderate would understand that the present tension of the South is merely a necessary phase of the transition from an obnoxious negative peace, where the Negro passively accepted his unjust plight, to a substance-filled positive peace, where all men will respect the dignity and worth of human personality. Actually, we who engage in nonviolent direct action are not the creators of tension. We merely bring to the surface the hidden tension that is already alive. We bring it out in the open where it can be seen and dealt with. Like a boil that can never be cured as long as it is covered up but must be opened with all its pus-flowing ugliness to the natural medicines of air and light, injustice must likewise be exposed, with all of the tension its exposing creates, to the light of human conscience and the air of national opinion before it can be cured.

In your statement you asserted that our actions, even though peaceful, must be condemned because they precipitate violence. But can this assertion be logically made? Isn't this like condemning the robbed man because his possession of money precipitated the evil act of robbery? Isn't this like condemning Socrates because his unswerving commitment to truth and his philosophical delvings precipitated the misguided popular mind to make him drink the hemlock? Isn't this like condemning Jesus because His unique God-Consciousness and never-ceasing devotion to His will precipitated the evil act of crucifixion? We must come to see, as federal courts have consistently affirmed, that it is immoral to urge an individual to withdraw his efforts to gain his basic constitutional rights because the quest precipitates violence. Society must protect the robbed and punish the robber.

I had also hoped that the white moderate would reject the myth of time. I received a letter this morning from a white brother in Texas which said: "All Christians know that the colored people will receive equal rights eventually, but it is possible that you are in too great of a religious hurry. It has taken Christianity almost 2000 years to accomplish what it has. The teachings of Christ take time to come to earth." All that is said here grows out of a tragic misconception of time. It is the strangely irrational notion that there is something in the very flow of time that will inevitably cure all ills. Actually time is neutral. It can be used either destructively or constructively. I am coming to feel that the people of ill will have used time much more effectively than the people of goodwill. We will have to repent in this generation not merely for the vitriolic words and actions of the bad people, but for the appalling silence of the good people. We must come to see that human progress never rolls in on wheels of inevitability. It comes through the tireless efforts and persistent work of men willing to be co-workers with God, and without this hard work time itself becomes an ally of the forces of social stagnation. We must use time creatively, and forever realize that the time is always ripe to do right. Now is the time to make real the promise of democracy, and transform our pending national elegy into a creative psalm of brotherhood. Now is the time to lift our national policy from the quicksand of racial injustice to the solid rock of human dignity.

You spoke of our activity in Birmingham as extreme. At first I was rather disappointed that fellow clergymen would see my nonviolent efforts as those of the extremist. I started thinking about the fact that I stand in the middle of two opposing forces in the Negro community. One is a force of complacency made up of Negroes who, as a result of long years of oppression, have been so completely drained of self-respect and a sense of "somebodiness" that they have adjusted to segregation, and, of a few Negroes in the middle class who, because of a degree of academic and economic security, and because at points they profit by segregation, have unconsciously become insensitive to the problems of the masses. The other force is one of bitterness and hatred, and comes perilously close to advocating violence. It is expressed in the various black nationalist groups that are springing up over the nation, the largest and best known being Elijah Muhammad's Muslim movement. This movement is nourished by the contemporary frustration over the continued existence of racial discrimination. It is made up of people who have lost faith in America, who have absolutely repudiated Christianity, and who have concluded that the white man is an incurable "devil." I have tried to stand between these two forces, saying that we need not follow the "do-nothingism" of the complacent or the hatred and despair of the black nationalist. There is the more excellent way of love and nonviolent protest. I'm grateful to God that, through the Negro church, the dimension of nonviolence entered our struggle. If this philosophy had not emerged, I am convinced that by now many streets of the South would be flowing with floods of blood. And I am further convinced that if our white brothers dismiss as "rabble rousers" and "outside agitators" those of us who are working through the channels of nonviolent direct action and refuse to support our nonviolent efforts, millions of Negroes, out of frustration and despair, will seek solace and security in black nationalist ideologies, a development that will lead inevitably to a frightening racial nightmare.

Oppressed people cannot remain oppressed forever. The urge for freedom will eventually come. This is what happened to the American Negro. Something within has reminded him of his birthright of freedom; something without has reminded him that he can gain it. Consciously and unconsciously, he has been swept in by what the Germans call the *Zeitgeist,* and with his black brothers of Africa, and his brown and yellow brothers of Asia, South America and the Caribbean, he is moving with a sense of cosmic urgency toward the promised land of racial justice. Recognizing this vital urge that has engulfed the Negro community, one should readily understand public demonstrations. The Negro has many pent-up resentments and latent frustrations. He has to get them out. So let him march sometime; let him have his prayer pilgrimages to the city hall; understand why he must have sit-ins and freedom rides. If his repressed emotions do not come out in these nonviolent ways, they will come out in ominous expressions of violence. This is not a threat; it is a fact of history. So I have not said to my people "get rid of your discontent." But I have tried to say that this normal and healthy discontent can be channelized through the creative outlet of nonviolent direct action. Now this approach is being dismissed as extremist. I must admit that I was initially disappointed in being so categorized.

But as I continued to think about the matter I gradually gained a bit of satisfaction from being considered an extremist. Was not Jesus an extremist in love—"Love your enemies, bless them that curse you, pray for them that despitefully use you." Was not Amos an extremist for justice—"Let justice roll down like waters and righteousness like a mighty stream." Was not Paul an extremist for the gospel of Jesus Christ—"I bear in my body the marks of the Lord Jesus." Was not Martin Luther an extremist—"Here I stand; I can do none other so help me God." Was not John Bunyan an extremist—"I will stay in jail to the end of my days before I make a butchery of my conscience." Was not Abraham Lincoln an extremist—"This nation cannot survive half slave and half free." Was not Thomas Jefferson an extremist—"We hold these truths to be self-evident, that all men are created equal." So the question is not whether we will be extremist but what kind of extremist will we be. Will we be extremists for hate or will we be extremists for love? Will we be extremists for the preservation of injustice—or will we be extremists for the cause of justice? In that dramatic scene on Calvary's hill, three men were crucified. We must not forget that all three were crucified for the same crime—the crime of extremism. Two were extremists for immorality, and thusly fell below their environment. The other, Jesus Christ, was an extremist for love, truth and goodness, and thereby rose above his environment. So, after all, maybe the South, the nation and the world are in dire need of creative extremists.

I had hoped that the white moderate would see this. Maybe I was too optimistic. Maybe I expected too much. I guess I should have realized that few members of a race that has oppressed another race can understand or appreciate the deep groans and passionate yearnings of those that have been oppressed and still fewer have the vision to see that injustice must be rooted out by strong, persistent and determined action. I am thankful, however, that some of our white brothers have grasped the meaning of this social revolution and committed themselves to it. They are still all too small in quantity, but they are big in quality. Some like Ralph McGill, Lillian Smith, Harry Golden and James Dabbs have written about our struggle in eloquent, prophetic and understanding terms. Others have marched with us down nameless streets of the South. They have languished in filthy roach-infested jails, suffering the abuse and brutality of angry policemen who see them as "dirty nigger lovers." They, unlike so many of their moderate brothers and sisters, have recognized the urgency of the moment and sensed the need for powerful "action" antidotes to combat the disease of segregation.

Let me rush on to mention my other disappointment. I have been so greatly disappointed with the white church and its leadership. Of course, there are some notable exceptions. I am not unmindful of the fact that each of you has taken some significant stands on this issue. I commend you, Rev. Stallings, for your Christian stand on this past Sunday, in welcoming Negroes to your worship service on a non-segregated basis. I commend the Catholic leaders of this state for integrating Springhill College several years ago.

But despite these notable exceptions I must honestly reiterate that I have been disappointed with the church. I do not say that as one of the negative critics who can always find something wrong with the church. I say it as a minister of the gospel, who loves the church; who was nurtured in its bosom; who has been sustained by its spiritual blessings and who will remain true to it as long as the cord of life shall lengthen.

I had the strange feeling when I was suddenly catapulted into the leadership of the bus protest in Montgomery several years ago that we would have the support of the white church. I felt that the white ministers, priests and rabbis of the South would be some of our strongest allies. Instead, some have been outright opponents, refusing to understand the freedom movement and misrepresenting its leaders; all too many others have been more cautious than courageous and have remained silent behind the anesthetizing security of the stained-glass windows.

In spite of my shattered dreams of the past, I came to Birmingham with the hope that the white religious leadership of this community would see the justice of our cause, and with deep moral concern, serve as the channel through which our just grievances would get to the power structure. I had hoped that each of you would understand. But again I have been disappointed. I have heard numerous religious leaders of the South call upon their worshippers to comply with a desegregation decision because it is the *law,* but I have longed to hear white ministers say, "Follow this decree because integration is morally *right* and the Negro is your brother." In the midst of blatant injustices inflicted upon the Negro, I have watched white churches stand on the sideline and merely mouth pious irrelevancies and sanctimonious trivialities. In the midst of a mighty struggle to rid our nation of racial and economic injustice, I have heard so many ministers say, "Those are social issues with which the gospel has no real concern," and I have watched so many churches commit themselves to a completely other-worldly religion which made a strange distinction between body and soul, the sacred and the secular.

So here we are moving toward the exit of the twentieth century with a religious community largely adjusted to the status quo, standing as a tail-light behind other community agencies rather than a headlight leading men to higher levels of justice.

I have traveled the length and breadth of Alabama, Mississippi and all the other southern states. On sweltering summer days and crisp autumn mornings I have looked at her beautiful churches with their lofty spires pointing heavenward. I have beheld the impressive outlay of her massive religious education buildings. Over and over again I have found myself asking: "What kind of people worship here? Who is their God? Where were their voices when the lips of Governor Barnett dripped with words of interposition and nullification? Where were they when Governor Wallace gave the clarion call for defiance and hatred? Where were their voices of support when tired, bruised and weary Negro men and women decided to rise from the dark dungeons of complacency to the bright hills of creative protest?"

Yes, these questions are still in my mind. In deep disappointment, I have wept over the laxity of the church. But be assured that my tears have been tears of love. There can be no deep disappointment where there is not deep love. Yes, I love the church; I love her sacred walls. How could I do otherwise? I am in the rather unique position of being the son, the grandson and the great-grandson of preachers. Yes, I see the church as the body of Christ. But, oh! How we have blemished and scarred that body through social neglect and fear of being nonconformists.

There was a time when the church was very powerful. It was during that period when the early Christians rejoiced when they were deemed worthy to suffer for what they believed. In those days the church was not merely a thermometer that recorded the ideas and principles of popular opinion; it was a thermostat that transformed the mores of society. Wherever the early Christians entered a town the power structure got disturbed and immediately sought to convict them for being "disturbers of the peace" and "outside agitators." But they went on with the conviction that they were "a colony of heaven," and had to obey God rather than man. They were small in number but big in commitment. They were too God-intoxicated to be "astronomically intimidated." They brought an end to such ancient evils as infanticide and gladiatorial contest.

Things are different now. The contemporary church is often a weak, ineffectual voice with an uncertain sound. It is so often the arch supporter of the status quo. Far from being disturbed by the presence of the church, the power structure of the average community is consoled by the church's silent and often vocal sanction of things as they are.

But the judgment of God is upon the church as never before. If the church of today does not recapture the sacrificial spirit of the early church, it will lose its authentic ring, forfeit the loyalty of millions, and be dismissed as an irrelevant social club with no meaning for the twentieth century. I am meeting young people every day whose disappointment with the church has risen to outright disgust.

Maybe again, I have been too optimistic. Is organized religion too inextricably bound to the status quo to save our nation and the world? Maybe I must turn my faith to the inner spiritual church, the church within the church, as the true *ecclesia* and the hope of the world. But again I am thankful to God that some noble souls from the ranks of organized religion have broken loose from the paralyzing chains of conformity and joined us as active partners in the struggle for freedom. They have left their secure congregations and walked the streets of Albany, Georgia, with us. They have gone through the highways of the South on tortuous rides for freedom. Yes, they have gone to jail with us. Some have been kicked out of their churches, and lost support of their bishops and fellow ministers. But they have gone with the faith that right defeated is stronger than evil triumphant. These men have been the leaven in the lump of the race. Their witness has been the spiritual salt that has preserved the true meaning of the Gospel in these troubled times. They have carved a tunnel of hope through the dark mountain of disappointment.

I hope the church as a whole will meet the challenge of this decisive hour. But even if the church does not come to the aid of justice, I have no despair about the future. I have no fear about the outcome of our struggle in Birmingham, even if our motives are presently misunderstood. We will reach the goal of freedom in Birmingham and all over the nation, because the goal of America is freedom. Abused and scorned though we may be, our destiny is tied up with the destiny of America. Before the pilgrims landed at Plymouth we were here. Before the pen of Jefferson etched across the pages of history the majestic words of the Declaration of Independence, we were here. For more than two centuries our foreparents labored in this country without wages; they made cotton king; and they built the homes of their masters in the midst of brutal injustice and shameful humiliation—and yet out of a bottomless vitality they continued to thrive and develop. If the inexpressible cruelties of slavery could not stop us, the opposition we now face will surely fail. We will win our freedom because the sacred heritage of our nation and the eternal will of God are embodied in our echoing demands.

I must close now. But before closing I am impelled to mention one other point in your statement that troubled me profoundly. You warmly commended the Birmingham police force for keeping "order" and "preventing violence." I don't believe you would have so warmly commended the police force if you had seen its angry violent dogs literally biting six unarmed, nonviolent Negroes. I don't believe you would so quickly commend the policemen if you would observe their ugly and inhuman treatment of Negroes here in the city jail; if you would watch them push and curse old Negro women and young Negro girls; if you would see them slap and kick old Negro men and young boys; if you will observe them, as they did on two occasions, refuse to give us food because we wanted to sing our grace together. I'm sorry that I can't join you in your praise for the police department.

It is true that they have been rather disciplined in their public handling of the demonstrators. In this sense they have been rather publicly "nonviolent." But for what purpose? To preserve the evil system of segregation. Over the last few years I have consistently preached that nonviolence demands that the means we use must be as pure as the ends we seek. So I have tried to make it clear that it is wrong to use immoral means to attain moral ends. But now I must affirm that it is just as wrong, or even more so, to use moral means to preserve immoral ends. Maybe Mr. Connor and his policemen have been rather publicly nonviolent, as Chief Pritchett was in Albany, Georgia, but they have used the moral means of nonviolence to maintain the immoral end of flagrant racial injustice. T. S. Eliot has said that there is no greater treason than to do the right deed for the wrong reason.

I wish you had commended the Negro sit-inners and demonstrators of Birmingham for their sublime courage, their willingness
to suffer and their amazing discipline in the midst of the most inhuman provocation. One day the South will recognize its real
heroes. They will be the James Merediths, courageously and with
a majestic sense of purpose facing jeering and hostile mobs and
the agonizing loneliness that characterizes the life of the pioneer.
They will be old, oppressed, battered Negro women, symbolized in
a seventy-two year old woman of Montgomery, Alabama, who rose
up with a sense of dignity and with her people decided not to ride
the segregated buses, and responded to one who inquired about her
tiredness with ungrammatical profundity: "My feet is tired, but
my soul is rested." They will be the young high school and college
students, young ministers of the Gospel and a host of their elders
courageously and nonviolently sitting-in at lunch counters and
willingly going to jail for conscience's sake. One day the South will
know that when these disinherited children of God sat down at
lunch counters they were in reality standing up for the best in the
American dream and the most sacred values in our Judeo-Christian
heritage, and thusly, carrying our whole nation back to those
great wells of democracy which were dug deep by the founding
fathers in the formulation of the Constitution and the Declaration
of Independence.

Never before have I written a letter this long (or should I say a
book?). I'm afraid that it is much too long to take your precious
time. I can assure you that it would have been much shorter if I
had been writing from a comfortable desk, but what else is there
to do when you are alone for days in the dull monotony of a narrow jail cell other than write long letters, think strange thoughts,
and pray long prayers?

If I have said anything in this letter that is an overstatement of
the truth and is indicative of an unreasonable impatience, I beg
you to forgive me. If I have said anything in this letter that is an
understatement of the truth and is indicative of my having a patience that makes me patient with anything less than brotherhood,
I beg God to forgive me.

I hope this letter finds you strong in the faith. I also hope that
circumstances will soon make it possible for me to meet each of
you, not as an integrationist or a civil-rights leader, but as a fellow

clergyman and a Christian brother. Let us all hope that the dark clouds of racial prejudice will soon pass away and the deep fog of misunderstanding will be lifted from our fear-drenched communities and in some not too distant tomorrow the radiant stars of love and brotherhood will shine over our great nation with all of their scintillating beauty.

Yours for the cause of Peace and Brotherhood,
Martin Luther King, Jr.

CIVIL RIGHTS AND DISOBEDIENCE TO LAW

Harrison Tweed, Bernard G. Segal, and Herbert L. Packer

One of the most troubling aspects of the current crisis in race relations is the frequency with which it seems the law is being violated by those active in the struggle on both sides.

This is a serious matter because no one can doubt that this country must solve the civil-rights problem not by a resort to lawlessness and disorder but by reliance upon the administration of the law through due process in the courts and fair enforcement by the appropriate authorities.

Thus the spectacle of repeated violations of law, actual or apparent, by those who are pressing the fight for civil rights is deeply troubling to many thoughtful persons who reject the notion that the end justifies the means and who insist that those who work for good ends must remain morally accountable for the methods they use to work toward those ends.

What is the difference, these people ask, between the Southern governor who violates the law by standing in the schoolhouse door to prevent the court-directed entry of Negro pupils, and the Negro demonstrator who violates the law by participating in a "sit-in" at a segregated lunch counter in a Southern city that has an ordi-

Reprinted by permission of the authors and publisher from *Presbyterian Life,* February 1, 1964, pp. 6–9. © 1964 by Presbyterian Life, Inc.

nance making it illegal for him to do so? Is there a meaningful distinction between these two cases? And what can be said about the position of an eminent clergyman who attacks segregation by taking part in a demonstration that ends in his arrest on the charge of having wrongfully trespassed on another's property; or the people who delay construction of a hospital by physically obstructing the movement of men and materials at the construction site during a protest against discriminatory hiring practices by the builder of the hospital? These and many similar instances that continue to recur require careful thought if we are to be clear about the bounds within which the struggle for civil rights may legitimately proceed.

In this article we shall not venture into the deep waters of philosophic speculation about the moral justifiability of disobeying an unjust law. Our concern is with the legal issues involved, and our purpose is to call attention to some aspects of the legal system that are often overlooked in discussions of this subject, to the detriment of clear thinking about it.

Let us start with a relatively easy case. On the one hand we have Governor Wallace vowing to "stand in the schoolhouse door." On the other hand we have a Negro demonstrator who sits at a lunch counter in Greenville, South Carolina, that is required by local law to be segregated. We think that these two cases are easy to differentiate; but there are obviously erroneous answers to the problem. It is no answer to say that in one case the objective is "bad" and in the other it is "good." Orderly social living would be impossible if people only obeyed laws they happened to like. And it is not much more helpful to say that in the first case the law being disobeyed was constitutional, while in the second case it was not. Whether a law is constitutional involves a prediction as to how a court will decide the question. We know now that laws and ordinances directing racial segregation in places of public accommodation are unconstitutional. The Supreme Court, to whom belongs the power of final decision, has so held. But we did not know it before the Court so held, although it may not have required great learning in constitutional doctrine to enable one to guess the outcome. The point is that Negro demonstrators who staged sit-ins before those laws and ordinances were held unconstitutional appeared on the surface to be engaging in conduct just as defiant of law as that of Governor Wallace in Tuscaloosa and of Governor

Barnett in Oxford. The distinction between the cases plainly involves something more than a difference in accuracy of predicting the course of judicial decision.

The crucial difference lies in the fact that the Negro demonstrators were not violating any court order, but rather laws which had not been tested, which the Negro demonstrators *in good faith believed were invalid,* and which they were determined to challenge *through the processes of law.* Under our system a person is entitled to challenge the validity of a law being applied against him by resisting its enforcement *in court* on a plea of invalidity. That kind of lawful resistance to law is a cornerstone of our liberties. A free society would be doomed unless it provided the citizen with means for asserting the invalidity of laws and other official acts as measured against the fundamental law of the Constitution. When the law being challenged provides criminal penalties, as these segregation laws do, the challenger runs the risk of going to jail if his challenge is not ultimately upheld by the courts. In the face of that danger, it is a courageous and commendable act for a man to defy a law in order to attack its validity through the processes of law. That is what the Negro demonstrators against segregation laws have done, and we should honor them for it.

The conduct of Governor Wallace and of Governor Barnett stands in sharp contrast to this kind of lawful resistance to law. Both sought to resist the execution of Federal court decrees ordering their respective state universities to admit Negro students. We may assume that both of them believed that the Federal court decrees were unconstitutional, that desegregation by law is an invasion of the rightful sphere of the states. But that belief, if it existed, was not accompanied by a determination to challenge desegregation through the processes of law. Quite the contrary. Both Governor Wallace and Governor Barnett did everything they could to avoid submitting their dispute about the validity of the law they were resisting to the orderly and due processes of law. Instead, they did everything they could to delay and defeat the execution of the court orders without involving themselves in a legal contest; and they acted after the validity of the desegregation orders had been fully and unsuccessfully challenged in the courts.

Governor Wallace's brief show of defiance at Tuscaloosa was evidently calculated to avoid subjecting himself to being held in contempt of the Federal court's order. His evident purpose was to harass by diversionary tactics, not to contest by law. His conduct was, simply and literally, lawless. The Negro demonstrators, on the other hand, were disobeying laws they believed to be invalid in order to invite rather than to evade a lawful resolution of their contentions. There may have been no other way to contest the validity of segregation laws. Defiance of a court order, however, is both unnecessary (since other means are available to test its validity) and subversive of the orderly processes of government. Such conduct by one who is sworn to uphold the law is particularly deplorable.

It is of course true that it does not require a multiplicity of sit-in cases to establish the legal proposition that state and municipal segregation laws are invalid. In the case of many sit-ins, freedom rides, and other demonstrations against segregation laws and other forms of discrimination, a somewhat different issue is presented. The purpose of mass demonstrations such as those that took place in Birmingham, Alabama, last spring was not primarily to provide an opportunity for court attack on segregation but rather to dramatize the contentions of the Negro community, to focus public attention on the pattern of racial inequality, and to bring pressure on the white community to alter their ways. Inevitably, these demonstrations appeared to involve violations of laws other than the admittedly invalid segregation ordinances. Demonstrators were arrested for such offenses as holding a parade without a permit, disorderly conduct, and trespassing upon private property. The same pattern of demonstration, disorder, and resulting arrests has taken place in many Northern cities.

Now, of course, there is nothing invalid about a statute or ordinance that prohibits disorderly conduct, or trespass, or that imposes reasonable requirements on the holding of public meetings in the interest of maintaining order. That is to say, there is nothing invalid about such a statute or ordinance on its face, as lawyers say. Many people leap from that fact to the erroneous conclusion that conduct in violation of such an ordinance necessarily is unlawful and should therefore be condemned. That conclusion overlooks the well-established proposition of law that a statute or ordinance that is valid on its face may be administered in an unfair way and may consequently be invalid as applied. For example, let us assume that it is unobjectionable for a city to have an ordinance requiring persons wishing to use public thoroughfares or parks for a parade or a meeting to obtain a license to do so from the chief of police. Such an ordinance may be used so that traffic will not be disrupted at inconvenient hours, or so that there will not be a conflict between two or more groups seeking to use the same location for a meeting at the same time, or for some other valid and nondiscriminatory municipal purpose. Such an ordinance can be valid on its face: that is to say, in its normal application it presents no problems, as opposed to an ordinance that requires segregation of the races, which has no valid application at all and is therefore invalid on its face.

Now let us suppose that the chief of police uses the ordinance to deny access to public facilities to Negro groups but not to whites. There is no question but that the ordinance is then being applied in an invalid manner to deny to the Negro groups the rights of speech and assembly to which they are entitled under the Bill of Rights. They are caught in a familiar dilemma. If they stand on their rights, they are disobeying the local law; if they obey the local law (and do not parade without the license that they cannot get), then they are deprived of rights to which they are constitutionally entitled. That dilemma is dissolved by decisions of the Supreme Court holding that people may not be punished for violating a local law which, however fair on its face, has been applied in a way that violates their constitutional rights.

Of course, it is not always easy to tell when people's constitutional rights are being violated by the application of local laws and when they are not. For example, suppose that it is perfectly clear that the holding of a public meeting on a controversial issue is going to provoke an outbreak of disorder, and the authorities therefore try to prevent the meeting from taking place. Are civil-rights demonstrators justified in going ahead with a meeting even though they know that the result is likely to be violence? Perhaps it would be more prudent for them to abstain, but our American tradition of protection for free speech suggests that they may assert their right to go ahead and hold the meeting despite the threat of violence. It is the duty of law-enforcement authorities to protect freedom of speech by making arrangements for the safety of those who urge unpopular causes. Needless to say, that ideal is often not realized in practice, and never more obviously than in the failure of law-enforcement authorities in the South to protect the rights of Negroes and others who demonstrate for civil rights. In an extremity, the police may stop a meeting in order to protect the participants from violence and to prevent a general eruption of disorder. But that reserve power should not be used as an excuse to do nothing in advance to protect the rights of the speakers or demonstrators. It would be a strange legal system that held those who violently interfere with the freedom of others equally accountable with those who are their hapless victims. And our system is not in any ultimate way open to that reproach, whatever the views to the contrary of state and local police, prosecutors, and judges.

One of the most difficult questions in the civil-rights area that the Supreme Court has to face is whether segregation by private owners of facilities open to the public-at-large may be enforced by criminal prosecutions for trespass in the absence of any state law or policy requiring or favoring segregation. The Court has on its current docket cases that may force it to deal with the question. And the question was put dramatically in July, 1963, when a group of Protestant clergymen, including Dr. Eugene Carson Blake of the United Presbyterian Church, were arrested for criminal trespass while accompanying a group of Negroes who sought admission to a segregated amusement park in Maryland.* It seems to us that Dr. Blake and his colleagues were well within the justifying principles that we have been discussing in this article. It is perfectly true as a general proposition that you may be subjected to criminal prosecution for going upon another's property against his will. There is nothing illegal on their face about laws that protect private property rights by penalizing people who willfully violate those rights. But it is fairly open to question whether the state may back up a private preference for segregation, at least when the premises in question are normally open to the public-at-large, by lending the aid of its criminal process to enforce the will of the would-be segregator.

To put it another way, the state's criminal trespass law may be invalid as it is applied to the case of the public facility whose owner seeks state aid in enforcing segregation. Valid or invalid, it seems

*[See the case of *Griffin et al.* v. *Maryland,* 378 U.S. 131 (1964). Ed.]

entirely appropriate, until the question is finally decided for those who have a *good-faith belief* that the law is being invalidly applied in these circumstances, to challenge the law by acting as Dr. Blake and his colleagues did. If the courts were finally and definitively to rule against the argument that the trespass laws were being invalidly applied in this situation, continued defiance of the law would not have the justification that can presently be made for it. Then Dr. Blake and Governor Wallace would indeed be in the same boat insofar as the lack of legal justification for their conduct is concerned. Continued resistance to law that has been fully and fairly settled, whatever the appeal to conscience or to history may produce in the way of an answer, is no part of the American tradition and is in the deepest sense subversive of the legal process. But as matters stand today, whatever judgment men of the world might reach on prudential grounds about this sort of social protest, it cannot be labeled as lawless.

We do not want to leave the impression that the mere fact that demonstration is carried on in behalf of civil rights can serve as a legal justification for it. There is much civil-rights activity that merits the condemnation of all who prize the ideal of liberty under law. When valid laws are broken simply to create sympathy for the civil-rights position or, even less defensibly, simply to dramatize the contentions of the demonstrators, it seems clear that important values are being unjustifiably sacrificed. The demonstrators who were convicted of breach of the peace for camping in Governor Rockefeller's office could offer no justification of the kind we have been discussing for the violation of law. The law they violated was not invalid, either on its face or as applied to them. Other instances of civil-rights demonstrations that have involved totally unjustifiable violations of law come also to mind. Last summer's blockade of the approaches to Jones Beach in New York by demonstrators lying down in the road can hardly be condoned, even assuming the correctness of the demonstrators' view that Negroes were being discriminated against in employment there. The same is true of the demonstrations that led to a halt in construction work on the Downtown Medical Center in Brooklyn, New York. The distinction between peaceful picketing and interference with the rights of others is not always an easy one to draw, as the history of labor relations in this country demonstrates; but both of these incidents violated well-accepted standards of behavior in labor disputes.

Even when demonstrations may not in themselves involve illegal conduct, there is a question of judgment involved if they are used indiscriminately. Primary reliance should be placed, we believe, upon quiet and orderly processes of conciliation and negotiation to resolve specific civil-rights disputes. Demonstrations which expose their participants to situations that may involve violations of law should be a last resort.

Disobedience to law is always prima facie unjustifiable. It can be justified, as we have shown, particularly in situations in which obeying the law defeats the enjoyment of constitutionally guaranteed civil liberties. But the burden is always on the person who claims that his violation of law is legally justifiable. And that burden applies just as strongly in the court of public opinion as it does in a court of law, a fact that makes it incumbent on proponents of the great struggle for civil rights to go about their important task with a keen awareness of the value of preserving the respect for law upon which any social order must ultimately depend.

CIVIL DISOBEDIENCE: OBSERVATIONS ON THE STRATEGIES OF PROTEST

William L. Taylor

When I was first asked to discuss civil disobedience from a law-yer's standpoint, it seemed to me that there was something incon-gruous about the assignment. If a person, following the dictates of his conscience, chooses to disobey a law and then to accept the penalty rather than to contest his rights in court, the lawyer is al-most irrelevant to the process. He may feel impelled as a citizen to take a position on the issues which gave rise to the act of civil disobedience or on the act itself, but as a lawyer he has no role to play.

On reflection, however, there may be a few observations that a lawyer can make about civil disobedience which will help to pro-mote a useful discussion of the issues. For example, there is a ques-tion of definition. Civil disobedience is a term that is being bandied about a good deal in connection with protests against racial in-justice and it is obvious that not all who use it mean the same thing. Segregationists tend to use civil disobedience as a catch-all phrase to cover any protest against the practice of racial discrimi-nation. But civil rights' advocates may disagree even among them-

Reprinted from *Legal Aspects of the Civil Rights Movement,* pp. 227–235, edited by Donald B. King and Charles W. Quick, by permission of the Wayne State Uni-versity Press. Copyright ©1965 by Wayne State University Press.

selves about what they mean when they talk about civil disobedience. Arriving at definitions can be a tedious and sometimes unproductive process, but if we agree on what we are talking about it may be possible at least to avoid some needless arguments about our conclusions.

One aspect of civil disobedience has already been alluded to—*a willingness to accept the penalty*. Gandhi, talking about his first essay into civil disobedience, said, "None of us had to offer any defence. All were to plead guilty to the charge of disobeying the order . . ."[1] Martin Luther King, drawing on Gandhi, says, "Most important, they [the violators of law] willingly accept the penalty, whatever it is."[2] This willingness to accept the penalty is based upon a principle crucial to the philosophy of civil disobedience: that the violation of pernicious laws is justified by the fact that these laws themselves violate a higher law, which may be called moral law, natural law or divine law, depending on the point of view of the interpreter. But if the appeal of the law violator is not simply to moral law, but to positive, articulated law such as the Constitution of the United States, it is not civil disobedience we are dealing with, but something else.

What I am suggesting is that not every violation of law is an act of civil disobedience. If a violation is committed under a claim of legal right with the intention of seeking redress in the courts, it can hardly be termed civil disobedience. In fact, under our judicial system, it is frequently necessary to violate the law to vindicate one's legal rights. If the person challenging a law as unconstitutional cannot show that he has violated it, the courts may say that the case is a hypothetical one which is not ripe for decision.[3]

By this test, sit-ins in places of public accommodation, the most popular and effective means of direct community action, are not acts of civil disobedience. The great majority of the sit-inners have not pleaded guilty; they have acted under a claim of legal right, or at least, of immunity from prosecution for their acts.[4]

The character of sit-ins as appeals to law rather than acts of civil disobedience is not changed by the fact that large numbers of protesters have been involved. While the ordinary test case may involve a single violation of a law by one person or a small group, there is no reason that a law cannot be tested by larger groups in a more dramatic manner as long as they are willing to incur the additional legal expense that these larger protests entail. Nor do the sit-ins become acts of civil disobedience simply because they are direct appeals to the conscience of the community as well as to the law of the land. One of the proudest aspects of our heritage is the part that legal controversies play in educating and stirring the conscience of the nation even while they are being resolved in the courts.

This is not to suggest that sit-ins could not become civil disobedience. If Congress fails to pass a public-accommodations law[5] and if the Supreme Court were to rule that state trespass laws can be validly applied to enforce the racially discriminatory policies of proprietors of public places, sit-ins might then become acts of civil disobedience. Or if sit-ins suddenly become an effort to fill the jails rather than to test the law, they would take on a different character. But these things have not happened yet.

It is even clearer that the freedom rides were appeals to law, rather than acts of civil disobedience. The right to equal treatment in interstate transportation terminals had been established for many years at the time the freedom rides took place,[6] and the violators of law were not the riders who sought to exercise their rights, but the police and bus-company officials who sought to deny them.[7] The result of the freedom rides was federal action to vindicate the law by putting a halt to these violations.[8]

Similarly, it would be grossly inaccurate to characterize many of the street demonstrations and marches to protest discrimination that have taken place during the past months as acts of civil disobedience. For the most part these protests have been marked by restraint; they have been peaceful and orderly, and there has been no effort to obstruct traffic. As such, the protesters, far from violating any law, have been exercising their rights of free speech, free assembly and freedom to petition for a redress of grievances, all protected by the First and Fourteenth amendments to the Constitution. This was made clear by the Supreme Court just last year when it reversed the breach of peace convictions of 187 Negroes who marched on the South Carolina state house to make their grievances known to the public and to the legislature. The Court said that this was "an exercise of basic constitutional rights in their most pristine and classic form."[9]

Picketing and other noncoercive efforts to persuade the public not to patronize business establishments which follow policies of racial discrimination are also expressions of free speech protected by the Constitution. When properly conducted, they violate no valid law and thus cannot be classed as a form of civil disobedience.[10]

One of the newest types of direct action, the rent strikes in New York, is also more appropriately classified as an appeal to legal processes rather than as a form of civil disobedience. The protesters there have argued that when a landlord violates the housing codes by permitting his apartments to become breeding places for blight and disease, he has in effect evicted his tenants and relieved them of any obligation to pay rent. A court in New York recently recognized this claim and ordered the rents due to be paid into court as security for the landlord's making the necessary repairs.[11]

Thus, almost all of the major forms of direct community action —sit-ins, freedom rides, demonstrations, picketing and rent strikes— in my judgment are properly understood as actions well within the framework of our legal system, rather than as civil disobedience.

There have been, however, random activities by civil-rights groups which have not been conducted under any claim of legal right or immunity. When in New York demonstrators physically block the access of trucks to a construction project in protest[12] against the discriminatory practices of management and unions; when in California they rearrange the shelves of a supermarket in protest against employment policies;[13] when they sit down on the Triborough Bridge during rush hour,[14] it is generally acknowledged that they are acting in defiance of admittedly valid laws and not pursuant to any constitutional right or immunity. Are these then acts of civil disobedience? Reverend King says that civil disobedience is the violation of unjust laws—laws which are "out of harmony with the moral law of the universe." On the other hand, he says, the devotee of nonviolent social action feels a "moral responsibility to obey *just* laws."[15]

Gandhi defines civil disobedience more broadly to encompass not only a refusal to obey bad laws, but also a violation of laws which work no hardship where the breach "does not involve moral turpitude and is undertaken as a symbol of revolt against the State."[16] But in Gandhi's view, such resistance is justified only in a corrupt or tyrannical state. The Triborough-Bridge type of demonstrations have taken place in northern states which not only have

rid themselves of unjust racial laws, but have adopted laws to pro-
hibit discrimination. In such states, the protest is not directed
against the power of the state to enforce unjust laws, but against
its weakness in failing to act vigorously enough to remedy unjust
conditions. It is questionable at least whether the government in
such states can be ranked with Britain's iron rule of India or the
slavery-sanctioning United States which Thoreau found tyrannical
and unendurable.

It is also questionable whether some of the activities mentioned
would fit Gandhi's requirement of deeds which do not involve
moral turpitude. Gandhi condemned mass picketing which ob-
structed traffic and damage to property as acts of violence rather
than disobedience. Thus, on two counts, questions may be raised
about characterizing these interferences with traffic and communication as acts of civil disobedience. It is possible that some of these
activities are more properly understood simply as defiance of law
rather than civil disobedience.

What then *is* civil disobedience? Is it possible to have true civil
disobedience in a society in which unjust racial laws are almost
always unconstitutional also? Two situations may warrant closer
examination. The first is the developing technique of school boycotts in the North to protest against *de facto* segregation and second-
class education. The theory of the boycotts must be that, although
compulsory attendance laws are valid, it is unjust to use them to
compel children to attend schools in which they receive unequal
and inferior education. The objection to such schools does not depend on whether a court would say they are operated in an unconstitutional manner.[17] In the circumstances, we would appear to
be dealing with a situation of civil disobedience.

But in practice, the school boycotts have not really been boycotts at all, but one-day stay-outs, designed to protest substandard
educational conditions in a dramatic way. Thus, whatever one may
think of their wisdom in particular circumstances, the boycotts at
least until now have been more closely akin to exercises of free
speech and assembly than to acts of civil disobedience. It is true
that an unexcused absence even for one day may be a violation
of the law, but it is the kind of technical violation that goes on
all the time and that school administrators prudently overlook.

The second situation involves the violation of court injunctions in the South. Increasingly, southern officials have resorted to local courts to obtain orders prohibiting all forms of protest and demonstration, including those clearly protected by the First and Fourteenth amendments to the Constitution. It is clear that these injunctions violate the Constitution and that ultimately they will be dissolved in the courts of legal appeal. The issue is whether protesters have a legal obligation to obey them until they are overturned. There are conflicting theories in American law on this question. On the one hand, there is the opinion expressed by Mr. Justice Frankfurter that no one is entitled to be the judge in his own case and that even invalid court injunctions must be obeyed as long as there are orderly legal processes for testing them.[18] On the other hand, it is generally recognized that rights can be as effectively destroyed by restraining their exercise during the period of time it takes to test a court order as by prohibiting their exercise altogether.[19]

If violation of an unconstitutional statute may not be punished, why should an unconstitutional court order be any more sacrosanct? This question is particularly relevant to a situation in which courts are being used as instruments of lawlessness. When, in the past, injunctions against labor unions were prevalently used as instruments of repression, means were found to remedy that situation.[20] So here we have a challenge to the judicial system and perhaps to Congress to respond so quickly to lawless injunctions as to make violation unnecessary or else to define more precisely the rights and obligations of people faced with such invalid orders.

Until this happens the law is not certain enough to enable us to characterize violation of an unconstitutional injunction as either a legal right or an act of civil disobedience.

These distinctions are important for several reasons. The fact that all of the major forms of protest against racial discrimination have been well within the scope of legally protected activity enables us to avoid some tough problems we would face if they were not. At least since 1954, the case for justice has been built not simply on its moral rightness but upon the principle of respect for law. It is true that there has been a great deal of defiance of law, but there has also been progress which has resulted in large measure from our tradition of obeying even those laws with which we do not agree.

We have come to appreciate that it is not necessary to secure changes in attitudes in order to secure changes in actions, and that acceptance may come simply from habitual obedience to a law which is sound and just and workable. Again last year, when Congress passed the civil-rights bill, thousands of employers and proprietors will be asked to give at least grudging acceptance to laws which many of them will think unjust.

It is difficult to see how we can have it both ways. To embrace a philosophy which says that each man must decide for himself which laws he will obey is to forfeit a major instrument for achieving justice under law. This is not to equate all acts which violate the law. Obviously there are important differences between the obstruction-by-any-means tactics of some of those bent on defying desegregation laws and acts of civil disobedience which are based in their execution as well as in theory on a set of ethical concerns and standards. But while we recognize these distinctions, there is no escaping the fact that a philosophy of disobedience implies that the rule of law is bankrupt and that each man should be the judge of his own case.

To say this in no way suggests that man must resign his conscience or forfeit his right to revolution against a despotic government. It merely says there are principles of forbearance that qualify Thoreau's observation that "the only obligation which I have a right to assume is to do at any time what I think is right," and that he was seriously wrong in saying that "Law never made a man a whit more just."[21]

The distinctions drawn between various forms of protest may also help us to assess their effectiveness. There is little argument that the most successful form of protest thus far has been the sit-in in places of public accommodation. The sit-ins are simultaneous appeals to conscience, to law and to economic self-interest. Although it is difficult to assign a value to each of these appeals, I think it is true to say that if any had been lacking the sit-ins would have been much less effective. At the other end of the scale, I would question the effectiveness of such violations of admittedly valid laws as are exemplified by the Triborough-Bridge sit-down. These are clearly not appeals to law and, if they are appeals to conscience, the message may be lost on most of the public by the remoteness of the act from the injustice protested and by the harm, ranging from petty annoyance to serious injury, which may flow from the protest. More and more such demonstrations tend to play upon society's fear of disorder, rather than on its conscience or even its economic self-interest. It is at least doubtful that such techniques can prove effective and, even if they can, whether the victory will be anything more than pyrrhic.

Finally, by distinguishing among protests which are legally protected, those which may be termed civil disobedience and those which are simply lawless, we may help to define better the obligations of government. If civil disobedience in a Gandhian sense ever comes to the United States, it will be a protest not against a national government so strong and tyrannical that it enforces unjust laws, but so weak that it is unable to enforce its just laws. It will come because there are places in the United States where the writ of federal law does not run, where federal officers ignore their oaths of office and where lawless local officials violate the constitutional rights of citizens with impunity. It will come because in these and other places in the United States, government has been unable to establish the basic conditions for economic and social justice. But all of us who have lived through the past decade are witnesses to the changes that law and conscience can work in American society. And many of us retain the faith that the conditions for justice can be established by all of the legitimate techniques available to a free people, rather than by those which are symbols only of despair, revolt or lawlessness.

CIVIL RIGHTS—YES:
CIVIL DISOBEDIENCE—NO
(A Reply to Dr. Martin Luther King)

Louis Waldman

On Wednesday, April 21, 1965, Dr. Martin Luther King, Jr. addressed a meeting of the Association of the Bar of the City of New York on the subject "The Civil Rights Struggle in the United States Today." In that address Dr. King made a strong and eloquent plea for civil rights for our fellow citizens of the Negro race. He also dealt with another subject of far-reaching importance, not only to Negroes, but to every single American and to our nation as such, a subject on which he has spoken and written before: his program for civil disobedience as a means of achieving not only civil rights but to remedy all injustice.

In so far as Dr. King made a plea for Negro civil rights, I say with emphasis: Civil Rights—Yes. In so far, however, as Dr. King advocated civil disobedience, I say with equal emphasis: Civil Disobedience—No.

For myself, long before Dr. King was born, I espoused, and still espouse, the cause of civil rights for all people along with causes aimed at abolishing poverty and lifting the standards of working-men, regardless of race or color, to a higher level of civilized ex-

Reprinted by permission of the author and publisher from *New York State Bar Journal*, XXXVII (August 1965), pp. 331–37.

istence, and providing for equality before the law, human dignity, and social and economic justice. In my world we were, and are, color blind. I have never ceased believing in the rightness of these causes. I am happy to say that more and more Americans, not only in the profession of the law, but in every walk of life are enlisting in the realization of these dreams, which are at the heart of the American dream.

The nation's response, and the ever-growing support for civil rights for the Negro, is reflected by the actions of all three branches of our Federal Government, by the United States Supreme Court, beginning with *Brown* v. *Board of Education* in 1954, by the Executive, from the White House down, and by Congress' enactment of new legislation, a process continuing up to the present. And this, it should be recorded in the interest of truth, is also the fact in the overwhelming number of our states, going back many years.

But this must be proclaimed for all to remember: The unanimous decision in *Brown* v. *Board of Education*, which is the foundation for the progress made in the last 10 years, was not achieved by civil disobedience, sit-ins, lie-ins, or marches. On the contrary, it was achieved by reason and the appeal to traditional constitutional principles.

Now the rights of Negroes to enjoy the same civil rights as do other Americans, to equality before the law, to equal opportunity, to an education, to a job, to vote under a system of voter qualifications applied uniformly to all citizens, are all based on our constitutional system of government, and the laws enacted under the Constitution. Those who assert rights under the Constitution and the laws made thereunder must abide by that Constitution and the law, if that Constitution is to survive. They cannot pick and choose; they cannot say that they will abide by those laws which they think are just and refuse to abide by those laws which they think are unjust. And the same is true of decisions on constitutional principles.

The country, therefore, cannot accept Dr. King's doctrine that he and his followers will pick and choose, knowing that it is illegal to do so. I say, such doctrine is not only illegal and for that reason alone should be abandoned, but that it is also immoral, destructive of the principles of democratic government, and a danger to the very civil rights Dr. King seeks to promote.

Stripped of all pejorative rhetoric, what is this program of civil disobedience which Dr. King advocates? In his address on April 21st, Dr. King said the following:

> "Before I close I feel compelled to comment briefly on the oft-heard charge that we who urge non-cooperation with evil in the form of civil disobedience are equally lawless."

And, continuing, he said:

> ". . . the devotees of nonviolent action . . . feel a moral responsibility to obey just laws. But they recognize that there are also unjust laws."

Dr. King then performs intellectual acrobatics by jumping from the premise—that he and his "devotees" . . . "recognize that there are also unjust laws"—to the asserted right to violate such laws "that conscience tells him [are] unjust," that is, in the sole judgment of the violator. He defines "an unjust law" as

> ". . . One in which people are required to obey a code that they had no part in making because they were denied the right to vote

and also as being

> ". . . One in which the minority is compelled to observe a code that is not binding on the majority."

According to this logic, every person under 21 or the millions of non-citizens, all denied the right to vote, have no obligation to obey the law. Now, as to the minority logic. There are thousands of laws throughout the land which apply only to minorities, and are "not binding on" the majorities. For example, we are all familiar with laws which provide that application is limited to "cities of 1,000,000 or more," or "cities of less than 100,000," or just "cities" as opposed to "towns" or "villages." We all know of laws that apply only to bankers, farmers, trade unions, manufacturers, sailors, or electricians, or other trades or groups, but do not apply to the great bulk of the rest of the nation, to the "majority." May all such laws be ignored by the affected minority because they do not bind the majority?

These glib generalizations in Dr. King's advocacy of civil disobedience are as bad as they are illogical. For when literally applied by many of his followers, who do not have the sophistication and training of Dr. King, such shibboleths lead to an intellectual, religious, and moral justification for doing illegal acts of which violence and lawlessness are but the extreme expressions.

"In disobeying such unjust laws," continues Dr. King, "we do so peacefully, openly, and non-violently. Most important, we willingly accept the penalty, whatever it is."

Apparently Dr. King thinks that in violating laws "openly," he and his followers are more virtuous than those who violate laws secretly. As a matter of fact, the reverse is true. The open violation of law is an open invitation to others to join in such violation. Disobedience to law is bad enough when done secretly, but it is far worse when done openly, especially when accompanied by clothing such acts in the mantle of virtue and organizing well-advertised and financed plans to carry out such violations. The secret violator of law recognizes his act for what it is: an antisocial act; he may even be ashamed of what he is doing and seek to avoid disapprobation of his neighbors. But the open violator, the agitating violator, acts shamelessly, in defiance of his neighbor's judgment and his fellow man's disapproval.

After his address Dr. King was asked questions and he gave answers, all recorded. The answers to some of these questions are most illuminating.

Dr. King was asked whether he thought "there is a right to disobey an unjust law" in those places "where the Negroes actually have the right to vote." This is Dr. King's answer:

"There may be a community where Negroes have the right to vote, but there are still unjust laws in that community. There may be unjust laws in a community where people in large numbers are voting, and I think wherever unjust laws exist people on the basis of conscience have a right to disobey those laws."

There we have it. If this philosophy were accepted and carried out by the twenty million American Negroes, it would be enough to disorganize our entire society and produce an intolerable chaos and a denial of individual liberty to every other American.

But, note carefully, Dr. King does not limit his philosophy to Negroes. He says "wherever unjust laws exist *people* on the basis of conscience have a right to disobey those laws." To this I say that we are all fully aware that human beings, being what they are, "conscience" can be, and sometimes is, elastic, conforming to what people want, both overtly and subconsciously. But, as Dr. King must know, civil disobedience cannot end with Negroes alone. You cannot build a fence around this kind of program. Other people become involved.

The consequences of Dr. King's program, if allowed to continue, would be disastrous to our nation. For example, if Dr. King's erroneous and ill-founded advocacy of civil disobedience were applied, let us say, to the Labor Movement and its fifteen million organized members, think of what it would mean. It is common knowledge that the Labor Movement is convinced, and in good conscience believes, that Section 14 (b) of the Taft-Hartley Law discriminates in favor of states having the so-called "Right-to-Work" laws, and is unjust. What if in the last 18 years the Labor Movement had proceeded with a program of civil disobedience as outlined by Dr. King, and had used its organizational power to stage marches, "non-violent marches" of course, sit-ins, "non-violent sit-ins" of course, and other activities—would not such actions tend to disorient our politically organized society? Let us suppose further that George Meany, his Executive Council, and the AFL-CIO unions did all of these things not only with respect to Section 14(b) of the Taft-Hartley Law, but also with respect to other laws, city, state, or federal, which they honestly and in good conscience believe to be unjust to labor. What would happen to our country, to our industries, to our commerce, to our trade, to our existence as a civilized community?

The same applies to all other segments of the nation, to farmers, to merchants, to bankers, to manufacturers, to pacifists, to Catholics, to Protestants or to Jews. Whatever the group, if they decide in the name of religion, morality or personal conscience that certain laws are unjust, then, according to Dr. King's program, they would be justified in carrying out civil disobedience.

Again I ask: If this be so, where would our nation be? Where would our freedom be? Where would our civil rights be?

Dr. King has, not only at this meeting, but at other meetings recently, referred to Hitler's Germany and said that "everything that Hitler did in Germany was legal."

Apart from the fact that in this bare assertion Dr. King is telling only part of Hitler's role in relation to law, he is making an invidious comparison between Hitler's Germany and the United

States. I deeply resent it. Most Americans in their right senses should resent it as well. Hitler's Germany was the product of a vicious meglomaniac who was a curse to Germany and the German people, as he turned out to be a curse to other people, and the world at large.

But I want to remind Dr. King, whenever he makes his next speech and compares Hitler and Hitler's Germany to the United States, to tell his audience also that Hitler, when he began in the middle 20's and until he finally escalated himself into becoming the Chancellor of that unhappy nation, followed a philosophy and practice of direct action and civil disobedience. To Hitler and his devotees the laws of the Weimar Republic and the treaties made thereunder were unjust. And from small beginnings of violating one law after another, he built a movement which was prepared to accept and obey the laws he thought were just and to defy and violate the laws he thought were unjust.

Hitler's Germany and all that it represents in modern experience, with all its tragic consequences, is a most potent argument against civil disobedience. There are any number of other experiences in the world in this century alone, where those who advocated and organized movements to defy the laws made by their governments, particularly democratic governments, have brought evil to their countries and to the world. Numerous Communist as well as Fascist examples come to mind and should not be passed over.

And let us not think that Dr. King's advocacy of civil disobedience is just for the South. He was asked what are the main differences between North and South in so far as civil rights are concerned, and his answer came in a flash:

> "Let me say that the problem in a sense is the same. There may be a difference in degree, but not a difference of kind."

And so, civil disobedience applies to the North as it does to the South, in Dr. King's view. The reason why the North is to be included in the civil disobedience program, according to Dr. King, is that the North is guilty of broad injustice in three areas: unemployment, housing and education. Yet, it is patently obvious, that these three problems involve broad social and economic policies, on the justice or injustice of which thousands of laws, touching on these questions, honest men may in good conscience differ.

Then, as if to cap the climax of the April 21st meeting, came the last question:

> "Dr. King, does your concept of civil disobedience include such tactics as obstructing sites where Negroes are not employed, where those who use such means are willing to accept the consequences, but are not quarreling with the justice of any law?"

Dr. King's answer, which is self-revealing, I set forth in full, as follows:

> "I think all of our demonstrations and all civil disobedience must be centered on something. In other words, the goals must be clearly stated. I think we have to face the fact that there are instances where in the process of frustration with the structure of things, people find themselves in positions of not quite being able to see the unjust law. But they see injustice in a very large sense existing. Consequently, they feel the need to engage in civil disobedience to call attention to overall injustice. At that point they are not protesting against an unjust law. I would say that there are very few unjust laws in most of our northern communities. There are some unjust laws, I think, on the housing question and some other, but on the whole the laws are just. But there is injustice, and there are communities which do not work with vigor and with determination to remove that injustice. In such instances I think men of conscience and men of good will will have no alternative but to engage in some kind of civil disobedience in order to call attention to the injustices, so that the society will seek to rid itself of that overall injustice. Again I say that there must be a willingness to accept the penalty.
>
> "I think there must be, always, in a nonviolent movement, a sense of political timing. I do not believe in the indiscriminate use of any form of demonstration. I think we must be well disciplined and think through our moves, and we must clearly define our goals. I think some of us, for example, felt that the stall-in at the World's Fair didn't quite meet that test because certain goals had not been clearly defined. On the other hand we understood the discontent and the impatience and the frustration, and the disappointment, that led individuals to feel that in an unfair world, maybe people should not be finding it too easy to get to a World's Fair. But at the same time we must set clearly defined goals, in calling for demonstrations and practicing civil disobedience."

This answer, like many others, is full of holes and dodges. For example, according to Dr. King, as long as there is "discontent" and "disappointment" individuals have a right to "feel that in an unfair world, maybe people should not be finding it too easy to get to a World's Fair." And thus stall-ins to block the road between New York City and the World's Fair on opening day in 1964, instead of being condemned, get to be *"understood."*

From the same sources came the suggestion that, as a further demonstration of "discontent" and "disappointment" with "an unfair world" people should open their faucets in their private homes and let water run to waste. A simpler name for this conduct is sabotage. Where is the end to this type of civil disobedience? It seems that private sabotage, stall-ins on the highway, lie-ins in the White House, in the offices of governors and mayors, and in the offices of other governmental agencies, do not suggest that the end is in sight.

There is also implied in Dr. King's last answer, that if once you state your goal, then you are justified in proceeding with marches and demonstrations, a point which, it seems to a lawyer, is constitutionally indefensible. Let me illustrate with a graphic example that has only come to the fore in Chicago this very month. In the June 13, 1965, *New York Times,* there appeared a story under the head of "150 Jailed in Chicago Sitdown over Rehiring of School Chief." The repeated demonstrations in Chicago were designed to compel Mayor Richard J. Daley to discharge Dr. Benjamin C. Willis as Superintendent of Schools. The demonstrators stated their goal, "Ben Willis must go." Their demonstrations included laying on the streets to obstruct traffic, sit-ins at City Hall and other familiar techniques.

The demonstrators, according to the *Times,*

". . . were led today by the Rev. John Porter, a Negro minister who is head of the Chicago affiliate of the Rev. Dr. Martin Luther King's Southern Christian Leadership Conference, and by Robert Lucas, also a Negro and chairman of the Chicago branch of the Congress of Racial Equality."

Unfortunately, we have reached a point where, if you can gather a large enough group who will chant and sing loud enough, and if that group can obstruct the normal operations of life in the community or of agencies of government and that group's actions are carried out repeatedly, then they seem to feel that they have acquired a legal right to do so. Police are "brutal" when they stop such actions; mayors are "unfair" if they seek to protect life and property; and judges and the law are denounced.

Now, why?

Dr. King has written a book called *Why We Can't Wait,* in which he tells us his philosophy and purpose: "The purpose of our direct-action program is to create a situation so crisis-packed that it will inevitably open the door to negotiation."

At another point, he says:

"... Actually, we who engage in nonviolent direct action are not the creators of tension. We merely bring to the surface the hidden tension that is already alive. We bring it out in the open, where it can be seen and dealt with. ..."

Thus, we have the philosophy and purpose of Dr. King's program. It is to produce "crisis-packed" situations and "tensions." Such a purpose is the very opposite of non-violence, for the atmosphere-of-crisis policy leads to violence by provoking violence. And the provocation of violence is violence. To describe such provocations as "non-violent" is to trifle with the plain meaning of words.

The perpetual crisis technique has been used by the Communist movement throughout the world. Both Communist governments and parties follow it. As I said, it was also used by Hitler in Germany, both on his road to power and after power came to him, as a means of justifying his arbitrary, brutal and barbarous policy. It has been used by every Fascist country we learned to know and abhor in this century. It is disruptive of democratic society and institutions.

Whether Dr. King knows it or not, or wills it or not, the policy of perpetual crisis, of provoking "tensions," as he calls it, and of civil disobedience, are disastrous to the Negro people themselves, to civil liberties and to constitutional government. Such a policy flies in the teeth of the very purpose of our Constitution, which is clearly stated in the preamble to be, among other things, "to insure domestic tranquillity."

It is time that the organized Bar is heard on this question. It is time that we tell Dr. King and his devotees of civil disobedience that the rule of law will and must prevail, that violators of the law, however lofty their aims or position in society, are not above the law. Correction of injustices by intimidation, by extra-legal means, or inspired by fear of violence cannot longer be continued. And law enforcement authorities must make it clear that we are a constitutional government and the laws enacted pursuant to our Constitution must be obeyed whether the individuals or groups affected by those laws believe they are just or not.

In absolute as well as relative terms, we in the United States have built a democratic constitutional system second to none. We have done so by recognizing the proper roles, assigned by our history and governmental philosophy, to the separation of powers in our government. This separation recognizes the sovereignty of states and distributes the political and governmental authorities and functions at the Federal level. It lays down the fundamental principles which regulate the relations of government with citizens and inhabitants of our land. It establishes the rule of law through constitutions and the Bill of Rights.

Our nation has survived because of the dedication to these principles. Our nation will continue to live as long as all of us, from lawyer to ditch digger, from judge to police officer, insist on according respect and obedience to these basic values of our society.

Part Three:

———

AGAINST WAR

———

INTRODUCTION

We have already had occasion to notice how civil disobedience can be the act of a person who conscientiously refuses to obey an unjust law, as well as the act of someone who seeks out his government and violates the law so as to hurl this challenge: "Either change the system or throw me in prison, because I break your law not as a common criminal nor even because otherwise I would be required to do something against my moral convictions, but because in this way only can I sufficiently protest the crying injustice you inflict through your authority, injustice you seem not to see." Nowhere is this contrasting conception of civil disobedience more evident than in the resistance to war and the preparation for war since World War II. In the United States, there have been two distinct phases in this resistance, the first provoked by the development and deployment of thermonuclear weapons, and the second in response to our government's escalation of its military effort to repress a "war of national liberation" in South Vietnam. The civil disobedience described and interpreted below, therefore, includes acts of nonparticipation (passive resistance, noncooperation) and also acts of direct resistance (direct action, confrontation politics) directed against both of these threats to world peace.

"In prosecuting war, the Government demands only two things of its people: warm bodies and cold cash. So we have the draft and taxes." Thus states a recent pamphlet (one of several now circulating) on "war tax resistance." The first two selections below present the case for civil disobedience in the form of tax resistance and draft resistance. I have chosen excerpts from the writings of Milton Mayer and A. J. Muste because both are known to thousands of Americans as pacifist spokesmen of many years' standing, and because they practiced and preached years ago what only now has become fashionable in radical circles.

Tax resistance in the United States is extraordinarily difficult, because in most cases the federal government simply attaches the bank account of the resister or proceeds to obtain its revenues at their source from his employer. The government in the end always gets its money, plus a surcharge of 6% per annum. In the resolute determination not to have taxable income, some resisters have simply refused to earn income above the limit set by their legal deductions and exemptions. A booklet distributed by The Peacemakers, who have been most active in organizing tax resistance, is full of personal histories of those who have for as long as twenty years either paid no tax, filed no returns, or otherwise declined to let their money do what they refuse to do themselves. Milton Mayer's own case, though not typical, is worth recounting.

> He claimed that at least 50% of taxes go for armaments, and that if he paid these taxes it would jeopardize his rights as a conscientious objector in the eyes of the government which has through its courts held several times that any substantial contribution for war by an individual is legal proof that he is not a genuine conscientious objector. He also maintained that the government denies the "freedom of worship" part of the First Amendment whenever it compels people to pay for armaments against their religious belief.
>
> These were the grounds on which he sought to recover what the IRS collected from him. In 1955 he instituted a suit to recover one half of his 1952 taxes. First, the district court in March 1957 refused to hear it. Then in 1958 the Circuit Court of Appeals held that he had erred in making a refusal, that what he should have done was to pay the tax and file a suit for recovery. A lawyer had given his services, but the expenses of the suit had, nevertheless, already cost $1600. Expense of taking the matter to the Supreme Court was estimated at another $1600. It looks like a lot of money to spend on trying to win a legal point, but Milton Mayer said, half jokingly: "In the end, the government spent about $3394 to keep the $33.94; the government, like me, is not interested in the nickel, but in the principle of the thing."[1]

Whether tax refusal in this country will ever become widespread and therefore influential on national policy is, given the penalties and energies of the Internal Revenue Service, unlikely. Since the popular folksinger and founder of the Institute for the Study of Nonviolence, Joan Baez, undertook tax withholding in 1964, refusal to pay all or part of one's federal income tax as a matter of principled protest against the "warfare state" has become not only more widely publicized but also almost respectable. For several years, *The New York Times* each spring has refused to publish a paid advertisement urging tax refusal, on the ground that to accept such an ad might place the newspaper in violation of the Internal Revenue Code. Still, it did not find the news unfit to print that, as of January 1968, the "Writers and Editors War Tax Protest" group had more than four hundred persons signed in support of this form of civil disobedience.[2] The special difficulties posed by tax resistance—difficulties of justification as well as difficulties of effective execution —are even greater than they were in Thoreau's day. Milton Mayer's essay is refreshingly direct in arguing for this most momentous form of civil disobedience.

Muste's argument, as stated in his oft-cited essay, "Of Holy Disobedience," portions of which are reprinted below, is framed by reference to the special history in this country of the development of the concept of a "conscientious objector" to military conscription. The Civil War and World War I caused many men to spend months (and in some cases, years) behind bars rather than accept conscription; harsh treatment was usually their lot at the hands of unsympathetic authorities. Before America's entry into World War II, however, a special draft classification of "conscientious objector" (C.O.) provided a way for most pacifists to assert the supremacy of their religious scruples against war without thereby violating the draft law, provided they were willing to register and perform either noncombatant or civilian "alternative" service, e. g., in federal forestry programs. A very small number refused these options, and served out the war years in federal prison. The prevailing moral acceptability of the war against Germany and Japan and of the Korean War, plus the category of C.O., accounts for the fact that only a few out of millions chose to commit civil disobedience rather than enter uniform.[3] Muste's argument, although it is addressed particularly to pacifists in the so-called "historic peace churches" (Friends, Mennonites, Jehovah's Witnesses), has a wider relevance because he argues that *any* draft status, in the end, provides just that kind of cooperation which enables the war machine to continue to operate smoothly; it co-opts the dissenter and nullifies resistance in a subtle but effective way.

If the essays of Mayer and Muste bring forward the classic argument against rendering tribute and service in the employ of Caesar, in recent years the most publicized acts of anti-war civil disobedience have been mass direct action against military installations, especially those involving the use or construction of nuclear weaponry. The next two selections, from Albert Bigelow and Bertrand Russell, convey the quality of these protests which became increasingly common in the later 1950's. One of the best known and most successful ventures of this sort was the protest in New York City against Civil Defense air-raid drills. Starting in 1955 with a dozen who refused to "take cover" when so ordered, in protest at the futility of conventional shelters for the civilian population in a nuclear war, the resisters grew to a thousand by 1960. They effectively caused the authorities to discontinue all further local drills for the general public, and their civil disobedience played a part in defeating the nationwide shelter-building program promoted in the first year of President John F. Kennedy's administration. But by far the most dramatic single act of civil disobedience in this period was the attempt of four Americans in March 1958 to sail their ketch, *Golden Rule,* into the Marshall Islands of the Central Pacific, to protest the scheduled nuclear bomb tests there by the U. S. Atomic Energy Commission. Their voyage failed: it was halted at Honolulu and the crew was imprisoned when they refused to obey an injunction against continuing on their projected course.[4] Yet it was a tremendous success; no other event so well signified the efforts of individual persons to try to influence their governments by direct and sacrificial action outside the normal political processes, to try to halt the threat of war and the testing of nuclear weapons. The brief statement reprinted here by Albert Bigelow, captain of *Golden Rule,* explaining "Why I am Sailing This Boat into the Bomb-Test Area," is one of the best first-hand statements from this period on record. The voyage of the *Golden Rule* was only the most publicized of the efforts organized by such groups as CNVA and its affiliates. Trespassing on missile sites

(Omaha) and at the launching of nuclear-powered, missile-armed submarines (New London, Newport News), as well as demonstrations in the form of "Peace Walks," were among the many "peace actions" involving civil disobedience in the late 1950's and early 1960's.

The essay by Bertrand Russell is one of several he has written in the past decade supporting mass civil disobedience.[5] Russell, though not a pacifist as such, did oppose his country's entry into World War I and was imprisoned during 1918 for refusing to silence his protest. In recent years, he has been one of the organizers of the Campaign for Nuclear Disarmament (CND) and its militant off-shoot, The Committee of 100, in England. Russell has become both a "nuclear pacifist" and a "unilateralist," i.e., one who believes it is an unmitigated crime for any nation to use nuclear weapons either aggressively or defensively, strategically or tactically, against military or civilian targets, and who also believes that his own country must take the first step toward foreswearing all use of such weapons. Nuclear pacifism and unilateralism have had their exponents in this country, too, and Russell's argument has a special relevance for Americans, even though his audience and the venue of his civil disobedience have been British throughout. A common theme runs through all his writings on this subject: Britain is a helpless hostage to the decisions in Washington, and therefore can gain nothing and could lose everything by a policy which allowed Polaris missile bases and nuclear weapons sites on its territory as the front line of defense against nuclear war between East and West.[6] National pride, not sound military judgment, together with the unwillingness of the United States to restrict its allies in Europe in its permanent Holy War against Communism to West Germany, Spain, and Portugal is the cause of Britain's nuclear posture. Such are Russell's views, and they have brought upon him bitter denunciations at home and in this country. Be that as it may, his position shows how mass civil disobedience in Great Britain against nuclear weapons has been understood by its leading defender to be a protest ultimately aimed at another country's military policy. Russell's position is also instructive in that, more than most theorist-practitioners of civil disobedience, he has justified such acts on the ground not that they will of themselves cause the government to change or reconsider its policies, but that this is the only way in which publicity can be obtained for anti-Establishment views and that only through widespread publicity can the case for unilateral nuclear disarmament hope to persuade the public and thus influence the government. In February 1961, immediately before one of the largest mass demonstrations in London (a protest which led directly to Russell's own arrest), he wrote:

> . . . the life of every inhabitant of Britain, old and young, man, woman and child, is at every moment in imminent danger and . . . this danger is caused by what is mis-named defence and immensely aggravated by every measure which governments pretend will diminish it—to make this known has seemed to some of us an imperative duty which we must pursue with whatever means are at our command. The Campaign for Nuclear Disarmament has done and is doing valuable and very successful work in this direction, but the press is becoming used to its doings and beginning to doubt their news value. It has therefore seemed to some of us necessary to supplement its campaign by such actions as the press is sure to report.[7]

More American men have defied their government in more different ways, with more sympathy and active support from the rest of the community, because of the war in Vietnam than on account of any other military adventure in a century. The remaining selections represent only a small fraction of the literature discussing civil disobedience on this issue.

Even before the first bombs fell on North Vietnam in February 1965, a "Declaration of Conscience Against the War in Vietnam" was circulated in this country, sponsored mainly by leading pacifists (including Milton Mayer and A. J. Muste). It was modeled on the "Declaration of the 121," drawn up in the summer of 1960 by leading French intellectuals as an attack on their government's conduct of the Algerian War.[8] Unlike their French counterparts, the American protesters had little or no effect on curbing the increasing tempo of the war. They and their "Declaration" (with over 4,000 signatures on it) were received at the White House in April 1965 and were politely ignored by the government and the public. In August 1967, a far more militant statement was circulated as "A Call to Resist Illegitimate Authority." It was sent out over the signatures of Professor Noam Chomsky, Reverend William Sloan Coffin, Jr., Dwight Macdonald, and Dr. Benjamin Spock; its sponsors included many others who were not conventional pacifists. Within a few months this statement was a key item in the indictment against Coffin, Spock and three others for conspiracy to violate the Selective Service Act.[9] When they were convicted in June 1968, the "Call to Resist" became a document of uncommon significance.

Were Thoreau alive today, he undoubtedly would think no better of the Vietnam war than he did of the Mexican war. His draft status, in any case, would be subject to the decisions of Local Board No. 114, in Middlesex County, Massachusetts. The letter reprinted below from Richard Boardman was sent to this same draft board late in 1967, and is one of hundreds drawn up out of disgust and shame over American involvement in the Vietnam conflict. Boardman's letter presents with great cogency the application to his own predicament of the general argument set forth in the earlier selection from Muste. Since Boardman's position is not typical of the views of all young men who have decided to refuse to cooperate with the Selective Service System at the present time, it is accompanied below by a quite different kind of testimonial written by Tom Jarrell and originally published on the front page of Boston's leading "underground" newspaper, *Avatar.* By way of reply to Boardman and Jarrell, the next selection is as good as one is likely to find. It is from the hand of the distinguished federal judge, Charles E. Wyzanski, Jr., also a Bostonian; it originally appeared on the newsstands shortly after the indictment against Spock *et al.* was announced. These three selections, while they do not ex-exhaust what is, and is to be, said on draft resistance at the present time, do effectively convey the moods and quality of the debate.

The essay by Carl Cohen is an extended comment on a mass sit-in at the Selective Service office in Ann Arbor,

Michigan. Cohen addresses himself to the brief for the defense, as it were, which raised on behalf of the protesters two increasingly popular arguments: (a) their civil disobedience is in fact a form of protected dissent under the First Amendment,[10] and (b) their civil disobedience is protected (indeed, required) under the holdings in the Nuremberg trials.[11] Both these contentions will undoubtedly continue to receive serious and weighty advocacy in cases now (or soon to come) before the courts. In his article, Cohen rejects both contentions, but not the protesters' convictions against the draft and the war, or their demand for the broadest possible scope to civil liberties.

The final selections are drawn from a baker's dozen of responses to a set of questions drawn up by *The New York Times* late in 1967. There is space to reprint only those which seemed most representative of the extremes of debate as advanced by those whose participation in it was most instructive: Noam Chomsky, theoretical linguist and the leading academic spokesman against the Vietnam War; Lewis Feuer, social philosopher and a frequent critic of the "New Left" style of confrontation politics; Paul Goodman, author and lecturer and perhaps the foremost interpreter and critic of American life, especially to college audiences (and one of the few original sponsors of both the "Declaration" and "Call to Resist"); and Irving Kristol, editor and frequent spokesman for the older radicalism. Brief though these four statements are, their contradictions and disagreements perhaps convey as well as anything could the misgivings which intelligent observers have over civil disobedience and over the sort of warfare this country has been waging in Vietnam.[12]

THE TRIBUTE MONEY

Milton Mayer

In 1949 a man named Veepings came to see me and stayed for a week. He was a nice man, from the Bureau of Internal Revenue, and he had come, he said, to audit my 1948 income-tax return. When he got through auditing, my home, my work, and I were a homogeneous shambles, and I owed the government one dollar. I thought of paying Veepings only 65.4 cents, but then I decided to pay him the whole dollar. The reason for the 65.4 was that I had undertaken, in my 1948 return, to refuse to pay 34.6 per cent of my income tax, that being the percentage of the United States Budget which was going directly into guns in that happy-go-lucky year. I had not, however, succeeded in refusing to pay, because, being, like most peaceable persons, an optimist, I had overestimated my income and paid-as-I-went 65.4 per cent of the overestimate, and at the end of the year, the government owed me money anyway. The government did not, naturally, refund me everything above 65.4 per cent of the tax due; it refunded me everything above 100 per cent of the tax due. Since I could not very well sue the government, in its own courts, for the 34.6 per cent that, under its own laws, it had taken, my refusal looked as if it would remain an empty gesture until such time as I would stop being either optimistic or peaceable.

Reprinted by permission of the author and publisher from *The Progressive*, March 1953, pp. 22–5. Copyright 1953 by The Progressive magazine, Madison, Wisconsin.

In 1950 my telephone rang and a man said: "I am Veepings. You wouldn't remember me."

"I wouldn't," I said bitterly, "but I do."

"I have been ordered," he said, "to audit your 1949 income-tax return."

"You already did," I said, "and I gave you a dollar."

"That," he said, "was your *1948* return. This is your *1949* return."

"Do you mean," I asked, "that you are going to move in for a week again, gouge my eyeballs, pull my fingernails, and all for another dollar? I'll give you *two* dollars to stay away."

"I'm afraid, Mr. Mayer," said Veepings, in his double-breasted blue-serge voice, "that you do not understand me. I am *ordered* to audit your return. I am only obeying orders."

"That," I snapped, "was General Keitel's defense at Nürnberg. You know, of course," I added, "what happened to General Keitel."

"I never meddle in politics," said Veepings. "When may I see you?"

"Any time," I said, affecting lightheartedness, "I have nothing to conceal and, incidentally, nothing to show you, either. You remember last time. I had no records for 1948, and we had to start from scratch. I have none for 1949, either. I'm the type that always assumes that the bank knows how to add."

"Then," said Veepings, evenly, "we'll have to start from scratch."

"Now see here, Veepings," I said, unevenly, "I'm a busy man. And besides, I'm a proletarian. Do you know what a proletarian is, you cad?"

"I told you," said Veepings, ignoring the epithet, "that I never meddle in politics."

"Proletarianism isn't politics; it's economics," I said, my voice like a knife. "A proletarian is a man who has nothing to sell but his labor. I have nothing to sell but my labor, and you want another week of my labor and a dollar on top of it. *You* ought to be paying *me*."

"Mr. Mayer," he said, "you don't understand my position."

"You don't understand *mine*," I said. "Last year you found that in 1948 I cheated the government by mistake. You also found that I paid five quarterly installments that year by mistake. The whole thing came to a dollar. Was it worth it? What good is a dollar to you? Eggs were 89 cents a dozen today. That's a dozen eggs and 11 cents. What can you do with 11 cents? You can make a telephone call and throw the penny away. You're throwing my money away," I concluded, fighting mad. "I won't stand for it."

"Mr. Mayer," he said, "you have what we here at the Bureau call an unmathematical mind. You have no head for figures, and you are, for that reason, a lovable fellow and you know it. You are also honest, at least as far as your income tax is concerned. You are painfully honest. You make so much noise about being honest that, if I hadn't audited your 1948 return, I'd be suspicious of you."

"Flattery will get you nowhere," I said, "I want to be let alone. I'm a busy man. I'm a proletarian. My labor is—"

"Mr. Mayer," said Veepings, "may I speak to you unofficially?"

"Sit down," I said, gesturing with the telephone receiver. "Sit down and tell me your troubles. Maybe I can help you or send you to someone who can."

"Unofficially, Mr. Mayer," said Veepings, "I think you bring this all on yourself."

"Bring what?"

"This auditing. It's extremely unusual—unofficially, Mr. Mayer— for an ordinary citizen like you—"

"An ordi—"

"I mean, for a man of modest income to have his return audited two years in a row. Extremely unusual. Especially when the first audit failed to disclose any—"

"Any what?"

"Any—substantial discrepancy, shall we say?"

"We shall," I said, icily, "unless we want to be sued for slander. Veepings," I said, "why don't you let me alone?"

"I have no choice, Mr. Mayer. I am under orders, and I don't want to hear about Keitel, or Sheitel, or whoever it is. But I wouldn't be surprised—unofficially, Mr. Mayer—if this extremely unusual procedure wasn't the consequence of your writing those long letters to the collector of internal revenue."

"'Those long letters,' Veepings," I said, "are my reasons for refusing, or trying to refuse, to pay 34.6 per cent of my income tax.

That's politics, and you told me yourself that you never meddle in politics."

"*I* don't, myself," said Veepings, "but—"

"But what?"

"Nothing," he said, "nothing at all. But I wouldn't be surprised—strictly unofficially, Mr. Mayer—if you weren't bringing all this on yourself."

So I was being harassed—unofficially—by the government of the United States—the biggest, busiest government on earth. I was not being put in prison, like Thoreau. I was not being shot, like Nathan Hale. I was not being hanged, like John Brown. I was being harassed. There is no money and no martyrdom in being harassed. There is only harassment.

In 1951 and 1952, Veepings couldn't find me; I was moving too fast around Europe. Besides, I was being paid in German money, on which I had to pay German taxes, and having no head for figures *or* German, I let the thing ride. But this is 1953, and I am back home, and the 34.6 per cent that the government was buying guns with a few years ago has risen to 60 per cent or 80 per cent or 110 per cent. I am settling for 50 per cent. (My grandfather used to say that the Mayers were early settlers—fifty cents on the dollar). I am paying 50 per cent of my 1952 income tax and sending the balance to people who will buy something fit for human consumption with it.

I cannot see why I should not persist in my folly. Like every other horror-stricken American I keep asking myself, "What can a man do? What weight does a man have, besides petition and prayer, that he isn't using to save his country's soul and his own?" The frustration of the horror-stricken American as he sees his country going over the falls without a barrel is more than I can bear just now. He tries to do constructive work, but all the while he is buying guns. I have thought as hard as I can think. I have thought about, for example, anarchy. Not only am I not an anarchist, but I believe in taxes, in very high taxes, and especially in a very high graduated income tax. I realize that a man who believes in taxes cannot pick and choose among them and say he will not spend 50 per cent of them on guns just because he doesn't need guns. I realize that anarchy is unworkable and that that is why the state came into being. And I realize, too, that the state cannot be maintained without its authority's being reposed in its members' representatives. I realize all that. But in this state—and a very good state it is, or was, as states go, or went—I cannot get anybody to represent me. My senators will not represent me. My congressman will not represent me. I am opposed to taxation without representation.

Don't tell me that I am represented by my vote. I voted against the national policy. Having done so, I am constrained in conscience to uphold my vote and not betray it. If my offense is anarchy—which I dislike—I can't help it. If the preservation of society compels me to commit worse evils than anarchy, then the cost of preserving society is too high. Society is not sacred; I am. My first responsibility is not to preserve the state—that is Hitlerism and Stalinism—but to preserve my soul. If you tell me that there is no other way to preserve the state than by the implicit totalitarianism of Rousseau's "general will," I will reply that that is the state's misfortune and men must not accept it. I have surrendered my sovereignty to another Master than the general will—I do not mean to be sanctimonious here—and if the general will does not serve Him it does not serve me or any other man.

In so far as there is any worldly sovereign in the United States, it is not the general will, or the Congress, or the President. It is I. I am sovereign here. I hold the highest office of the land, the office of citizen, with responsibilities to my country heavier, by virtue of my office, than those of any other officer, including the President. And I do not hold my office by election but by inalienable right. I cannot abdicate my right, because it is inalienable. If I try to abdicate it, to the general will, or to my representatives or my ministers, I am guilty of betraying not only democracy but my nature as a man endowed with certain inalienable rights.

I have thought about all this, in the large and in the little. I have thought about my wife and children and my responsibility to them. War will not even save them their lives, not even victorious war this time. And it will lose them their most precious possession, their souls, if they call a man husband and father who has lightly sold his own. I have thought of the fact that better men than I, much better men, disagree with me. That grieves me. But I am not, in this instance, trying to emulate better men.

I have thought about my effectiveness. A man who "makes

trouble for himself," as the saying is, is thought to reduce his effectiveness, partly because of the diversion of his energies and partly because some few, at least, of his neighbors will call him a crank, a crook, or a traitor. But I am not very effective anyway, and neither, so far as I can see, is anyone else. If anything is effective in matters of this sort, it is example. I go up and down the land denying the decree of Caesar that all able-bodied men between eighteen and twenty-five go into the killing business and urging such men as are moved in conscience to decline to do so. If a million young men would decline, in conscience, to kill their fellow men, the government would be as helpless as its citizens are now. Its helplessness then would, I think, be at least as contagious abroad as its violence is now. Other governments would become helpless, including the Russian, and thus would we be able to save democracy at home *and* abroad. Victorious war has failed to do it anywhere.

But how can a million old men who themselves will not decline to hire the killing expect a million young men to do it? How can I urge others to do what I do not care to do myself? Of course the government doesn't want me for military service. I am overage, spavined, humpbacked, bald, and blind. The government doesn't want me. Men are a dime a dozen. What the government wants is my dime to buy a dozen men with. If I decline to buy men and give them guns, the government will, I suppose, force me to. I offer to pay all of my taxes for peaceable purposes, the only purposes which history suggests will defend democracy; the government has, I believe, no way, under the general revenue system, to accept my offer. I like the out-of-doors and I do not want to go to jail. I could put my property in my wife's name and bury my money in a hole or a foreign bank account. But I am not Al Capone. I am, as Veepings himself said of me, an honest man. And I am not mathematically minded; if I did try deceit, I'd be caught.

There is only one other alternative, and that is no alternative either. That is to earn less than $500 a year and be tax-free. I'd be paying taxes anyway on what I bought with $500, but that doesn't bother me, because the issue is not, as long as I am only human, separation from war or any other evil-doing but only as much separation as a being who is only human can achieve within his power. No, the trouble with earning less than $500 a year is that it doesn't support a family. Not a big family like mine. If I were a subsistence farmer I might get by, but I'm a city boy.

I would be hard put to answer if you asked me whether a man should own property in the first place, for a government to tax. If I said, "No, he should not," I should stand self-condemned as a Christian Communist. It is illegal, under the McCarran Act, to be either a Christian *or* a Communist, and I don't want to tangle with both the Internal Revenue Act and the McCarran Act at the same time, especially on the delicate claim to being a Christian. Still, the Christian Gospels are, it seems to me, passing clear on the point of taxes. When the apostle says *both* that "we should obey the magistrates" *and* that "we should obey God rather than man," I take it that he means that we should be law-abiding persons unless the law moves us against the Lord.

The problem goes to the very essence of the relationship of God, man, and the state. It isn't easy. It never was. History, however, is on the side of us angels. The primitive Christians, who were pacifists, refused to pay taxes for heathen temples. They were of course, outlaws anyway. The early Quakers, who were pacifists, refused to pay tithes to the established church and went to prison. But the war tax problem seems not to have arisen until 1755, when a considerable number of Quakers refused to pay a tax levied in Pennsylvania for the war against the red Indians.

The Boston (and New York and Baltimore and Charleston) "tea parties" of the 1700's were, of course, a vivid and violent form of tax refusal endorsed, to this day, by the Daughters of the American Revolution. Seventy-five years after the Revolution, Henry David Thoreau refused to pay his poll tax because the government was waging both slavery against the Negroes and war against the Mexicans. Thoreau was put in jail overnight, and the next day Emerson went over to Concord and looked at him through the bars and said, "What in the devil do you think you're doing, Henry?" "I," said Thoreau, "am being free." So Emerson paid Thoreau's poll tax, and Thoreau, deprived of his freedom by being put out of jail, wrote his essay on civil disobedience. Seventy-five years later, Gandhi read Thoreau's essay and worked it into a revolution. It could happen here, but it won't. The place was propitious for Gandhi, a slave colony whose starving people had no money or status to lose, just as the time was propitious for

Thoreau, a time of confidence and liberality arising from confidence. Totalitarianism was unthinkable and parliamentary capitalism was not in danger. The appeal to the rights of man was taken seriously, and McCarthyism, McCarranism, and MacArthurism were all as yet unborn.

I doubt that anybody will be able to bring me more light in this matter than I now have. The light I need will come to me from within or it won't come at all. When George Fox visited William Penn, Penn wanted to know if he should go on wearing his sword. "Wear it," said Fox, "as long as thou canst." I hasten to say that I feel like Penn, not like Fox. I know I can't say that you ought to do what I can't do or that I'll do it if you do it. But I don't know if I can say that you ought to do what I do or even if I ought to do it. I am fully aware of the anomaly of refusing to pay 50 per cent of my taxes when 50 per cent of the 50 per cent I do pay is used for war. I am even fuller aware of the converse anomaly of refusing to pay 50 per cent of my taxes when 50 per cent of the 50 per cent I won't pay would be used for peaceable purposes. In addition, if the government comes and gets it, and fines me, as I suppose it might, it will collect more for war than it would have in the first place.

Worst of all, I am not a good enough man to be doing this sort of thing. I am not an early Christian; I am the type that, if Nero threw me naked into the amphitheatre, would work out a way to harass the lions. But somebody over twenty-five has got to perform the incongruous affirmation of saying, "No," and saying it regretfully rather than disdainfully. Why shouldn't it be I? I have sailed through life, up to now, as a first-class passenger on a ship that is nearly all steerage. By comparison with the rest of mankind, I have always had too much money, too many good jobs, too good a reputation, too many friends, and too much fun. Who, if not I, is full of unearned blessings? When, if not now, will I start to earn them? Somebody will take care of me. Somebody always has. The only thing I don't know is who it is that does it. I know who feeds the young ravens, but I know, too, that the Devil takes care of his own.

OF HOLY DISOBEDIENCE   *(abridged)*

A. J. Muste

A book which the French writer, George Bernanos, wrote in Brazil
—to which he had exiled himself because he would not remain in
France under Nazi occupation—has just been published in this
country. It is entitled *Tradition of Freedom* and is a hymn to freedom,
an impassioned warning against obedience and conformity, especially obedience to the modern State engaged in mechanized,
total war.

In the closing pages of this work, Bernanos writes:

> I have thought for a long time now that if, some day, the in-
> creasing efficiency of the technique of destruction finally causes our
> species to disappear from the earth, it will not be cruelty that will
> be responsible for our extinction and still less, of course, the indig-
> nation that cruelty awakens and the reprisals and vengeance that
> it brings upon itself . . . but the docility, the lack of responsibility
> of the modern man, his base subservient acceptance of every com-
> mon decree. The horrors which we have seen, the still greater hor-
> rors we shall presently see, are not signs that rebels, insubordinate,
> untameable men, are increasing in number throughout the world,
> but rather that there is a constant increase, a stupendously rapid
> increase, in the number of obedient, docile men.

Reprinted from *Of Holy Disobedience* by A. J. Muste, Pendle Hill Pamphlet 64,
copyright © 1952 by Pendle Hill, Wallingford, Penna., 19086, by permission of
the publisher.

It seems to me that this is a true and timely warning. It might serve as a text for a general appeal to American youth to adopt and practice the great and urgent virtues of Holy Disobedience, non-conformity, resistance toward Conscription, Regimentation and War. For the present I want to use Bernanos' words as an introduction to some observations on the discussion regarding the absolute and relative role of these "virtues" which goes on chiefly among pacifists, members of the Historic Peace Churches and other such groups. I think it will be readily apparent, however, that the principles set forth have a wider bearing and merit consideration by all who are concerned about the maintenance of freedom in our time and the abolition of war.

Most believers in democracy and all pacifists begin, of course, with an area of agreement as to the moral necessity, the validity and the possible social value of No-saying or Holy Disobedience. Pacifists and/or conscientious objectors all draw the line at engaging in military combat and most of us indeed at any kind of service in the armed forces. But immediately thereupon questions arise as to whether we should not emphasize "positive and constructive service" rather than the "negative" of refusal to fight or to register; or questions about the relative importance of "resistance" and "reconciliation," and so on. It is to this discussion that I wish to attempt a contribution. It may be that it will be most useful both to young men of draft age and to other readers if we concentrate largely on the quite concrete problem of whether the former should register, conform to other requirements of the Selective Service Act which apply to conscientious objectors and accept or submit to the alternative service required of them under the law as amended in June, 1951; or whether they shall refuse to register, or if they do register or are "automatically" registered by the authorities, shall refuse to conform at the next stage; and in any event refuse to render any alternative service under conscription. We deal, in other words, with the question whether young men who are eligible for it shall accept the IV-E classification or take the more "absolutist," non-registrant position. (For present purposes, consideration of the I-A-O position, the designation used for draftees who are willing to accept service in the armed forces provided this is non-combatant in character, may be omitted. The IV-E classification is the designation used for persons who are on grounds of religious training and belief opposed to participation in any war. Those who are given this classification are required to render alternative service, outside the armed forces and under civilian auspices, and designed to serve "the health, safety and interest of the United States.")

Two preliminary observations are probably necessary in order to avoid misunderstanding. In the first place, in every social movement there are varied trends or emphases, and methods of working. Those who hold to one approach are likely to be very critical of those who take another. Disagreements among those within the same movement may be more intense or even bitter than with those on the outside. I suppose it can hardly be denied that every movement has in it individuals whose contribution is negative, and that such individuals do not all come from within one wing of the movement. Objective evaluation also leads to the view that the cause is forwarded by various methods and through the agency of diverse individuals and groups. But this does not mean that discussion within the movement of trends and methods of work is not useful and essential. Even if it were true that each of several strategies was *equally* valid and useful, it would still be necessary that each be clearly and vigorously presented and implemented in order that the movement might develop its maximum impact.

Secondly, in what I shall have to say I am not passing moral judgment on individual draftees. But from the fact that a pacifist minister should not pass moral condemnation on the young man in his congregation who in obedience to his conscience enlists or submits to conscription, we do not deduce that this minister should abandon his pacifism or cease to witness to it. Similarly, the fact that in the pacifist movement we support various types of COs in following the lead of conscience does not rule out discussion as to the validity and usefulness of various strategies. It is one thing for a young and immature draftee to follow a course which amounts to "making the best of a bad business" and for others to give him sympathetic understanding and help. It is a very different thing for pacifist organizations or churches to advocate such a course or to rationalize it into something other than it really is.

As some of the readers of this statement are likely to be aware, the writer has advocated the non-registrant position. The majority in the pacifist movement probably believe that it is preferable for

COs to accept or submit to the alternative civilian service which was required under the World War II Selective Service Act and is now again required under "peacetime conscription."

The varied considerations and arguments which currently enter into the discussion of this choice confronting the youth of draft age tend, as I see it, to fall into three categories, though there is a good deal of overlapping. One set of considerations may be said to center largely around the idea of Christian or human "vocation"; a second set has to do with the problem of "the immature 18-year-old"; the third with the relation of the pacifist and citizens generally to military conscription and the modern Power-State.*

Participation in alternative service is quite often defended on the ground that our opposition is to war rather than conscription; except in the matter of war we are as ready to serve the nation as anybody; therefore, as long as we are not drafted for combat or forced against our will into the armed services, we are ready to render whatever service of a civilian character may be imposed upon us.

Is this a sound position? Let me emphasize that it is conscription for war under the conditions of the second half of the twentieth century that we are talking about. The question as to whether sometime and under some circumstances we might accept conscription for some conceivable purpose not related to war, is not here at stake. It is academic and irrelevant. The question with which we are dealing is that of conscripting youth in and for modern war.

As pacifists we are opposed to all war. Even if recruitment were entirely on a voluntary basis, we would be opposed. It seems to me we might infer from this that we should be *a fortiori* opposed to military conscription, for here in addition to the factor of war itself, the element of coercion by government enters in, coercion which places young boys in a military regime where they are deprived of freedom of choice in virtually all essential matters. They may not have the slightest interest in the war, yet they are made to kill by order. This is surely a fundamental violation of the human spirit which must cause the pacifist to shudder.

The reply is sometimes made that pacifists are *not* being con-

---

*[The author's discussion of the first two of these three topics is omitted here. Ed.]

scripted for military purposes and therefore—presumably—*they* are not faced with the issue of the nature of military conscription. I shall later contend that it is not really possible to separate conscription and war, as I think this argument does. Here I wish to suggest that even if the question is the conscription of non-pacifist youth, it is a fundamental mistake for pacifists ever to relent in their opposition to this evil, ever to devote their energies primarily to securing provisions for COs in a draft law or to lapse into a feeling that conscription has somehow become more palatable if such provisions are made by the State. It is not our own children if we are pacifist parents, our fellow-pacifist Christians if we are churchmen, about whom we should be most deeply concerned. In the first place, that is a narrow and perhaps self-centered attitude. In the second place, pacifist youths have some inner resources for meeting the issue under discussion. The terrible thing which we should never lose sight of, to which we should never reconcile our spirits, is that the great mass of 18-year olds are drafted for war. They are given no choice. Few are at the stage of development where they are capable of making fully rational and responsible choice. Thus the fathers immolate the sons, the older generation immolates the younger, on the altar of Moloch. What God centuries ago forbade Abraham to do even to his own son—"Lay not thy hand upon the lad, neither do thou anything unto him"—this we do by decree to the entire youth of a nation.

We need to ask ourselves whether such conscription is in any real sense a lesser evil. As we have already said, the pacifist is opposed to war and we have all sensed the danger of arguing against conscription *on the ground that* the nation could raise all the troops it needed by voluntary enlistment. Nevertheless, there is a point to an impassioned argument which Georges Bernanos makes in the book we mentioned at the outset. He states that the man created by western or Christian civilization "disappeared in the day conscription became law . . . the principle is a totalitarian principle if ever there was one—so much so that you could deduce the whole system from it, as you can deduce the whole of geometry from the propositions of Euclid."

To the question as to whether France, the Fatherland, should not be defended if in peril, he has the Fatherland answer: "I very much doubt whether my salvation requires such monstrous behavior" as defense by modern war methods. If men wanted to die on behalf of the Fatherland, moreover, that would be one thing but "making a clean sweep, with, one scoop of the hand, of an entire male population" is another matter altogether: "You tell me that, in saving me, they save themselves. Yes, if they can remain free; no, if they allow you to destroy, by this unheard of measure, the national covenant. For as soon as you have, by simple decree, created millions of French soldiers, it will be held as proven that you have sovereign rights over the persons and the goods of every Frenchman, that there are no rights higher than yours and where, then, will your usurpations stop? Won't you presently presume to decide what is just and what is unjust, what is Evil and what is Good?"

It is pretty certainly an oversimplification to suggest, as Bernanos here does, that the entire totalitarian, mechanized "system" under which men today live or into which they are increasingly drawn even in countries where a semblance of freedom and spontaneity remains, can be traced to its source in the military conscription which was instituted by the French Revolution in the eighteenth century. But what cannot, it seems to me, be successfully denied is that today totalitarianism, depersonalization, conscription, war, and the conscripting, war-making power-state are inextricably linked together. They constitute a whole, a "system." It is a disease, a creeping paralysis, which affects all nations, on both sides of the global conflict. Revolution and counter-revolution, "peoples' democracies" and "western democracies," the "peace-loving" nations on both sides in the war, are cast in this mold of conformity, mechanization, and violence. This is the Beast which, in the language of the Apocalypse, is seeking to usurp the place of the Lamb.

We know that "war will stop at nothing" and we are clear that as pacifists we can have nothing to do with it. But I do not think that it is possible to distinguish between war and conscription, to say that the former is and the latter is not an instrument or mark of the Beast.

Non-conformity, Holy Disobedience, becomes a virtue and indeed a necessary and indispensable measure of spiritual self-preservation, in a day when the impulse to conform, to acquiesce, to go along, is the instrument which is used to subject men to totalitarian rule and involve them in permanent war. To create the impression at least of outward unanimity, the impression that there is no "real" opposition, is something for which all dictators and military leaders strive assiduously. The more it seems that there is no opposition, the less worthwhile it seems to an ever larger number of people to cherish even the thought of opposition. Surely, in such a situation it is important not to place the pinch of incense before Caesar's image, not to make the gesture of conformity which is involved, let us say, in registering under a military conscription law. When the object is so plainly to create a situation where the individual no longer has a choice except total conformity or else the concentration camp or death; when reliable people tell us seriously that experiments are being conducted with drugs which will paralyze the wills of opponents within a nation or in an enemy country, it is surely neither right nor wise to wait until the "system" has driven us into a corner where we cannot retain a vestige of self-respect unless we say No. It does not seem wise or right to wait until this evil catches up with us, but rather to go out to meet it—to *resist*—before it has gone any further.

As Bernanos reminds us, "things are moving fast, dear reader, they are moving very fast." He recalls that he "lived at a time when passport formalities seemed to have vanished forever." A man could "travel around the world with nothing in his wallet but his visiting card." He recalls that "twenty years ago, Frenchmen of the middle class refused to have their fingerprints taken; fingerprints were the concern of convicts." But the word "criminal" has "swollen to such prodigious proportions that it now includes every citizen who dislikes the Regime, the System, the Party, or the man who represents them. . . . The moment, perhaps, is not far off when it will seem natural for us to leave the front-door key in the lock at night so that the police may enter at any hour of the day or night, *as it is to open our pocket-books to every official demand.* And when the State decides that it would be a practical measure . . . to put some outward sign on us, why should we hesitate to have ourselves branded on the cheek or on the buttock, with a hot iron, like cattle? The purges of 'wrong-thinkers,' so dear to the totalitarian regimes, would thus become infinitely easier."

To me it seems that submitting to conscription even for civilian service is permitting oneself thus to be branded by the State. It makes the work of the State in preparing for war and in securing the desired impression of unanimity much easier. It seems, therefore, that pacifists should refuse to be thus branded.

In the introductory chapter to Kay Boyle's volume of short stories about occupied Germany, *The Smoking Mountain*, there is an episode which seems to me to emphasize the need of Resistance and of not waiting until it is indeed too late. She tells about a woman professor of philology in a Hessian university who said of the German experience with Nazism: "It was a gradual process." When the first *Jews Not Wanted* signs went up, "there was never any protest made about them, and, after a few months, not only we, but even the Jews who lived in that town, walked past without noticing any more that they were there. Does it seem impossible to you that this should have happened to civilized people anywhere?"

The philology professor went on to say that after a while she put up a picture of Hitler in her class-room. After twice refusing to take the oath of allegiance to Hitler, she was persuaded by her students to take it. "They argued that in taking this oath, which so many anti-Nazis had taken before me, *I was committing myself to nothing, and that I could exert more influence as a professor than as an outcast in the town.*"

She concluded by saying that she now had a picture of a Jew, Spinoza, where Hitler's picture used to hang, and added: "Perhaps you will think that I did this ten years too late, and perhaps you are right in thinking this. *Perhaps there was something else we could all of us have done, but we never seemed to find a way to do it, either as individuals or as a group, we never seemed to find a way.*" A decision by the pacifist movement in this country to break completely with conscription, to give up the idea that we can "exert more influence" if we conform in some measure, do not resist to the uttermost—this might awaken our countrymen to a realization of the precipice on the edge of which we stand. It might be the making of our movement.

Thus to embrace Holy Disobedience is not to substitute Resistance for Reconciliation. It is to practice both Reconciliation and Resistance. In so far as we help to build up or smooth the way for American militarism and the regimentation which accompanies it, we are certainly not practising reconciliation toward the millions of people in the Communist bloc countries against whom American war preparations, including conscription, are directed. Nor are we practising reconciliation towards the hundreds of millions in Asia and Africa whom we condemn to poverty and drive into the arms of Communism by our addiction to military "defense." Nor are we practising love toward our own fellow-citizens, including also the multitude of youths in the armed services, if against our deepest insight, we help to fasten the chains of conscription and war upon them.

Our works of mercy, healing, and reconstruction will have a deeper and more genuinely reconciling effect when they are not entangled with conscript service for "the health, safety and interest" of the United States or any other war-making State. It is highly doubtful whether Christian mission boards can permit any of their projects in the Orient to be manned by men supposed to be working for "the health, safety and interest" of the United States. The Gospel of reconciliation will be preached with a new freedom and power when the preachers have broken decisively with American militarism. It can surely not be preached at all in Communist lands by those who have not made that break. It will be when we have gotten off the back of what someone has called the wild elephant of militarism and conscription on to the solid ground of freedom, and only then, that we shall be able to live and work constructively. Like Abraham we shall have to depart from the City-which-is in order that we may help to build the City-which-is-to-be, whose true builder and maker is God.

It is, of course, possible, perhaps even likely, that if we set ourselves apart as those who will have no dealing whatever with conscription, will not place the pinch of incense before Caesar's image, our fellow-citzens will stone us, as Stephen was stoned when he reminded his people that it was they who had "received the law as it was ordained by angels, and kept it not." So may we be stoned for reminding our people of a tradition of freedom and peace which was also, in a real sense, "ordained by angels" and which we no longer keep. But, it will thus become possible for them, as for Paul, even amidst the search for new victims to persecute, suddenly to see again the face of Christ and the vision of a new Jerusalem.

Someone may at this point reflect that earlier in this paper I counseled against people too readily leaving the normal path of life and that I am now counseling a policy which is certain to create disturbance in individual lives, families, and communities. That is so. But to depart from the common way in response or reaction to a conscription law, in the attempt to adapt oneself to an abnormal state of society, is one thing. To leave father, mother, wife, child, yea and one's own life also, at the behest of Christ or conscience is quite another. Our generation will not return to a condition under which every man may sit under his own vine and fig tree, with none to make him afraid, unless there are those who are willing to pay the high cost of redemption and deliverance from a regime of regimentation, terrors and war.

Finally, it is of crucial importance that we should understand that for the individual to pit himself in Holy Disobedience against the war-making and conscripting State, wherever it or he be located, is not an act of despair or defeatism. Rather, I think we may say that precisely this individual refusal to "go along" is now the beginning and the core of any realistic and practical movement against war and for a more peaceful and brotherly world. For it becomes daily clearer that political and military leaders pay virtually no attention to protests against current foreign policy and pleas for peace when they know perfectly well that when it comes to a showdown, all but a handful of the millions of protesters will "go along" with the war to which the policy leads. All but a handful will submit to conscription. Few of the protesters will so much as risk their jobs in the cause of "peace." The failure of the policy-makers to change their course does not, save perhaps in very rare instances, mean that they are evil men who want war. They feel, as indeed they so often declare in crucial moments, that the issues are so complicated, the forces arrayed against them so strong, that they "have no choice" but to add another score of billions to the military budget, and so on and on. Why should they think there is any reality, hope, or salvation in "peace advocates" who when the moment of decision comes also act on the assumption that they "have no choice" but to conform?

Precisely in a day when the individual appears to be utterly helpless, to "have no choice," when the aim of the "system" is to convince him that he is helpless as an individual and that the only way to meet regimentation is by regimentation, there is absolutely no hope save in going back to the beginning. The human being, the child of God, must assert his humanity and his sonship again. He must exercise the choice which he no longer has as something accorded him by society, which he "naked, weaponless, armourless, without shield or spear, but only with naked hands and open eyes" must create again. He must understand that this naked human being is the one *real* thing in the face of the mechanics and the mechanized institutions of our age. He, by the grace of God, is the seed of all the human life there will be on earth in the future, though he may have to die to make that harvest possible. As *Life* magazine stated in its unexpectedly profound and stirring editorial of August 20, 1945, its first issue after the atom bombing of Hiroshima: "Our sole safeguard against the very real danger of a reversion to barbarism is the kind of morality which compels the individual conscience, be the group right or wrong. The individual conscience against the atomic bomb? Yes. There is no other way."

WHY I AM SAILING THIS BOAT
INTO THE BOMB-TEST AREA

Albert Bigelow

My friend Bill Huntington and I are planning to sail a small vessel westward into the Pacific H-bomb test area. By April we expect to reach nuclear testing grounds at Eniwetok. We will remain there as long as the tests of H-bombs continue. With us will be two other volunteers.

Why? Because it is the way I can say to my government, to the British government, and to the Kremlin: "Stop! Stop this madness before it is too late. For God's sake, turn back!"

How have I come to this conviction? Why do I feel under compulsion, under moral orders, as it were, to do this?

The answer to such questions, at least in part, has to do with my experience as a Naval officer during World War II. The day after Pearl Harbor was attacked, I was at the Navy recruiting offices. I had had a lot of experience in navigating vessels. Life in the Navy would be a glamorous change from the dull mechanism of daily civilian living. My experience assured me of success. All this adventure ahead and the prospect of becoming a hero into the bargain.

I suppose, too, that I had an enormous latent desire to conform,

Reprinted by permission of the author and publisher from *Liberation,* February 1958, pp. 4–6.

to go along with the rest of my fellows. I was swayed by the age-old psychology of meeting force with force. It did not really occur to me to resist the drag of the institution of war, the pattern of organized violence, which had existed for so many centuries. This psychology prevailed even though I had already reflected on the fantastic wastefulness of war—the German *Bismarck* hunting the British *Hood* and sending it to the bottom of the sea, and the British Navy hunting the *Bismarck* and scuttling it.

I volunteered, but instead of being sent to sea, I was assigned to 90 Church Street in New York and worked in project "plot" establishing the whereabouts of all combat ships in the Atlantic. In a couple of months I escaped from this assignment and was transferred to the Naval Training Station at Northwestern University.

I had not been at Northwestern very long when I sensed that because of my past experience I would be made an instructor there and still not get to sea. So I deliberately flunked an examination in navigation and before long was assigned to a submarine chaser in the Atlantic.

From March to October of 1943, I was in command of a submarine chaser in the Solomon Islands, during the fighting. It was during this period that more than 100 Japanese planes were shot down in one day. This was called "the Turkey Shoot." The insensitivity which decent men must develop in such situations is appalling. I remember that the corpse of a Japanese airman who had been shot down was floating bolt upright in one of the coves, a position resulting from the structure of the Japanese life belts, which were different from our Mae Wests. Each day as we passed the cove we saw this figure, his face growing blacker under the terrific sun. We laughingly called him Smiling Jack. As a matter of fact, I think I gave him that name myself and felt rather proud of my wit.

Later in World War II, I was captain of the destroyer escort *Dale W. Peterson*—DE 337—and I was on her bridge as we came into Pearl Harbor from San Francisco when the first news arrived of the explosion of an atomic bomb over Hiroshima. Although I had no way of understanding what an atom bomb was I was absolutely awestruck, as I suppose all men were for a moment. Intuitively it was then that I realized for the first time that morally war is impossible.

I don't suppose I had the same absolute realization with my whole being, so to speak, of the immorality and "impossibility" of nuclear war until the morning of August 7, 1957. On that day, I sat with a score of friends, before dawn, in the Nevada desert just outside the entrance to the Camp Mercury testing grounds. The day before, eleven of us, in protest against the summer-long tests, had tried to enter the restricted area. We had been arrested as we stepped one after another over the boundary line, and had been carried off to a ghost town which stands at the entrance to Death Valley. There we had been given a speedy trial under the charge of trespassing under the Nevada laws. Sentencing had been suspended for a year, and later in the afternoon we had returned to Camp Mercury to continue the Prayer and Conscience Vigil along with others who had remained there during our civil disobedience action.

In the early morning of August 7, an experimental bomb was exploded. We sat with our backs to the explosion site. But when the flash came I felt again the utterly impossible horror of this whole business, the same complete realization that nuclear war must go, that I had felt twelve years before on the bridge of U. S. S. *Dale W. Peterson*, off Pearl Harbor.

I think also that deep down somewhere in me, and in all men at all times, there is a realization that the pattern of violence meeting violence makes no sense, and that war violates something central in the human heart—"that of God," as we Quakers sometimes say. For example, when each of us at the trial the afternoon before had told why we were committing civil disobedience against nuclear tests, our attorney, Francis Heisler, said: "There isn't one of us in this courtroom who doesn't wish that he had walked into the testing grounds with these people this morning." Everybody, including the police and court officers, nodded assent.

However, I am ahead of my story. At the close of the War, in spite of what I had felt on the bridge of that destroyer, I did not break away from my old life. For a time I was Housing Commissioner of Massachusetts. Like many other people who had been through the War, I was seeking some sort of unified life-philosophy or religion. I did a good deal of religious "window-shopping." I became impressed by the fact that in one way or another the saints, the wise men, those who seemed to me truly experienced, all pointed in one direction—toward nonviolence, truth, love, toward a way and a goal that could not be reconciled with war. For quite a while, to use a phrase of Alan Watts', I "sucked the finger instead of going where it pointed." But finally I realized that I did have to move in that direction, and in 1952 I resigned my commission in the Naval Reserve. It was promptly and courteously accepted. I felt a bit proud of doing it a month before I would have come into a pension. Such little things we pride ourselves on!

I came into contact with the Quakers, the Society of Friends. My wife, Sylvia, had already joined the Society in 1948. As late as 1955 I was still fighting off joining the Society, which seemed to me to involve a great, awesome commitment. I suppose I was like the man in one of Shaw's plays who wanted to be a Christian— but not yet.

Then came the experience of having in our home for some months two of the Hiroshima maidens who had been injured and disfigured in the bombing of August 6, 1945. Norman Cousins and other wonderful people brought them to this country for plastic surgery. There were two things about these girls that hit me very hard and forced me to see that I had no choice but to make the commitment to live, as best I could, a life of nonviolence and reconciliation. One was the fact that when they were bombed in 1945 the two girls in our home were nine and thirteen years old. What earthly thing could they have done to give some semblance of what we call justice to the ordeal inflicted upon them and hundreds like them? What possible good could come out of human action—war—which bore such fruits? Is it not utter blasphemy to think that there is anything moral or Christian about such behavior?

The other thing that struck me was that these young women found it difficult to believe that *we,* who were not members of their families, could love *them.* But *they* loved *us;* they harbored no resentment against us or other Americans. How are you going to respond to that kind of attitude? The newly-elected president of the National Council of Churches, Edwin T. Dahlberg, said in his inaugural talk that instead of "massive retaliation" the business of Christians is to practice "massive reconciliation." Well, these Hiroshima girls practiced "massive reconciliation" on us, on me, who had laughed derisively at "Smiling Jack." What response can one make to this other than to give oneself utterly to destroying the evil, war, that dealt so shamefully with them and try to live in the spirit of sensitivity and reconciliation which they displayed?

As I have said, I think there is that in all men that abhors and rejects war and knows that force and violence can bring no good thing to pass. Yet men are bound by old patterns of feeling, thought, and action. The organs of public opinion are almost completely shut against us. It seems practically impossible, moreover, for the ordinary person by ordinary means to speak to, and affect the action of, his government. I have had a recent experience of this which has strengthened my conviction that it is only by such acts as sailing a boat to Eniwetok and thus "speaking" to the government right in the testing area that we can expect to be heard.

I was asked by the New England office of the American Friends Service Committee to take to the White House 17,411 signatures to a petition to cancel the Pacific tests. Ten thousand signatures had previously been sent in. I realized that even a President in good health cannot see personally everyone who has a message for him. Yet the right of petition exists—in theory—and is held to be a key factor in democratic process. And the President presumably has assistants to see to it that all serious petitions are somehow brought to his attention. For matters of this kind, there is Maxwell Rabb, secretary to the cabinet.

Twenty-seven thousand is quite a few people to have signed a somewhat unusual petition. The A. F. S. C. is widely known and recognized as a highly useful agency. I am known to Maxwell Rabb with whom I worked in Republican politics in Massachusetts. I was a precinct captain for Eisenhower in the 1952 primaries. Yet a couple of days work on the part of the staff of the Friends Committee on National Legislation failed to secure even an assurance that some time on Tuesday, December 31, the day I would be in Washington, Max Rabb would see me to receive the petitions. On that day I made five calls and talked with his secretary. Each time I was assured that she would call me back within ten minutes. Each time the return call failed to come and I tried again. The last time, early in the afternoon, I held on to the telephone for ten minutes, only to be told finally that the office was about to close for the day.

Each time I telephoned, including the last, I was told I could, of course, leave the petitions with the policeman at the gate. This I refused to do. It seems terrible to me that Americans can no longer speak to or be seen by their government. Has it become their master, not their servant? Can it not listen to their humble and reasonable pleas? This experience may in one sense be a small matter but I am sure it is symptomatic—among other things—of a sort of fear on the part of officials to listen to what in their hearts they feel is right but on which they cannot act without breaking with old patterns of thought. At any rate, the experience has strengthened in me the conviction that we must, at whatever cost, find ways to make our witness and protest heard.

I am going because, as Shakespeare said, "Action is eloquence." Without some such direct action, ordinary citizens lack the power any longer to be seen or heard by their government.

I am going because it is time to *do something* about peace, not just *talk* about peace.

I am going because, like all men, in my heart I know that *all* nuclear explosions are monstrous, evil, unworthy of human beings.

I am going because war is no longer a feudal jousting match; it is an unthinkable catastrophe for all men.

I am going because it is now the little children, and, most of all, the as yet unborn who are the front line troops. It is my duty to stand between them and this horrible danger.

I am going because it is cowardly and degrading for me to stand by any longer, to consent, and thus to collaborate in atrocities.

I am going because I cannot say that the end justifies the means. A Quaker, William Penn, said, "A good end cannot sanctify evil means; nor must we ever do evil that good many come of it." A Communist, Milovan Djilas, says, "As soon as means which would ensure an end are shown to be evil, the end will show itself as unrealizable."

I am going because, as Gandhi said, "God sits in the man opposite me; therefore to injure him is to injure God himself."

I am going to witness to the deep inward truth we all know, "Force can subdue, but love gains."

I am going because however mistaken, unrighteous, and unrepentant governments may seem, I still believe all men are really good at heart, and that my act will speak to them.

I am going in the hope of helping change the hearts and minds of men in government. If necessary I am willing to give my life to help change a policy of fear, force, and destruction to one of trust, kindness, and help.

I am going in order to say, "Quit this waste, this arms race. Turn instead to a disarmament race. Stop competing for evil, compete for good."

I am going because I have to—if I am to call myself a human being.

When you see something horrible happening, your instinct is to do something about it. You can freeze in fearful apathy or you can even talk yourself into saying that it isn't horrible. I can't do that. I have to act. This is too horrible. We know it. Let's all act.

CIVIL DISOBEDIENCE AND THE THREAT OF NUCLEAR WARFARE

Bertrand Russell

The Committee of 100, as your readers are aware, calls for non-violent civil disobedience on a large scale as a means of inducing the British Government (and others, we hope, in due course) to abandon nuclear weapons and the protection that they are supposed to afford. Many critics have objected that civil disobedience is immoral, at any rate where the government is democratic. It is my purpose to combat this view, not in general, but in the case of non-violent civil disobedience on behalf of certain aims advocated by the Committee of 100.

It is necessary to begin with some abstract principles of ethics. There are, broadly speaking, two types of ethical theory. One of these, which is exemplified in the Decalogue, lays down rules of conduct which are supposed to hold in all cases, regardless of the effects of obeying them. The other theory, while admitting that some rules of conduct are valid in a very great majority of cases, is prepared to consider the consequences of actions and to permit breaches of the rules where the consequences of obeying the rules are obviously undesirable. In practice, most people adopt the second point of view, and only appeal to the first in controversies with opponents.

Reprinted by permission of the author and publisher from Clara Urquhart, ed., *A Matter of Life* (London: Jonathan Cape, 1963), pp. 189–96.

Let us take a few examples. Suppose a physically powerful man, suffering from hydrophobia, was about to bite your children, and the only way of preventing him was to kill him. I think very few people would think you unjustified in adopting this method of saving your children's lives. Those who thought you justified would not deny that the prohibition of murder is *almost* always right. Probably they would go on to say that this particular sort of killing should not be called "murder." They would define "murder" as "unjustifiable homicide." In that case, the precept that murder is wrong becomes a tautology, but the ethical question remains: "What sort of killing is to be labelled as murder?" Or take, again, the commandment not to steal. Almost everybody would agree that in an immense majority of cases it is right to obey this commandment. But suppose you were a refugee, fleeing with your family from persecution, and you could not obtain food except by stealing. Most people would agree that you would be justified in stealing. The only exceptions would be those who approved of the tyranny from which you were trying to escape.

There have been many cases in history where the issue was not so clear. In the time of Pope Gregory VI, simony was rife in the Church. Pope Gregory VI, by means of simony, became Pope and did so in order to abolish simony. In this he was largely successful, and final success was achieved by his disciple and admirer, Pope Gregory VII, who was one of the most illustrious of Popes. I will not express an opinion on the conduct of Gregory VI, which has remained a controversial issue down to the present day.

The only rule, in all such doubtful cases, is to consider the consequences of the action in question. We must include among these consequences the bad effect of weakening respect for a rule which is usually right. But, even when this is taken into account, there will be cases where even the most generally acceptable rule of conduct should be broken.

So much for general theory. I will come now one step nearer to the moral problem with which we are concerned.

What is to be said about a rule enjoining respect for law? Let us first consider the arguments in favour of such a rule. Without law, a civilized community is impossible. Where there is general disrespect for the law, all kinds of evil consequences are sure to follow. A notable example was the failure of prohibition in America. In this case it became obvious that the only cure was a change in the law, since it was impossible to obtain general respect for the law as it stood. This view prevailed, in spite of the fact that those who broke the law were not actuated by what are called conscientious motives. This case made it obvious that respect for the law has two sides. If there is to be respect for the law, the law must be generally considered to be worthy of respect.

The main argument in favour of respect for law is that, in disputes between two parties, it substitutes a neutral authority for private bias which would be likely in the absence of law. The force which the law can exert is, in most such cases, irresistible, and therefore only has to be invoked in the case of a minority of reckless criminals. The net result is a community in which most people are peaceful. These reasons for the reign of law are admitted in the great majority of cases, except by anarchists. I have no wish to dispute their validity save in exceptional circumstances.

There is one very large class of cases in which the law does not have the merit of being impartial as between the disputants. This is when one of the disputants is the state. The state makes the laws and, unless there is a very vigilant public opinion in defence of justifiable liberties, the state will make the law such as suits its own convenience, which may not be what is for the public good. In the Nuremberg trials war criminals were condemned for obeying the orders of the state, though their condemnation was only possible after the state in question had suffered military defeat. But it is noteworthy that the powers which defeated Germany all agreed that failure to practise civil disobedience may deserve punishment.

Those who find fault with the particular form of civil disobedience which I am concerned to justify maintain that breaches of the law, though they may be justified under a despotic régime, can never be justified in a democracy. I cannot see any validity whatever in this contention. There are many ways in which nominally democratic governments can fail to carry out principles which friends of democracy should respect. Take, for example, the case of Ireland before it achieved independence. Formally, the Irish had the same democratic rights as the British. They could send representatives to Westminster and plead their case by all the received democratic processes. But, in spite of this, they were in a minority which, if they had confined themselves to legal methods, would have been permanent. They won their independence by breaking the law. If they had not broken it, they could not have won.

There are many other ways in which governments, which are nominally democratic, fail to be so. A great many questions are so complex that only a few experts can understand them. When the bank rate is raised or lowered, what proportion of the electorate can judge whether it was right to do so? And, if anyone who has no official position criticizes the action of the Bank of England, the only witnesses who can give authoritative evidence will be men responsible for what has been done, or closely connected with those who are responsible. Not only in questions of finance, but still more in military and diplomatic questions, there is in every civilized state a well-developed technique of concealment. If the government wishes some fact to remain unknown, almost all major organs of publicity will assist in concealment. In such cases it often happens that the truth can only be made known, if at all, by persistant and self-sacrificing efforts involving obloquy and perhaps disgrace. Sometimes, if the matter rouses sufficient passion, the truth comes to be known in the end. This happened, for example, in the Dreyfus Case. But where the matter is less sensational the ordinary voter is likely to be left permanently in ignorance.

For such reasons democracy, though much less liable to abuses than dictatorship, is by no means immune to abuses of power by those in authority or by corrupt interests. If valuable liberties are to be preserved there have to be people willing to criticize authority and even, on occasion, to disobey it.

Those who most loudly proclaim their respect for law are in many cases quite unwilling that the domain of law should extend to international relations. In relations between states the only law is still the law of the jungle. What decides a dispute is the question of which side can cause the greatest number of deaths to the other side. Those who do not accept this criterion are apt to be accused of lack of patriotism. This makes it impossible not to suspect that law is only valued where it already exists, and not as an alternative to war.

This brings me at last to the particular form of non-violent civil disobedience which is advocated and practised by the Committee of 100. Those who study nuclear weapons and the probable course of nuclear war are divided into two classes. There are, on the one hand, people employed by governments, and, on the other hand, unofficial people who are actuated by a realization of the dangers and catastrophes which are probable if governmental policies remain unchanged. There are a number of questions in dispute. I will mention a few of them. What is the likelihood of a nuclear war by accident? What is to be feared from fall-out? What proportion of the population is likely to survive an all-out nuclear war? On every one of these questions independent students find that official apologists and policy-makers give answers which, to an unbiased inquirer, appear grossly and murderously misleading. To make known to the general population what independent inquirers believe to be the true answers to those questions is a very difficult matter. Where the truth is difficult to ascertain there is a natural inclination to believe what official authorities assert. This is especially the case when what they assert enables people to dismiss uneasiness as needlessly alarmist. The major organs of publicity feel themselves part of the Establishment and are very reluctant to take a course which the Establishment will frown on. Long and frustrating experience has proved, to those among us who have endeavoured to make unpleasant facts known, that orthodox methods, alone, are insufficient. By means of civil disobedience a certain kind of publicity becomes possible. What we do is reported, though as far as possible our reasons for what we do are not mentioned. The policy of suppressing our reasons, however, has only very partial success. Many people are roused to inquire into questions which they had been willing to ignore. Many people, especially among the young, come to share the opinion that governments, by means of lies and evasions, are luring whole populations to destruction. It seems not unlikely that, in the end, an irresistible popular movement of protest will compel governments to allow their subjects to continue to exist. On the basis of long experience, we are convinced that this object cannot be achieved by law-abiding methods alone. Speaking for myself, I regard this as the most important reason for adopting civil disobedience.

Another reason for endeavouring to spread knowledge about nuclear warfare is the extreme imminence of the peril. Legally legitimate methods of spreading this knowledge have been proved to be very slow, and we believe, on the basis of experience, that only such methods as we have adopted can spread the necessary knowledge before it is too late. As things stand, a nuclear war, probably by accident, may occur at any moment. Each day that passes without such a war is a matter of luck, and it cannot be expected that luck will hold indefinitely. Any day, at any hour, the whole population of Britain may perish. Strategists and negotiators play a leisurely game in which procrastination is one of the received methods. It is urgent that the populations of East and West compel both sides to realize that the time at their disposal is limited and that, while present methods continue, disaster is possible at any moment, and almost certain sooner or later.

There is, however, still another reason for employing non-violent civil disobedience which is very powerful and deserves respect. The programmes of mass extermination, upon which vast sums of public money are being spent, must fill every humane person with feelings of utter horror. The West is told that communism is wicked; the East is told that capitalism is wicked. Both sides deduce that the nations which favour either are to be "obliterated," to use Khrushchev's word. I do not doubt that each side is right in thinking that a nuclear war would destroy the other side's "ism," but each side is hopelessly mistaken if it thinks that a nuclear war could establish its own "ism." Nothing that either East or West desires can result from a nuclear war. If both sides could be made to understand this, it would become possible for both sides to realize that there can be no victory for either, but only total defeat for both. If this entirely obvious fact were publicly admitted in a joint statement by Krushchev and Kennedy, a compromise method of coexistence could be negotiated giving each side quite obviously a thousand times more of what it wants than could be achieved by war. The utter uselessness of war, in the present age, is completely obvious except to those who have been so schooled in past traditions that they are incapable of thinking in terms of the world that we now have to live in. Those of us who protest against nuclear weapons and nuclear war cannot acquiesce in a world in which each man owes such freedom as remains to him to the capacity of his government to cause many hundreds of millions of deaths by pressing a button. This is to us an abomination, and rather than seem to acquiesce in it we are willing, if necessary, to become outcasts and to suffer whatever obloquy and whatever hardship may be involved in standing aloof from the governmental framework. This thing is a horror. It is something in the shadow of which nothing good can flourish. I am convinced that, on purely political grounds, our reasoned case is unanswerable. But, beyond all political considerations, there is the determination not to be an accomplice in the worst crime that human beings have ever contemplated. We are shocked, and rightly shocked, by Hitler's extermination of six million Jews, but the governments of East and West calmly contemplate the possibility of a massacre at least a hundred times greater than that perpetrated by Hitler. Those who realize the magnitude of this horror cannot even *seem* to acquiesce in the policies from which it springs. It is this feeling, much more than any political calculation, that gives fervour and strength to our movement, a kind of fervour and a kind of strength which, if a nuclear war does not soon end us all, will make our movement grow until it reaches the point where governments can no longer refuse to let mankind survive.

DECLARATION OF CONSCIENCE AGAINST THE WAR IN VIETNAM

Because the use of the military resources of the United States in Vietnam and elsewhere suppresses the aspirations of the people for political independence and economic freedom;

Because inhuman torture and senseless killing are being carried out by forces armed, uniformed, trained, and financed by the United States;

Because we believe that all peoples of the earth, including both Americans and non-Americans, have an inalienable right to life, liberty, and the peaceful pursuit of happiness in their own way; and

Because we think that positive steps must be taken to put an end to the threat of nuclear catastrophe and death by chemical or biological warfare, whether these result from accident or escalation—

We hereby declare our conscientious refusal to cooperate with the United States government in the prosecution of the war in Vietnam.

This statement was sponsored originally in 1965 by the following organizations, all of New York City: Catholic Worker, Committee for Nonviolent Action, Student Peace Union, War Resisters League.

We encourage those who can conscientiously do so to refuse to serve in the armed forces and to ask for discharge if they are already in.

Those of us who are subject to the draft ourselves declare our own intention to refuse to serve.

We urge others to refuse and refuse ourselves to take part in the manufacture or transportation of military equipment, or to work in the fields of military research and weapons development.

We shall encourage the development of other nonviolent acts, including acts which involve civil disobedience, in order to stop the flow of American soldiers and munitions to Vietnam.

NOTE: *Signing or distributing this Declaration of Conscience might be construed as a violation of the Universal Military Training and Service Act, which prohibits advising persons facing the draft to refuse service. Penalties of up to 5 years imprisonment, and/or a fine of $5,000 are provided. While prosecutions under this provision of the law almost never occur, persons signing or distributing this declaration should face the possibility of serious consequences.*

A CALL TO RESIST
ILLEGITIMATE AUTHORITY

To the young men of America, to the whole of the American people, and to all men of good will everywhere:

1. An ever growing number of young American men are finding that the American war in Vietnam so outrages their deepest moral and religious sense that they cannot contribute to it in any way. We share their moral outrage.

2. We further believe that the war is unconstitutional and illegal. Congress has not declared a war as required by the Constitution. Moreover, under the Constitution, treaties signed by the President and ratified by the Senate have the same force as the Constitution itself. The Charter of the United Nations is such a treaty. The Charter specifically obligates the United States to refrain from force or the threat of force in international relations. It requires member states to exhaust every peaceful means of settling disputes and to submit disputes which cannot be settled peacefully to the Security Council. The United States has systematically violated all of these Charter provisions for thirteen years.

This statement was originally circulated in August, 1967, accompanied by a list of some one hundred and fifty sponsors. The signers, now in the thousands, are organized under the name of "Resist," with headquarters in Cambridge, Massachusetts.

3. Moreover, this war violates international agreements, treaties and principles of law which the United States Government has solemnly endorsed. The combat role of the United States troops in Vietnam violates the Geneva Accords of 1954 which our government pledged to support but has since subverted. The destruction of rice, crops, and livestock; the burning and bulldozing of entire villages consisting exclusively of civilian structures; the interning of civilian non-combatants in concentration camps; the summary executions of civilians in captured villages who could not produce satisfactory evidence of their loyalties or did not wish to be removed to concentration camps; the slaughter of peasants who dared to stand up in their fields and shake their fists at American helicopters—these are all actions of the kind which the United States and the other victorious powers of World War II declared to be crimes against humanity for which individuals were to be held personally responsible even when acting under the orders of their governments and for which Germans were sentenced at Nuremberg to long prison terms and death. The prohibition of such acts as war crimes was incorporated in treaty law by the Geneva Conventions of 1949, ratified by the United States. These are commitments to other countries and to Mankind, and they would claim our allegiance even if Congress should declare war.

4. We also believe it is an unconstitutional denial of religious liberty and equal protection of the laws to withhold draft exemption from men whose religious or profound philosophical beliefs are opposed to what in the Western religious tradition have been long known as unjust wars.

5. Therefore, we believe on all these grounds that every free man has a legal right and a moral duty to exert every effort to end this war, to avoid collusion with it, and to encourage others to do the same. Young men in the armed forces or threatened with the draft face the most excruciating choices. For them various forms of resistance risk separation from their families and their country, destruction of their careers, loss of their freedom, and loss of their lives. Each most choose the course of resistance dictated by his conscience and circumstances. Among those already in the armed forces some are refusing to obey specific illegal and immoral orders,

some are attempting to educate their fellow servicemen on the murderous and barbarous nature of the war, some are absenting themselves without official leave. Among those not in the armed forces some are applying for status as conscientious objectors to American aggression in Vietnam, some are refusing to be inducted. Among both groups some are resisting openly and paying a heavy penalty, some are organizing more resistance within the United States and some have sought sanctuary in other countries.

6. We believe that each of these forms of resistance against illegitimate authority is courageous and justified. Many of us believe that open resistance to the war and the draft is the course of action most likely to strengthen the moral resolve with which all of us can oppose the war and most likely to bring an end to the war.

7. We will continue to lend our support to those who undertake resistance to this war. We will raise funds to organize draft resistance unions, to supply legal defense and bail, to support families and otherwise aid resistance to the war in whatever ways may seem appropriate.

8. We firmly believe that our statement is the sort of speech that under the First Amendment must be free, and that the actions we will undertake are as legal as is the war resistance of the young men themselves. But we recognize that the courts may find otherwise, and that if so we might all be liable to prosecution and severe punishment.* In any case, we feel that we cannot shrink from fulfilling our responsibilities to the youth whom many of us teach, to the country whose freedom we cherish, and to the ancient traditions of religion and philosophy which we strive to preserve in this generation.

9. We call upon all men of good will to join us in this confrontation with immoral authority. Especially we call upon the universities to fulfill their mission of enlightenment and religious organizations to honor their heritage of brotherhood. Now is the time to resist.

*[In some later printings, this sentence was omitted. Ed.]

LAW, SPEECH, AND DISOBEDIENCE

Carl Cohen

When the elected leaders of a democracy behave unwisely or immorally, it is not only a citizen's right but his duty, owed to the community as a whole, to protest that conduct vigorously and publicly. Such protest may be unjustified or mistaken, but a citizen can be expected to inform himself only as fully as he can, and then act according to his best knowledge and belief. That such protest in general is proper and healthy most democrats are certain to agree.

But *how far* does the right to protest extend? To what limits should the courts protect conduct whose aim is clearly that of protesting established law or policy, or carrying on political debate? No questions are more serious than these in a democracy, and none more difficult to answer universally or unambiguously. The issues cannot be wholly avoided, however, and are now being pressed again in the Michigan courts.

It often happens, in the law, that matters of the highest consequence are argued and decided upon in connection with fact situations of relatively minor importance. A snail found in a bottle of ginger beer, a single student obliged to hear a prayer he does not share—such apparently small matters sometimes lead to land-

Reprinted, by permission of the author and publisher, from "Law, Speech and Disobedience," *The Nation* (March 28, 1966), pp. 357-62.

mark decisions in the courts. That, conceivably, may be the case with the conduct of those who, on October 15, 1965, refused to leave the Selective Service Office in Ann Arbor, Michigan, as a protest against United States policy in Vietnam. The facts surrounding this now notorious instance of civil disobedience are not in dispute. Some thirty-nine persons, mostly University of Michigan students, did "sit in" there and then, were taken from the office an hour or two after its normal time of closing, and did clearly understand that their act was a violation of the Michigan trespass statute. One of the most unhappy ramifications of the incident was the subsequent loss, by some dozen of the demonstrators, of their student draft deferments, on the alleged ground that they had impeded the operation of the Selective Service System. Much may be said about that (see: "Punishment by Conscription," *The Nation*, December 27, 1965), but the punitive use of the draft laws does not bear on the central issue now being raised.

That issue concerns the guilt of the demonstrators. Normally, the legal guilt of one who engages in civil disobedience is never seriously doubted. He disobeys the law openly to exhibit his deep concern on some issue, enters a guilty plea or one of no contest, and accepts his punishment publicly as further proof of his concern and as a further effort to focus public attention upon the injustice he protests. (See: "The Ethics of Civil Disobedience," *The Nation*, March 16, 1964.) Civil disobedience of this sort, again, may be foolish or unjustified, but normally it is practiced only by those with deep convictions, genuine public spirit and considerable courage.

The episode becomes tangled, however, when disobedient demonstrators claim—as is now being claimed by some twenty-nine of those at Ann Arbor—that *because their protest is clearly a form of political speech, it is protected—even though it is a deliberate violation of the state law—by the Constitution of the United States.* This is a strong and interesting claim, a matter of the highest interest to anyone concerned about the health and success of a democratic society, and I propose to examine it carefully.

I shall present the major arguments in support of this claim as plausibly and effectively as I can, at each step seeking to determine how well the argument stands up on examination. Before proceeding, I want to emphasize the fact that in this area no principles can be applied with absolute universality, and no set of facts can be interpreted in one and only one way. And I want to extol—what I know personally—the deep sincerity and moral goodness of the protesters in this case. By ordinary standards they are better persons than most of the rest of us.

Their arguments fall into two major divisions, as follows: (*1*) That this case of disobedient protest is a form of speech protected by the First Amendment to the Constitution; and (*2*) that because the object of their protest was the illegal character of the United States' actions in Vietnam, their individual conduct in that protest is protected by the principles of the Nuremberg Judgments. I take these arguments in turn.

(*1*) Speech, after all, is not restricted to verbal activity. It takes many forms, oral, written, or other; its essential element is the communication of an idea. Nonverbal acts often accomplish, as they are intended to accomplish, such communication. The classical example is that of picketing in a labor dispute, long held to be a violation of state law but in 1940 declared worthy of protection by the Supreme Court in *Thornhill* v. *Alabama.* Picketing was there recognized as a nonverbal act protected by the First Amendment, which reads, "Congress shall make no law . . . abridging the freedom of speech." Similarly, in very recent cases involving sit-ins and other forms of public protest against racial discrimination, convictions for the alleged violation of state trespass and other statutes have been repeatedly reversed. The Supreme Court has not upheld the conviction of any of the protesters in these civil rights cases.

Moreover, the protection of free communication and criticism is of such fundamental importance that conduct which falls under this category will be protected even when it may appear to fall also under categories otherwise illegal. So, for example, what might otherwise be thought libel will sometimes be protected by constitutional guarantees. There is, the Supreme Court said in 1964, "a profound national commitment to the principle that debate on public issues should be uninhibited, robust, and wide open, and that it may well include vehement, caustic, and sometimes unpleasantly sharp attacks on government and public officials." *(N. Y. Times Co.* v. *Sullivan.)* So, the Court went on, apparently libelous attacks on public figures will be protected. "Like insurrection, contempt, advocacy of unlawful acts, breach of the peace, obscenity, solicitation of legal business and the various other formulae . . . that have been challenged in this Court, libel cannot claim talismanic immunity from constitutional limitations." Why then should trespass not be treated likewise? Calling an act a trespass does not remove it automatically from First Amendment protection. The key question (according to this argument) is whether a given, deliberate trespass is a form of speech; if so, it is entitled to the same constitutional protection.

Of course real interests are safeguarded by state trespass laws, and these are, on the whole, good laws. But such interests must be balanced against the interests of the entire community in maximally free speech. And the Supreme Court has repeatedly recognized the need, in similar situations, to balance the one set of interests against the other. Such a balancing in this case (the argument continues) would surely result in the exculpation of a minor trespass, even if deliberate, providing it were carefully supervised and clearly intended as a political protest. It must be remembered that civil disobedience is normally performed under the public eye, that it carefully minimizes harm and inconvenience, and that (as in Ann Arbor) procedural details for the arrest are worked out with officials in advance. The relatively minute injury to the interests of the owner or occupants of the building clearly ought to be sacrificed as a matter of good public policy, when balanced against the interest of the entire community in having so grave a matter as war and peace argued effectively and dramatically. The right of peaceful, even if disobedient, protest must prevail. (For a further discussion of "balancing" and allied issues, see "Justice Black at 80: The Common Sense of Freedom," by Norman Redlich; *The Nation*, March 21, 1966.)

The defendants in this case do not maintain that the trespass law is invalid. Nor do they deny the facts of their technical violation of it. They argue that such a law, even a good law, cannot be used to suppress a "sit-in" protest under these special circumstances.

This is an appealing argument. Those of us who are eager to protect and extend the freedom of speech and political debate will naturally be inclined to view it with sympathy—a sympathy reinforced by our confidence in the good character and high purpose of the defendants. But is the argument sound? Reluctantly, I must say that I think it is not and that for strategic as well as jurisprudential reasons it is not the wisest position for disobedient demonstrators to adopt.

First on jurisprudential grounds. The central point, and one the defense attempts to gloss over, is that there are very great and even crucial *dis*analogies between cases of the present sort (deliberate disobedience to good trespass laws) and earlier cases before the Supreme Court protecting some demonstrators convicted of minor infractions of state law. These disanalogies are of two kinds:

(*a*) The first and most obvious is the disanalogy between violating a perfectly satisfactory statute, and violating an immoral and unconstitutional statute. The deliberate violation of segregation laws will be protected—because the act itself, whether it be called trespass or whatever, defies only a statute which should never have been in force, and which is rightly struck down when contested in the higher court. Such acts will be protected not as the result of a delicate balancing of interests but because, in a deep sense, the conduct never was wrongful. The Supreme Court reversals of the conviction of anti-segregation demonstrators provide no reasonable ground, then, for the protection of conduct which deliberately violates laws that are generally agreed to be proper and in the interests of the whole community.

(*b*) The second disanalogy is less obvious, but vitally important, and indeed the key to the present controversy. The defense argues that even good laws—libel laws, or breach of the peace laws, or anti-littering laws—will not suffice to condemn conduct in situations where the interests served by those laws are outweighed by the interests the First Amendment protects. But what is it in those situations (e.g., *N. Y. Times Co.* v. *Sullivan*, a clear and recent case) that demands a balancing? It is the almost inevitable conflict of certain *kinds* of interests. A community is well served by laws protecting its members from false and libelous defamation, but the community is also served by protecting uninhibited debate. The character and conduct of persons must be protected from vicious attack, and yet must often be kept open to attack. Conflict of real community interests arises unavoidably; the balancing of "libel" against "the freedom of speech" *must* sometimes be undertaken.

Normally, and rightly, the Court gives greater weight to freedom of speech. Similarly, the reasonable effort to keep the public peace comes naturally into conflict with freedom of speech when a speaker has an inflammatory manner and controversial things to say. In such instances the exercise of free speech *necessarily* offends against an otherwise valid law. In the event of such unavoidable conflict the courts must effect a balancing, and again unrestricted debate should and probably will prevail.

The enforcement of reasonable trespass laws (or other similar statutes), however, does not create any natural or unavoidable conflict with First Amendment freedoms. Protecting the interests of the owners or occupants of property normally has nothing whatever to do with the freedom to speak or protest. The courts will balance interests when they must, but will rightly refrain from doing so until they must. The defendants in the present case argue that their protest, being clearly a form of political speech, obliges the courts to undertake a balancing process with minor property interests on one side and the freedom to protest on the other. But the courts are likely to continue to deny that they have such an obligation. For to undertake such a balancing is to admit, in effect, that the defendants, by their deliberate choice in violating a trespass law, have the right to select which interests will be balanced against freedom of speech. If a deliberate trespass violation must be balanced against the need to preserve free speech, then the deliberate violation of any statute, minor or major, if intended as a protest, will have also to be balanced, and may claim the same protection. To allow the defendants' argument, in short, is to allow a First Amendment defense for any statute violation whatever, if it could reasonably be argued that the violation was intended as some form of protest. But this would carry the extension of First Amendment freedoms to the point of absurdity, giving that amendment as a protective weapon to whoever might wish to stage an illegal protest, whatever its form. A racial bigot protesting civil rights laws—or *any* person protesting *any* laws or policies he happens to think unjust—might then deliberately break the laws he thinks wrongful, or some other unrelated laws, and then go on to argue that his unlawful conduct is protected by the First Amendment. Clearly, that would be pushing the right to protected protest too far. The principle that the First Amendment protects whatever is claimed to be speech, whether normally so considered or not, is too strong to be reasonably adopted.

This is not to say that where the interests of free speech conflict with property interests of lesser importance the latter should prevail, but that unless there is a natural or normal conflict of interests the balancing process need not be undertaken. That, in effect, has been the decision of the lower courts in this case to date; they have held the defendants' contentions concerning their motives in trespassing as irrelevant and immaterial in determining their guilt on the specific charge of trespass. They have been found guilty on their first appeal (and given extraordinary sentences; ranging from fifteen to twenty days in jail, plus fines and court costs!) and now plan, with the guidance of attorney Ernest Goodman of Detroit, to take their case to the Michigan Court of Appeals.

Two further comments on this argument. First, note that the kinds of conduct which come naturally or normally into conflict with vigorous and open public debate cannot be antecedently clear beyond doubt, or permanently laid down. Conceivably, deliberate peaceful trespass in federal offices and buildings could become so common and normal a form of protest that its regular protection as a form of speech would seem less farfetched than it does at present. Until such a development, however, the balancing being requested is likely to be refused. Second, the defendants in this case might reply to my criticism by arguing that they are requesting a balancing not of kinds of interests but of actual interests in one specific fact situation. This is reasonable from their perspective, knowing as they do how genuine was their protest. But they cannot deny (nor would they want to if their case is to have an impact on future decisions) that to allow such a balancing in this case would be to set an important precedent in principle: that an individual, after choosing the form of deliberate disobedience he intends to employ as a form of speech, may seek protection for that disobedient conduct under the First Amendment. Any court would find it very difficult to allow such a position.

Put another way, my objection calls into question the premise upon which the appeal of these demonstrators is based: the claim that their deliberate disobedience was *essentially* an act of speech. Speech may indeed take many forms, and these demonstrators did wish, above all, to communicate an important idea. But whatever they may have wished to accomplish, their act had a clear outward form which cannot be denied. Human acts do not fall neatly into categories labeled "speech" and "non-speech," but are often of mixed character. Now, the deliberate violation of a trespass statute (or the like)—whatever the motivation of the violators —cannot reasonably be treated as one of the forms of speech deserving constitutional protection. The insistence that their act, regardless of its clear and specific nature, was at bottom speech (because of their aims) expands the notion of "speech" so extraordinarily that virtually nothing is left which it may not then be claimed to encompass. Such generalized protection was not the original intention, nor is it a proper present function, of the First Amendment to our Constitution.

Moreover, the result of this distorted expansion is likely to be the very opposite of these demonstrators' ultimate objective; it will weaken rather than strengthen First Amendment protections. For when the First Amendment provision that the freedom of speech is not to be abridged may be resorted to as a defense for virtually any kind of act, the need to qualify the protection it affords will be undeniable. The consequent efforts to define the limits of speech are likely to produce principles which can later be used to exclude from First Amendment protection marginal but effective varieties of speech now safeguarded. As long as "speech" be reasonably construed, the rigor of the First Amendment wording is clear and incontrovertible: "Congress shall make no law" which abridges its freedom. So soon as the concept of speech is unreasonably expanded, the infringements we all dread may enter through the back door, not by "abridging" the freedom of speech, but by carefully prescribing what "speech" may encompass. That would be a most unfortunate outcome. But if the present efforts to enlarge the notion of speech (to include even deliberate disobedience to law on some occasions) is unreasonable, as I believe, that may be the outcome to which such efforts eventually lead.

(2) Justification has also been sought in the Nuremberg Judgments. The principles of the Nuremberg convictions (the disobedient demonstrators argue) justify and protect even conduct in deliberate violation of state law, when that conduct is the protest of a citizen against the illegal acts of his government. For those,

like themselves, who deeply believe the present United States involvement in Vietnam to be a crass violation of treaties we have signed and international laws we profess to uphold, this argument appears quite plausible at first. The Nuremberg Tribunal, judging and punishing crimes against international law and against humanity—with vigorous American support—held clearly that "international law imposes duties and liabilities upon individuals as well as upon states," and that war crimes are "committed by men, not by abstract entities, and only by punishing individuals who commit such crimes can the provisions of international law be enforced." The United States Supreme Court (in another connection) has also shown that it has applied from its earliest history "the law of war as including that part of the law of nations which prescribes for the conduct of war the status, rights, and duties of . . . nations as well as . . . individuals." *(Ex Parte Quirin, 1942.)* And this American decision was cited by the International Military Tribunal at Nuremberg as authority for the proposition that individuals as well as states may be held responsible for the commission of international crimes. But if individuals are so responsible for their nation's conduct, individuals must act to repudiate that conduct (when illegal or immoral) if it is possible for them to do so.

The entire "Nuremberg argument," then, can be put concisely as follows: The conduct of these disobedient demonstrators did admittedly constitute a violation of a state statute. But the Judgments of Nuremberg, which our nation supported, were clear: ". . . the very essence [of the principles established here] is that individuals have duties which transcend the national obligation of obedience." In protesting against United States conduct in Vietnam these demonstrators claimed to be fulfilling those higher duties.

Many will find this defense appealing. A closer examination of it will show, however, that it does not correctly apply to cases of ordinary civil disobedience like the one at hand. There are a number of reasons for this, some of which are overwhelming.

First. That the principles of the Nuremberg Judgments have authority in state or federal courts is altogether very doubtful. Some jurisprudents reject them out of hand as having no legitimate authority whatever. But even if given support and respect it is hard to see how they can be made consistently effective within a national legal system.

Second. The right to protection under the Nuremberg principles (assuming that they do have authority) supposes that the national conduct repudiated *is* illegal and immoral. The defendants in this case (as well as some distinguished national leaders) are prepared to maintain that vigorously, but it remains to be proved to a court of proper jurisdiction. The demonstrators and their supporters may indeed believe our international involvement in Vietnam is criminal, both in substance and in manner, but most Americans and most American courts (rightly or wrongly) are not likely to accept their argument and are therefore not likely to allow that the Nuremberg principles apply in this case, even if they do allow their application as a theoretical possibility in some cases.

Third. One grave peculiarity of the "Nuremberg argument" is that any court in a national legal system which holds that its nation is acting illegally and immorally attacks thereby the legal and moral foundation of its own authority, of the court itself. This self-reflexive character of the judgment being asked for renders it a virtual impossibility for a national or state court to hold that the Nuremberg argument applies in any given case. To do so is to announce that the court is governed by a law other than, and in conflict with, the law the court is sworn to enforce. Of course one may insist that, as a purely moral matter, the court does have such an obligation to a higher law. But one must then seek ultimate protection under that higher law (against the state law) in a higher court—an international court perhaps, or the court of heaven. And these are the courts in which the civil disobedient may find, if ever, ultimate justification under Nuremberg principles.

These three considerations weigh against the technical merit of the appeal, but they do not weigh against the defendants' strategy in appealing or the moral basis of their appeal, and therefore do not dismay them at all. They believe that the Nuremberg Judgments *do* have legitimacy, and that present American conduct in Vietnam *is* immoral, and they are prepared to offer proof in defense of these claims.

Regarding any difficulty there may be in applying the Nuremberg principles in American courts, they maintain that a method *ought* to be worked out whereby these principles *can* be applied within our judicial system. For if we take these principles seriously enough to apply them to others, with ensuing capital punishment, we are morally obliged to make them applicable—at least in principle—to ourselves. One of the chief aims of their present appeal is to begin the process of legal adjustment which will make this internal application of the Nuremberg principles feasible. Ours is a legal system, they maintain, healthy enough and resilient enough to adopt and incorporate new principles governing national conduct, where the moral content of those principles is clear and accepted, and the principles themselves are badly needed to assist in the guidance of our nation's policies within the community of nations.

Fourth. There is, however, a most important reason why the Nuremberg principles could not apply in the present case (or cases like it), and this reason speaks directly against the substance of the protesters' defense. The point is that the Nuremberg Judgments could not reasonably be held to protect the kind of disobedient conduct of which these demonstrators are accused. Even supposing the Nuremberg Judgments could and should bind the state courts, they could do so only under circumstances in which the alternatives of obedience or disobedience forced a moral choice upon the defendants. If obedience to a statute would somehow have involved them in the alleged immoral activity, or would have clearly indicated their approval or acceptance of that immoral activity, they might plausibly have claimed that, forced to choose, they elected to disobey the state statute in obedience to a higher moral law. These were not the circumstances of the present case, however, nor are such circumstances likely to accompany this kind of civil disobedience.

It is important to guard against an easy but unfair criticism of the demonstrators in this connection. One cannot deny the applicability of the Nuremberg principles merely because the disobedients had not been specifically ordered to commit a criminal act. Had it been such an order they disobeyed, the Nuremberg argument would indeed seem applicable—for when the German war criminals defended their actions by showing that they had only been following orders, that defense was rejected on the ground that they had a higher obligation to disobey immoral orders. But the fact that these demonstrators had not faced specific immoral orders is not, as they rightly argued, the crucial issue. For the Nuremberg Judgments made it very plain that "the true test . . . is not the existence of the order, but whether moral choice was in fact possible." In this case, the defendants argue, they had a moral choice, and accordingly they felt obliged to make their option clear in this limited but dramatic way.

Nevertheless, the Nuremberg argument does not apply in cases of this sort. The key question is whether obedience, rather than disobedience, under the given circumstances, would in any way have implied participation or approval of the national conduct believed by the demonstrators to be immoral. Clearly it would not; obedience to trespass laws, and the like, indicates neither approval nor disapproval, tacit or explicit, of the nation's foreign policy. The defendants *chose* to exhibit their intense disapproval by such deliberate disobedience. But the Nuremberg principles, even if authoritative, cannot reasonably be extended to excuse any deliberate disobedience which the demonstrator selects as his instrument of protest. Only in circumstances where the alternatives of obedience or disobedience somehow compel the moral choice between participation and nonparticipation (or approval and disapproval) might the Nuremberg principles conceivably protect deliberate disobedient conduct. But where civil disobedience is indirect—i.e., where the law deliberately broken is clearly distinct from the law or policy being protested—it almost invariably takes place in a situation specially and carefully selected or created by the demonstrator. In such situations the Nuremberg principles—quite apart from all other difficulties in their application—could not govern.

Finally, there are important strategic reasons for not insisting that deliberate disobedience be protected either by constitutional guarantees, or by principles of international law. For the overriding aim of those who engage in civil disobedience is to make an effective protest to open grave issues to public debate, to register deep concern and vehement objection. To achieve this aim civil disobedience may prove reasonably effective when the depth of concern and commitment of the disobedients is beyond doubt or dispute. A willingness to accept public punishment for a deliberate public violation strongly reinforces the general belief in that commitment. But the effort to have the illegal conduct excused *because* it is a protest sharply reduces its effectiveness *as* a protest. If, after having disobeyed the law to make a dramatic self-sacrifice, one then seeks to avoid the penalty which makes it a sacrifice, the depth and completeness of one's commitment is likely to be questioned. Civil disobedience can be a powerful moral gesture; from the point of view of one who employs this tactic one very strong reason for not seeking legal immunity is that such a move would be self-defeating.

The defendants' reply to this strategic argument is twofold. First, they admit that seeking protection for their conduct may have the unfortunate consequence of raising some doubt about the depth of their convictions, but they maintain that that disadvantage is minor and is more than offset by advantages which would accrue from a successful appeal. For the effectiveness of civil disobedience, they argue, stems chiefly from its disruption of a complacent citizenry, and its capacity to force public attention to focus upon serious moral issues—whatever may come to be thought of the character of the disobedients. Second, they hope that if their appeal is successful many others might be encouraged to employ similar tactics where the issues are similarly grave, making moral protest all the more effective.

These are difficult claims to weigh, since they involve predictions about public reactions whose accuracy is virtually impossible to assess. If, as seems likely, their appeal is unsuccessful, some of their predictions will never be tested. In any case, the wisdom of alternative strategies, where the reactions of a large and varied citizenry must be estimated, is surely a matter upon which reasonable men may disagree. I am convinced, however, that these demonstrators under-estimate the moral force of the self-sacrificial element in disobedient protest, and underestimate, therefore, the deleterious effect upon any civilly disobedient protest which would result from the evasion of the punishment normally meted out to those who knowingly break the law.

One last observation. Whatever one may conclude about the legal guilt of these disobedient demonstrators, or the extent to which their disobedient protest should be protected by right, one must see that their position as defendants in a criminal case is a sad and ironic reflection upon our times. Given our laws, and the structure of our community, they must stand accused of a minor crime, as they do, in a court of justice. But who among the persons in that courtroom know better than they, or care more deeply, where justice lies?

LETTER TO LOCAL BOARD NO. 114

Richard M. Boardman

Local Board No. 114
Middlesex County
34 Commonwealth Ave.
West Concord, Mass.

Gentlemen:

I am writing to return my draft cards and to inform you that I am no longer able to comply with the Selective Service System. I will no longer carry a draft card or comply with any directives from the Selective Service System. To do so would be to violate the dictates of my conscience and thus do a disservice to myself, my country, and humanity.

I understand that by refusing to comply with the Selective Service System I will be breaking the law. I understand that the penalties imposed by the government on "non-cooperators" have not been light and for a long time this knowledge has prevented me from severing my connection with Selective Service. For a long time I thought that I could rest with an easy conscience if only I could establish recognition as a conscientious objector. I felt that

Reprinted by permission of the author, as originally published in *Hear Ye* (Acton, Mass.), June 1967, pp. 2–19.

it was participation in the military that I was rejecting and not conscription itself. I thought that as long as I was not compelled to participate directly in a system that has been established to do violence to human beings (like most violence, done in the name of freedom, justice, and self-defense), that as long as I could be assured of exemption from this system, I need not resist registration with the Selective Service System.

When my claim as a conscientious objector was recognized I was pleased and began to think that perhaps we had a very "reasonable" system of conscription after all. I found myself thinking that it's a very good system of conscription that "allows" a man to try to help his fellows to live constructively instead of destructively. I had failed to stop to question by what authority it came to be that a man should have to justify this creative inclination to his draft board. I had failed to realize that my deferment as a CO was a convenient way by which my resistance to conscription and the military (and the resistance of thousands like me) was effectively silenced. I had failed to acknowledge that my claim as a conscientious objector was only begrudgingly given to me because my "credentials" were good, because I was articulate, because my education had made it easy for me to produce a convincing defense of my desire to live peaceably and lovingly: in short, because I fell within a certain small, carefully defined group to whom the government felt it was both wise and safe to give deferments: wise, because otherwise this small group might raise some embarrassing questions about the legitimacy of conscription and militarism, and safe because the group is small enough so as to have little influence on the populace at large.

When I applied for recognition of my job as a draft counselor with the American Friends Service Committee as suitable civilian work in lieu of military service, I found myself trying to defend my request in terms of my work there being "in the national interest." I had compromised my own orientation, which is to do work in the interest of all of humanity, and had tried to defend my work on false grounds. False, not because my work is not in the "national interest," but because work in the interest of all humanity has a prior claim to work "in the national interest."

I didn't stop to ask how it is that the draft board's judgment about what constitutes "work in the national interest" should be considered any more legitimate than mine, or any more legitimate than that of the American Friends Service Committee, until my board decided to reject my proposed alternative service work. But even when I realized the arbitrariness of this unilateral decision by the board, I began to swallow my protest and my conscientious objection to such an undemocratic procedure, and for a month I looked for another, "more acceptable" job. I have found several jobs that would be acceptable to my board, but I have decided that the whole procedure is unacceptable to me and my value orientation. I have decided that the hypocrisy must end, that the inconsistency of my moral stance must be rectified and that I cannot accept an elitist I–O deferment from Selective Service any more than I can accept a IA–O, and for the same reason: to accept any classification is to tacitly accept the legitimacy of the system of conscription and the military for which conscription exists.

I cannot do this. As a pacifist I must totally reject both conscription and militarism. As one brought up to believe in the American principles of individualism and voluntarism I must reject any system of imposed and involuntary recruitment of manpower, and as one brought up to believe in the basic equality of all people and to respect the law only when it is equally administered to all citizens regardless of race, creed, color, social class, or education, I must reject a system of conscription that defers the most fortunate members of society and forces the least fortunate to bear the burden of responsibility and risk in the military.

It must be difficult for men in your position to understand why a man chooses to take a position in relation to the Selective Service System and the military that will result in his being considered foolish and unrealistically idealistic, and may result in his prosecution and imprisonment for violating the law. I would like to take this opportunity to try to give you an idea of the kind of thinking that has led me to take this position.

My thinking is both idealistic and very practical, religious and political, and I will try to acquaint you with some of the major considerations in both areas of my thinking.

The aspects of human existence that make life meaningful and fulfilling are psychological, social, and religious, and stem from the nature of men's relationships with each other. Mere existence is empty and barren, but human existence gains meaning and value through the development of loving human relationships. Material things have no intrinsic worth, they bring no satisfaction except in a social context. A rich man in isolation is miserable, but a poor man in love is filled with joy.

These observations lead me to conclude that the quality of human relations is always more important than the quantity of material things. And when we must choose between pursuing material things or human relations we are wisest and happiest when we choose the latter. This is also true in relation to politics, economics, and other spheres of human activity. We defeat ourselves when we place a higher value on any of these things than we do on loving human relations. Thus, I have come to believe that a man's first commitment must be to human values and not material things. Armies, wars, and violence are the means of achieving material, not spiritual or human ends, and must be rejected.

The implications of this kind of thinking related directly to the problem of determining what kinds of activities are "in the national interest." From this orientation, for example, we see that it is not in the national interest to place a higher value on material things than on human lives. It is not in the national interest to spend human lives in order to save dollars. It is not in the national interest to maintain "the balance of power," or to protect the "interests of the west" by sacrificing the prior claim of human values.

It is the development of better human relationships and social structures that is "in the national interest." This goal can only be achieved by bringing about conditions that will directly develop and enhance a creative human environment. I believe wholeheartedly that ends and means are inseparable: that, as Gandhi said, "the means is the end in the making." For this reason violence can never be successful in bringing about peace: coercion and tyranny will never work successfully in the "defense of freedom," and any contribution that one may make to supporting or cooperating with the system of organized violence we call "the military," will be directly opposing the human values, relationships, and social structures that men hope to develop in the world.

The weapons that one must use in the defense of freedom, or with which to build a better world, are the weapons that are commensurate with the ends they are used to achieve. These are the weapons of truth, of love, of charity, of equality, of understanding, of community. They are used to create rather than to destroy, to build a world devoted to developing the community of humanity rather than defending the divisive and limited interests of this or that individual, group, or nation.

The best place to begin creating a better world is at home. The first place for me to make a contribution to the goal of creating a better world is in my own behavior and way of life. It would seem that it should be easy for me to cooperate with the Selective Service System and the military. It would seem that it should be easy for me to accept one of a number of possible jobs as "civilian work in lieu of military service." I am a recognized conscientious objector. I will be engaged in work that is "in the national interest" for the rest of my life. Why then must I refuse to cooperate with my fellow citizens? Why do I insist on making myself difficult?

One way to answer these questions is by referring to the possible relevance of living one's life according to the dictates of an impossible ideal. Socrates, Christ, Gandhi, and others felt that they must live their lives in accordance with ideals that were seemingly irrelevant, impractical, and impossible under the prevailing conditions of the world in which they were living. The world would have lost much if these men had not seen fit to become impractical idealists and nuisances to their societies. Some groups of people, like the Quakers, have also tried to live their lives according to principles that demand actions that run contrary to the norms of the greater community, and they too have had to suffer the consequences of their nonconformity.

But these individuals and groups have persisted in living according to their principles—in a world that continually presses them to abandon principle and conform to the prevailing modes of behavior—because they have believed (as Isaac Pennington wrote in 1661, speaking of the peaceable kingdom foretold by prophecy) that,

> Whensoever such a thing shall be brought forth in the world it must have a beginning before it can grow and be perfected. And where should it begin but in some particulars [individuals] in a nation, and so spread by degrees? Therefore whoever desires to see this lovely state brought forth in the general, must cherish it in the particular.

The men who live their lives according to principle believe that they can most fully lend their support to the development of freedom and love by setting a living example of those qualities for their fellows. They know of no better way of achieving peace than by living peaceably with their neighbors; they know of no better way of developing a social climate in which men will be free and equal than by treating all men honestly and equally; they know of no better way of helping men to learn to love each other than by treating them lovingly. They know, in short, of no surer way of making the world a better place than by leading better lives themselves. And this they must do whether the laws permit it or not. For they realize, as Thoreau pointed out, that "Law never made men a whit more just; and, by means of their respect for it, even the well-disposed are daily made the agents of injustice."

I hope that my refusal to cooperate with Selective Service will be seen as an effort to continue in the tradition of the individuals and groups I have spoken of here. I have come to see that the law requires that I be less than just, less than honest, less than human. It has, indeed, made me an "agent of injustice," and I find that I must resist such a law with the full force of not only words, but also my actions. I hope that you will recognize the faith I have in the power that my example may have for helping others to work to make the world a better place. For this is the spirit in which my act is taken.

The political or practical basis for my disobedience relates, again, to my conception of work "in the national interest." As I see it the work that I am doing as a draft counselor with the American Friends Service Committee is not only in the national interest, it is in the interest of all of humanity. Resisting evil, in whatever form it takes, is in the best interest of mankind. By resisting the draft I am combatting the first ranks in the forces of an evil system—the military—that affects all young men throughout the United States.

I will try to make clear some of the more practical reasons why I feel that the military and conscription must be resisted. The evil effects of conscription are so numerous as to be impossible to catalog in detail, but some of its most destructive aspects are these:

1. The draft forces young men to become part of the military machine, the primary purpose of which is to kill human beings.

The draft forces young men—at a critical time in their lives, during which they are exploring values and trying to establish their own ethical orientations—to acquiesce to and participate in the military establishment which has its own uniquely pernicious value system that reverses most of the positive and creative values of humanity and undermines their influence in the lives of America's youth.

The best soldier, the Armed Forces teach us—contrary to our Christian tradition of values—is the most efficient murderer. The feeble voice of humanity's "Thou shalt not kill," is drowned out by the sergeants roaring "Thou shalt kill and kill well!"

"All men are brothers," we learn in our Sunday Schools. But the Army teaches, "The best soldier is the one who makes the clearest distinction between the 'good guys' and 'bad guys.'" The best soldier realizes soonest that "All men are brothers except the 'Japs,' the 'Krauts," the 'Commies,' the 'VC'."

The best soldier ignores religion, God, and his conscience and learns to "follow orders." The best soldier can kill without thinking twice about it because he realizes that it is "his job" to do so.

These are the values that our society has decided to instill into the minds, hearts, and reflexes of its youth. These are the values that I must reject. These are the values that are contrary to "the national interest." This is why draft resistance is work "in the national interest," and in the interest of all humanity.

2. The deferment system is an elitist system that serves the wealthy and privileged and feeds on the less prestigious. The draft obligation subtly forces the nation's youth into positions that a few power holders and policy makers deem to be "in the national interest," obliging them to move into professional and academic careers that they may not have chosen except for the fact that the military is their only alternative if they drop out of school. These inequities and manipulative "channeling" techniques are widely acknowledged and I need not expand on them here.

3. A curious double standard of social morality is introduced by our draft system—a double standard that should be examined.

There are only two small groups of draft registrants who are allowed to live according to the Judaeo-Christian principles and values which the great majority of registrants espouse. These groups are the ministers (IV–D) and the conscientious objectors (I–O or IA–O).

Ministers (though their prestige seems to have diminished in recent years) are held in high esteem by the community at large. They are looked to for ethical and spiritual guidance; their conduct is expected to be exemplary; they are highly respected members of the community.

The conscientious objector's position is much less prestigious. Indeed, the conscientious objector is generally regarded with suspicion or ridicule, particularly if he is not a member of a church with an historic peace tradition. The conscientious objector is often looked upon as a coward, a shirker, or some other kind of "draft dodger," by the general public. The law, however, respects the right of individual conscience (at least as long as it offers no substantial threat to the maintenance of the status quo) and, begrudgingly, respects the conscientious objector who claims a sincere refusal to "participate in war in any form" if he agrees to serve two years of civilian work (that his draft board determines is) "in the national interest."

Although it would seem quite laudable (from the religious perspective) for a Christian to refuse to "participate in war in any form," particularly in view of the Christian's professed commitment to adhere to the injunction to "turn the other cheek," and the imperative, "Thou shalt not kill," it is very difficult for a man to establish grounds for being recognized as a conscientious objector. Most men who imitate their ministers or follow their Christian commandments are discouraged in their moral consistency and distrusted by their society. Many are even punished for their attempts to live exemplary lives.

One would think (from the human perspective) that our society would demand that its young men should show cause why they can become soldiers—and if need be, to kill—in all good conscience. Instead, from the military perspective of our society, we insist that a young man must show cause why he should be allowed to refuse to kill, to refuse to participate in the Army.

4. The double standard referred to above is just one of the many paradoxes that plague our schizophrenic society. It is our dual commitment to humanitarian principles and militarism, to mercy and murder, that cripples our society spiritually and ethically, and contains the seeds of its destruction. For, as Christ said two thousand years ago, "Every kingdom divided against itself is laid waste, and

no city or house divided against itself will stand." (Matt: 12:25)

Because this saying is true, not only of nations, kingdoms, cities, and houses, but also of individuals, I find that I must refuse to comply further with the demands of the Selective Service System. I have tried my best to arrange a compromise—only to discover that by compromising my adherence to very basic, human, ethical principles—I defeat myself and do a disservice to mankind's best interest.

> No one can serve two masters; for either he will hate the one and love the other, or he will be devoted to the one and despise the other. You cannot serve God and Mammon. (Matt: 6:24)

I cannot truly serve the interests of humanity, and at the same time comply with the Selective Service System.

Yours in Peace,
Richard M. Boardman

CONFESSIONS OF A TWO-TIME DRAFT CARD BURNER

Tom Jarrell

Historically, my first offense against the draft was in August of '66, when a friend of mine was talking with me about Black Power, and how middle-class white suburbia was guilty of complicity with the overt racists, how America runs on institutional racism, how anyone not the black man's friend actively is his enemy passively, and how I was "a pimple on the ass of destiny" if I was no racist but did nothing to help end racism. I lit up my draft card, at 2 a.m. on a Greenwich Village street with no other witness than my friend, to show him that I could act on my convictions about the things *I* was hung up on, and I had been hung up on the draft for several years. As I threw the ashes into a trash can, he asked me if I felt any better for my little blaze; sadly, I felt no elation; the gesture being privatistic was lost in the empty street.

The symbolism became meaningful, however, at the Arlington Street Church on October 16th. The service united believer, agnostic, and atheist in a common faith of conscience, and made of the sacramental bread-breaking a full-course Meal of Reconciliation more divine in its secularity than any communion I have ever participated in. While 66 others burned "what they claimed were

Reprinted by permission of the author and publisher from *Avatar*, No. 18 (Feb. 2–15, 1968), p. 1.

Selective Service documents," I let the altar candle ignite a xerox of a draft card supplied by the Resistance marshals, one which the Boston Draft Resistance Group rubber-stamped in the space provided for the local board stamp.

I was only burning a xerox—because I had already mutilated the duplicate draft card I requested from Newton's local board 116, having gone around for some fourteen months violating the non-possession provisions of the Selective Service laws. Jeanette K. Tice, the civil service clerk who makes all the day-to-day board decisions, sent me a duplicate card after notifying the FBI, who called me the week following the church service:

"Mr. Jarrell, we'd like to talk to you sometime."

"Well, I don't know fellas, I'm kinda busy these days. And I work nights, so I'm not exactly available on your working hours."

"Oh, I'm sorry, did we wake you?"

"Yeah."

"I'm sure we can arrange a meeting at a time and place convenient to you."

"How about November 16th? A whole lot of us will have something to say then."

"Well, our investigation will be over by then."

"Too bad."

"So you can't talk to us . . ."

"I figure there's nothing I can tell you that you can't read in the papers. You know I burned my card a year ago, and I told the board of my intention to mutilate my card this week."

"Did you?"

"It's right here in my apartment now, antiqued and decollaged [sic] into an anti-draft thing that includes the paper the induction center sent me saying I'm 'unsuitable'."

"Well, it's a shame we can't get together . . ."

"Ain't it though. Well I'll tell you guys something, if you should ever come over here, you'd better come armed with good identification. Just flash a badge at me and I'll say nothing; anyone can have a badge—*I* got a badge. Means nothing, could be anybody."

"What would you consider proper identification?"

"Well you'd better have both your draft card and your classification notice, 'cause otherwise I'll get you on a citizen's arrest for nonpossession."

Then on Wednesday 10th of January, while marching as a marshal in the picket line supporting Marston and Brown, I lit up again. This time it was my 1-Y (morally unfit) classification notice. The immediate provocation came from Joseph Mlotz-Mroz, the "self-styled Polish Freedom Fighter" (fighting freedom wherever he can find it) and his supporters (super-patriotic longshoremen from Roslindale, according to the newspapers). Joe was carrying one of his usual thought-provoking picket signs: "Burn, Baby, Burn!" with the Victor Lundbergian suggestion that draft resisters should warm themselves in the glow of their citizenship papers and birth certificates ablaze; his supporters were tossing snowballs and eggs from the Boston Army Diner on the other side of Summer Street. An egg caught me on the left shoulder, creating the circumstances whereby the clean-cut virile counter-pickets casting aspersions on the manhood of the Samson-haired demonstrators could exercise their wit: "You're as yellow as the yolk of the egg." "Hey kid, you got egg on your face."

So I decided to turn pyromaniac once again. All those press photographers, and nothing dramatic (as far as *they* were concerned) going on. So why not force a little confrontation, let the stevedores foam at the mouth in front of the television cameras. Unfortunately, WGBH's TV crew, who might have given the event a little rational direction, had left, leaving WHDH (Ch. 5) alone on the scene. They were content to film the thing, to hell with conducting an interview or anything. So a Veteran For Peace made himself available for a rap of "complicity" by offering me his lighter since in the wind and zero-degree weather, ungloved and hands shaking, I had a hard time getting the flames to catch. Meanwhile, Joe on my left is screaming "He's a coward, he's a coward," and the longshoremen being restrained by the police on my right were into it with "You ought to be ashamed of yourself." So I ask them "Why?" while offering the burning classification notice to Joe to warm his hands. But the whole thing, this demonstration of symbolic what-for-lack-of-a-non-egotrip-word-I'll-have-to-call-"courage," really got me high on the sublimely-ridiculous incongruity bit when Joe, as the flames licked my freezing fingers, screams, "It's only a piece of paper!"

Exactly, it's only a piece of paper. It's not human, not the singed skin of a napalmed Vietnamese child, not the charred remains of the Buddhist self-immolator in identification with whom draft cards were burned at the Arlington Street Church. It's only a piece of paper, superfluous even to the bureaucracy that issues and establishes penalties for disrespect shown to their excreta. It's only a piece of paper, Joe, just as the flag you wave is only so much cloth and dye, and if you die for the cloth you are placing symbolic values before human ones. We, however, attach no significance to that piece of paper; if burning it means anything to me, it is only because it means so fucking much to you. Like the longhair told his parents when they approached him with scissors and asked why he could attach so much importance to such a trivial sign of defiance as long hair, "It means as much to me to keep it as it means to you to have it off." It's only a piece of paper, the burning of which in private, in Greenwich at 2 a.m., means nothing—only the context supplied by "them Red-baiters and race-haters" provides any meaning.

They called me coward. I identified myself fully to the newsmen, fully aware that such open activity makes me a "conspirator" liable to five years and/or $10,000 fine, while the man who threw the egg wouldn't identify himself, risking at most a mock charge of assault with a deadly dairy product.

But it took no courage, among 200 fellow demonstrators, colleagues in crime protected by the police (with only an occasional oversight, an occasional fist in a demonstrator's face unseen for lack of focus of hawkeyes that perhaps did not *want* to be focused on such a scene). It took only conscience, and a gut-level indignation.

And contrary to what the longshoremen think, it takes no courage to kill. Put yourself in a shoot-or-get-shot situation, gut-level self-preservation will give you all the trigger-finger you need. Granted, it may take some kind of physical courage to attack as opposed to returning fire, but physical courage is relative to the situation too; i.e., morale is group-courage transferred to individuals.

But moral courage is where it's at. That's what Nuremberg is all about; the willingness to act in public on what your conscience tells you in your private-most hours. The willingness to take the rap for what you believe, the ability to refuse to be put into situations where gut reactions take over contrary to your rational beliefs. It takes no courage to let the Army put you through the changes; it takes moral courage to tell the army to fuck off with the changes *they* want to put you through and let you be to put yourself through your own changes.

Which is where the whole anti-draft thing comes from, for me. I figure conscription is at least involuntary servitude, if not outright slavery, and therefore in violation of the thirteenth amendment: "Neither slavery nor involuntary servitude, except as a punishment for crime whereof the party shall have been duly convicted, shall exist within the United States. . . ."

When you cite this amendment to most people, they usually switch to a National Duty argument. "Don't you think you owe this country something?" At which point it becomes necessary to clue them in to a few psychological realities about Obligation. My reasoning runs like this: You're born into the United States arbitrarily (i.e., as opposed to as a result of your volition), granted the benefits of this grand country because your parents are good Americans who pay their taxes to secure the blessings of Freedom and Democracy for their progeny, one of these blessings being inculcated with the unofficial but damn-well-universal American religion of the Protestant Ethic, which includes the sacrifice-now-for-future-comfort notion which has as its bastard corollary the semi-fatalist, quasi-pragmatic doctrine of Necessary Evils.

Americans believe in Necessary Evils, and one of the Necessary Evils is the existence of Total Institutions, and one of these Total Institutions is American compulsory education, where one is inculcated in the myth of Necessary Evils. And since a belief in Necessary Evils is both a consequence and cause of a belief that there are no real alternatives, Americans never question the wisdom of sending their children to schools that stifle affect to enhance cognition, sacrifice creativity to the almighty Intelligence Quotient, and thus never hear of Summerhill. So the children graduate from grade to grade, homework becomes more and more a presence, the schools are more and more of a Total Environment, until the high school student feels himself to be a colonial subject. Kenneth Keniston and Paul Goodman and Edgar Z. Friedenberg and all the other social scientists concerned with the alienation of youth from and by the total institutions created to acculturate them, can only write books notionally about what each of us in the Pepsi Generation knows experientially: that American society is *not* free, democracy is still largely theoretical and every day becoming more academic and less actual, that our very existence as thinking individuals is co-opted by media poisoning, subverted by the Protestant Ethic which reveres Individualism but at the cost of Love.

It is useless, then, to tell us we owe something to our country. We have the country to thank for most of our hang-ups, and *that* debt we are paying interest on. And the way we serve this country is to educate its citizens—to *educate* them as to what's going on in Vietnam, what life is like in the ghetto, and what their mass education media poisoning society has done to our minds so that insanity-by-drugs is a truly attractive alternative to split-level closed-mind suburban living. Why get brainwashed in a high school civics course, when you can home-launder your mind by blowing it with STP? All these blessings conferred on us were unsolicited gifts—you owe no one thanks for what you never asked for, especially if it fucks you up. And certainly the way to serve your country is *not* to surrender to the ultimate Total Institution, the U.S. Army. Reading *U.S. News & World Reports* on the acculturation of beatniks into the ranks sounds like genocide ("A platoon that begins with three 'beatniks' will find that they disappear after a few weeks, never to be seen again."); reading the Selective Service Orientation Kit pamphlet on "Channeling" sounds like totalitarianism. And General Hershey, who refuses to be retired because he would then have nothing to do and he enjoys fucking American youth more than playing bingo, wants to draft Resistance people to punish them, while somehow believing that serving in the forces is a paramount honor. The President calls for a study of how to eliminate the draft, the Pentagon comes to the conclusion that a voluntary army is feasible but reverses that decision because we've got the draft already, and it's as American as apple pie.

Conscription is a way of life now, 20 years of the peace-time draft have sufficiently affected generations so that the father or older brother who had to serve "like-it-or-not" wants to inflict the same upon his son or younger brother. That the sacrifice they made was unnecessary is as repugnant to them as the idea that the Vietnam war is immoral is to the U.S. fighting man in Asia. (And if you think that all that pot-blowing indicates our guys are really turned on, you'd better get wise to the probability that reactions to a pot high are largely socially determined, and that the pot in Vietnam coupled with our military morale might just be making the front-line soldier *more* aggressive.)

We need to retire General Hershey—give him lots of money so's he can play the horses instead of bingo. We need to get the Pentagon to 'fess up about the voluntary army feasibility study. We need to back people like Milton J. Friedman (Goldwater's economic advisor, no less, but still a sound head), Mark Hatfield of Oregon, and Congressman Curtis—all of whom think the draft should be abolished.

And when we have a voluntary army, we can comfort ourselves with the thought that the government can no longer wage a war contrary to the wishes of the governed. Even when he's paid a reasonable wage, a soldier will not remain in the army if he disbelieves in the cause for which he is allegedly fighting.

If the country inspires commitment, it will be supported by its people. If the government resorts to conscription, it is an indicator that it governs not a free people, but a "country" that does not deserve to survive.

I am now guilty of five violations of the Selective Service laws, punishable by a maximum of 25 years in prison and/or $50,000. I intend to continue accumulating violations. When they indict Dr. Spock, they must also indict me. When they prosecute me for one transgression, they must prosecute me for all, or be guilty themselves of negligence and complicity. And if enough resisters are given life imprisonment for 20 counts each, maybe the country will discover that a draft card really *is* just a piece of paper.

ON CIVIL DISOBEDIENCE
AND DRAFT RESISTANCE

Charles E. Wyzanski, Jr.

Disobedience is a long step beyond dissent. In this country, at least in theory, no one denies the right of any person to differ with the government, or his right to express that difference in speech, in the press, by petition, or in an assembly.

But civil disobedience, by definition, involves a deliberate and punishable breach of a legal duty. However much they differ in other respects, both passive and violent resisters intentionally violate the law. So, in general, it is unnecessary in considering the moral qualities of disobedience to spend much time in determining what is the correct construction of the law. By hypothesis the law has been broken, and broken knowingly.

The virtual exclusion of legal topics makes it possible to discuss the morality of resistance to the Vietnam War without answering the question whether the President as Commander in Chief under the Constitution, or as the Chief Executive authorized by the Congress, or otherwise has power to send to Vietnam armed forces regularly enlisted or conscripted, or whether the Constitution gives power to draft men to serve in a conflict not covered by a formal declaration of war, or whether there is any rule of international or domestic law which inhibits the President or the Con-

Reprinted by permission of the author and publisher from "On Civil Disobedience", *The Atlantic Monthly*, CCXXI (Feb. 1968), pp. 58–60. © 1968, by the Atlantic Monthly Company, Boston, Mass.

gress or the armed forces either from conducting in Vietnam any operations whatsoever or any particular operations, or from using any specific methods of fighting or injuring other persons, military or civilian.

There cannot be an issue of civil disobedience unless there is a conscious choice to violate not merely a governmental policy but a technically valid law or order. Only such laws and orders as are ultimately held valid under our Constitution are subject to genuine civil disobedience.

Of course, until the Supreme Court has spoken, a person may not know whether a particular law or order is valid. If because he believes the law is invalid under the Constitution he refuses to obey it until the order has been upheld, he is not in the strictest sense engaged in civil disobedience. Thus many of the recent refusals of Negroes to obey segregation orders of local authorities, though they are popularly referred to as examples of civil disobedience, have been, in fact, nothing more than challenges to laws believed to be and often found to be unconstitutional.

If it turns out that the Supreme Court should hold that the government lacks power to order the induction of men into military training and service for the Vietnam War, then one who had refused to obey the induction order would not have been guilty of civil disobedience. He would merely have been vindicating his constitutional rights.

But if, as I suppose the majority of informed lawyers expect, the Supreme Court, at least during the continuation of hostilities, does not hold an induction order void on the ground of lack of legislative or éxecutive power, then one who continues willfully to disobey is engaged in civil disobedience. The same would be true of one who, on the ground that the funds were used for war, refused to pay taxes, or who in protesting war deliberately injured another's person or property, or who went beyond argument and persuasion to advocate resistance to lawful orders.

There are many people who have asserted that a man always has an undeniable moral claim to disobey any law to which he is conscientiously opposed. Antigone, Thoreau, and Gandhi are cited. It is contended that resistance to the law is the proper response to the still small voice of conscience.

That extreme position seems untenable. Every time that a law is disobeyed by even a man whose motive is solely ethical, in the sense that it is responsive to a deep moral conviction, there are unfortunate consequences. He himself becomes more prone to disobey laws for which he has no profound repugnance. He sets an example for others who may not have his pure motives. He weakens the fabric of society.

Those disadvantages are so serious that in *Principia Ethica* G. E. Moore, the English philosopher who set the tone for twentieth-century thought on ethics, concluded that in most instances civil disobedience is immoral. A dramatic precursor of Moore was Socrates. He swallowed hemlock pursuant to an arbitrary Athenian decree rather than refuse obedience to the law of the city-state which had formed and protected him.

However, it is not here suggested that disobedience is always morally wrong, or that it is never ethically proper for a man to organize opposition to an immoral law even before the state brings its command directly to his door.

There are situations when it seems plainly moral for a man to disobey an evil law promulgated by a government which is entirely lacking in ethical character. If a man has lost confidence in the integrity of his society, or if he fears that unless he acts forthwith there will not come a later day when he can effectively protest, or if (in terms reminiscent of Burke's metaphor) he seeks to terminate the partnership of the American dead, the American living, and the as yet unborn Americans, then there is much justification for his disobedience.

The gangster state operated by the Nazis presented such a picture to many conscientious men. But no unprejudiced observer is likely to see the American government in its involvement in Vietnam as in a posture comparable with that of the Nazi regime. Nor is there reason to suppose that men must act now or forever be silenced. We are not moving either torrentially or glacially toward despotism.

It is, of course, conceivable that if men resist forthwith, they may forestall grave consequences. It is certain that many, many Americans and Asians will lose their lives if the war continues. It is possible that if fighting is not promptly stopped, the scale will increase dramatically, and at worst, might produce a holocaust of worldwide dimensions.

But what is by no means assured is that resistance would avert those consequences. Historical prediction is clouded by ambiguities. Political developments move to a heterogeneity of ends. No one can tell whether, as the resisters would hope, they, by rallying widespread support, would prove that in a democracy substantial segments of public opinion have the residual power to terminate or veto a war, or, as less implicated observers fear, the resisters, by provoking the responsive passions of the belligerent, would set the stage for a revival of a virulent McCarthyism, an administrative system of impressment into the armed forces, and the establishment of a despotic tyranny bent on impairing traditional civil liberties and civic rights.

Most thoughtful men have always been aware how dangerous it is to go beyond persuasion and to defy the law by either peaceful or violent resistance. If the effort is successful, as with the Revolution of the American colonists, then history accepts the claims of the victors that they acted morally. But if the effort not merely fails but produces a horrible reaction, then history is likely to ask whether there were not other courses that could have been more wisely followed.

To illustrate how perplexing is the problem, nothing is more illuminating than the struggle in America in the 1850s and 1860s over the slavery question. Abraham Lincoln thought laws enforcing slavery were immoral. Yet he declared he would endure, and thus aid the enforcement of, slavery in the Southern states if that would preserve the Union. His position was shared by two great jurists of my state who were his contemporaries: Lemuel Shaw, Chief Justice of Massachusetts, and Benjamin Robbins Curtis, Associate Justice of the Supreme Court of the United States, both of whom enforced the Fugitive Slave Law.

But Lincoln's position was challenged by, among others, two men whom the city of Boston has honored by statues erected after their death—Wendell Phillips and William Lloyd Garrison, each of whom disobeyed the Fugitive Slave Law and wrote approvingly of the murderous violence of John Brown. What should give us even greater pause is that Oliver Wendell Holmes, Jr., the future Justice, in effect adhered to the Abolitionist cause when he joined the small group of Abolitionists who, during the winter of 1860–1861, made themselves responsible for securing the physical safety of Wendell Phillips agains the threats of the Boston mobs, a protection which the Boston police seemed unlikely to provide. The details are set forth in Professor Mark Howe's discriminating biography of Holmes.

If it was morally right to break the laws supporting slavery even when it cost the nation its unity and helped precipitate what, despite W. H. Seward, may not have been an "irrepressible conflict," one cannot be so certain that it is morally wrong to resist the war in Vietnam if one deeply believes its purposes or methods are wicked.

At any rate the Lincolnian analogy has not the final authority that it may seem to have on cursory inspection. In 1860 and 1861 our country was in immediate grave peril. Lincoln adhered to the ancient Roman maxim that the safety of the people is the highest law. But that maxim has no obvious application today. Even the most ardent supporters of our role in Vietnam would hardly aver that the threat they see in Communism or Asian nationalism is one of such immediacy as existed when the Civil War erupted. Perhaps there are long-term dangers from the Asian and other Communist powers, but one may wonder if Mr. Justice Holmes would have regarded them as either "clear" or "present." Would not President Lincoln have invoked our recollection not of 1860 or 1861 but rather of 1862 when, the battle of Antietam having made a change of policy practical, he issued the Emancipation Proclamation?

In support of the moral right of resistance, another, if cognate, point must be made, however uncongenial it is to me both temperamentally and officially. A man may conscientiously believe that his deepest obligation is to do his utmost to eradicate an evil, to stand athwart a wicked action, forcefully to promote reform, or to establish a new social or legal or religious order. Luther and Lenin serve as archetypes. They share to some degree the view Vanzetti on the eve of his electrocution expressed to his lawyer Thompson: "that, as he read history, every great cause for the benefit of humanity had to fight for its existence against entrenched power and wrong."

Perceptive observers may support Vanzetti's social theorem. Anguished souls may yield to its persuasiveness. Effective men may make that vision once again prove its reality.

Yet the fierce passion which moves men to rebel is often, not always, dangerously mixed with vanity, self-righteousness, and blindness to possible, nay probable, consequences far different from those sought. The voice of reason urges, in Cromwellian terms, "I beseech you, in the bowels of Christ, think it possible you may be mistaken."

Violent disorder once set in motion may spawn tyranny, not freedom. Rebellion may fail to gain its contemplated support, and as surely as in other human relations, result in "the expense of spirit in a waste of shame."

Or, what is far harder to bear, the rebellion may in form succeed but in substance impose a new oppressive yoke, a nihilistic world regime, or chaos instead of a community of nations. The wager on a finer, purer, more fraternal world order may be disastrously lost. Before one places all one's strength behind the rebel's cause, he should have not only naïve faith but that invincible insight which warrants martyrdom.

For men of conscience there remains a less risky but not less worthy moral choice. Each of us may bide his time until he personally is faced with an order requiring him as an individual to do a wrongful act. Such patience, fortitude, and resolution find illustration in the career of Sir Thomas More. He did not rush in to protest the Act of Henry VIII's Parliament requiring Englishmen to take an oath of supremacy attesting to the King's, instead of the Pope's, headship of the English Church. Only when attempt was made to force him to subscribe to the oath did he resist. In present circumstances the parallel to not resisting the Act of Supremacy before it has been personally applied is to await at the very least an induction order before resisting. Indeed, since, when inducted, one does not know if he will be sent to Vietnam, or if sent, will be called upon directly to do what he regards as an immoral act, it may well be that resistance at the moment of induction is premature.

This waiting until an issue is squarely presented to an individual and cannot further be avoided will not be a course appealing to those who have a burning desire to intervene affirmatively to save this nation's honor and the lives of its citizens and citizens of other lands. It seems at first blush a not very heroic attitude. But heroism sometimes lies in withholding action until it is compelled, and using the interval to discern competing interests, to ascertain their values, and to seek to strike a balance that marshals the claims not only of the accountant and of others in his society, but of men of distant lands and times.

Such restraint will in no way run counter to the rules applied in the judgment of the Nuremberg Tribunal. That judgment recognized that no one may properly be charged with a crime unless he personally participated in it by doing the wrong or by purposefully aiding, abetting, and furthering the wrong. As the Nuremberg verdicts show, merely to fight in an aggressive war is no crime. What is a crime is personally to fight by foul means.

Those who look upon Sir Thomas More as one of the noblest exemplars of the human spirit reflecting the impact of the love of God may find a delayed civil disobedience the response most likely to give peace of mind and to evidence moral courage.

A SYMPOSIUM ON CIVIL DISOBEDIENCE AND THE VIETNAM WAR

Editor's note: The New York Times *prefaced this symposium with the following statement. "Domestic critics of U.S. policy in Vietnam are increasingly advocating abandonment of 'mere' dissent for resistance, or civil disobedience. The Times Magazine asked a number of scholars and writers these questions: What justifies an act of civil disobedience? What are, or should be, the limits of civil disobedience? Is civil disobedience justified in the case of Vietnam? . . ."*

"Intolerable Evils Justify Civil Disobedience"
Noam Chomsky

Although I feel that resistance to United States policy is justified—in fact, a moral necessity—I do not think that dissent should be abandoned. Critical analysis of American policy can extend opposition to this war and can help modify the intellectual and moral climate that made it possible. Government propaganda has shifted to a new position: American self-interest. Correspondingly, critical analysis can now be directed to such questions as these: Whose interest is served by this war? What motivates the hysterical claim that if we do not stand fast in Vietnam we shall have to fight in Hawaii and California?—"a frivolous insult to the United States Navy," as Walter Lippmann rightly comments. Would the richest and most powerful nation in the world be justified in imposing such suffering and destruction even if this were in its "self-interest"?

From "On Civil Disobedience, 1967," *The New York Times Magazine,* November 26, 1967, pp. 27–28, 122–32. © 1967 by The New York Times Company, Reprinted by permission.

The other members of the symposium included William F. Buckley, Jr., John Dollard, James T. Farrell, John Cogley, Sidney Hook, Herbert C. Kelman, Dwight Macdonald, Richard Rovere, and Bayard Rustin.

What justifies an act of civil disobedience is an intolerable evil. After the lesson of Dachau and Auschwitz, no person of conscience can believe that authority must always be obeyed. A line must be drawn somewhere. Beyond that line lies civil disobedience. It may be quite passive, a simple refusal to take part in Government-initiated violence. An example is refusal to pay war taxes: refusal to serve in Vietnam is a far more meaningful, far more courageous example. It may involve symbolic confrontation with the war-making apparatus, as in the Washington demonstrations, a confrontation that becomes civil disobedience when the participant stands his ground in the face of Government force. It may go well beyond such symbolic acts.

Each citizen must ask himself whether he wishes to take part in the annihilation of the people of Vietnam. He has a range of actions available to him. Docility and passive acquiescence is one possible course. It is the course of full complicity in whatever the Government will do in his name.

The limits of civil disobedience must be determined by the extent of the evil that one confronts, and by considerations of tactical efficacy and moral principle. On grounds of principle and tactics, I think that civil disobedience should be entirely nonviolent, but space prevents a discussion of the reasons for, and the consequences of, this conclusion.

The final question posed is the crucial one. Those who defend American policy speak vaguely of Communist "aggression." Just when did the "aggression" take place? Was it in 1959, when Hanoi radio was urging that the leaders of the insurrection desist, when Diem spoke of having an Algerian war on his hands in the South while his agents were being parachuted into North Vietnam? Or was it perhaps in April 1965, when North Vietnamese troops were first discovered in the South, two months after the bombing of North Vietnam began—400 in the guerrilla force of 140,000, at a time when more than 30,000 American troops were helping protect the Saigon Government from its own population?

Or is it now, when a vast American army of occupation has taken over the conduct of the war, with about as many South Korean mercenaries as there are North Vietnamese troops in the South?

Or does Hanoi's "aggression" consist in the sending of supplies and trained South Vietnamese cadres to the South? By these standards our aggression in the South has always been incomparably greater in scale, and we are engaged in such aggression in half the countries of the world. It is pointless to continue. If an objective observer were to listen to American voices speaking of aggression from Hanoi or of the necessity for *America* to contain *China's* aggressive expansionism, he would not challenge our arguments but would question our sanity.

American Government sources freely admit that United States military force was introduced to prevent a political, organizational, agit-prop victory by the N.L.F. (see Douglas Pike, *The Vietcong*). The terrible consequences of the use of American military might are apparent to anyone with eyes and ears. I will not try to describe what everyone knows. To use inadequate words to tell what we have done is an insult to the victims of our violence and our moral cowardice. Yes, civil disobedience is entirely justified in an effort to bring to a close the most disgraceful chapter in American history.

I'll finish with two quotes, each very true, from opposite extremes of the moral spectrum.

(1) "Naturally the common people don't want war . . . it is the leaders of the country who determine the policy, and it is always a simple matter to drag the people along, whether it is a democracy, or a Fascist dictatorship, or a parliament, or a Communist dictatorship. Voice or no voice, the people can always be brought to do the bidding of the leaders. That is easy. All you have to do is to tell them that they are being attacked, and denounce the pacifists for lack of patriotism and exposing the country to danger. It works the same in every country."

(2) "Unjust laws and practices survive because men obey them and conform to them. This they do out of fear. There are things they dread more than the continuance of the evil."

The first quote is from Hermann Goering. Those who counsel civil disobedience are expressing their hope that it doesn't "work the same" in this country. The second quote is from A. J. Muste, paraphrasing Gandhi. These words have never been more appropriate than they are today.

"We Should Distinguish Between Disobedience and Resistance"

Lewis S. Feuer

We should distinguish between civil disobedience and civil resistance. The first is limited to dramatizing a particular issue; it retains a faith in representative democracy, and takes for granted that once the facts are known, and the people's sense of responsibility awakened, the necessary reforms will be made. Civil disobedience is justified when an oppressed group finds itself deprived of lawful channels for remedying its condition because of an arbitrary obstruction in the democratic workings.

Civil resistance, on the other hand, is total and unlimited, for it claims that the entire society is corrupt, that representative democracy is a failure, and that the resisters' weapon must be revolutionary. It regards each episode as part of a "guerrilla warfare" against society. It twists the vocabulary of civil disobedience to this purpose. The Student Nonviolent Coordinating Committee says it uses "nonviolent" in quotation marks, that is, meaninglessly, or deceptively. Civil resistance is advocated in the United States by two groups—the Ku Klux Klan (as in Meridian, Miss.) and the New Left, most recently in its demonstrations against the Vietnam war.

In the last analysis, we judge acts of civil disobedience and resistance in terms of what we think of the motives and rationality of their practitioners. The director of the Washington Pentagon demonstrators announced: "We are now in the business of wholesale and widespread resistance and dislocation of the American society." The New Resisters have an apocalyptic image of themselves as the successors to the abolitionists.

The wisest American of his time, Justice Holmes, knew the abolitionists well and as a youth, shared their madness. They "taught me a lesson," however, he said, as he recognized the basis of fanaticism. The abolitionists were often more intent on killing white men than on bettering the lot of the slaves. John Brown's favorite text was: "Without the shedding of blood, there is no remission of sins," and 20 years before the Civil War he was insisting that slavery could be ended only through a blood atonement. The New Resisters, as the Chicago Conference for New Politics last September made evident, are driven by a similar fanaticism; their resolutions reeked more of venom against Americans than of a desire for Asians' freedom.

To justify their civil resistance to the Vietnam war, the New Left claims that the American democracy has denied them a hearing. They fail to mention that their well-financed candidates in the last Congressional elections and primaries were rejected by the voters. The New Left, defeated by representative democracy, wants therefore to destroy and replace it with a "participatory democracy"—that is, the rule of its "guerrilla warriors" and activists.

Thus its civil disobedience has evolved into civil resistance, an antidemocratic ideology of rule by a dictatorial élite. No wonder that at the Chicago conference, some of its adherents began to awaken and to speak openly of its "fascism" and "totalitarianism." Benito Mussolini's march on Rome was also an act of massive civil resistance.

The New Resistance has tried to borrow the aura of the European resistance movements. The latter, however, were fighting the Nazis who had abrogated all constitutional processes, banned the opposition parties, and imprisoned their leaders. It makes no sense to describe the American democracy in such terms, and the efforts of the resisters to do so only accentuate their irrationality. At the same time, they remain strangely benign to the call of Lin Piao, Mao's defense minister in September 1965, for a "people's war" of Asia, Africa, and Latin America against North America and Western Europe.

Our entry into World War II was largely the outcome of our refusal to condone the expansion of the Japanese empire into Indochina and Southeast Asia. Our presence in Vietnam today is due to our similar refusal to condone a Chinese expansionism. An American departure, as Southeast Asians themselves generally recognize, would probably uproot such fragile growths of democracy as now exist. Draft evaders in World War II used much the same arguments as the draft-card burners today. The New Left is using all the worn arguments that the Old Left used against American involvement during 1939 to 1941. The draft-card burners and the New Left have just as little moral justification. This "prophetic minority" is one of false prophets.

"The Resisters Support U.S. Traditions and Interests"

Paul Goodman

The great majority of resisters do not consider themselves as lawless, whether they impede the draft, refuse war taxes, or try to bar recruiters and war contracts from the campuses. We hold that it is the Vietnam policy that is illegitimate. It has been created by a hidden government of military-industrial lobbyists and the C.I.A.; the Executive has gone beyond his mandate; there has been no genuine debate and voting in Congress; the public has been lied to and brainwashed. The Government is a usurper, so sovereignty reverts to the people more directly. It is the resisters who support American traditions and interests, and our behavior is itself traditional, not unlike the civil-rights movement, the labor movement, populism, abolitionism (and nullification), and the American Revolution itself. As in the previous cases, most action has been nonviolent though often disobedient to authorities, and there has also been sporadic violence, usually started by authorities.

Rather than "defying" the law, most resisters welcome a test of legitimacy in the courts, believing that, when everything is duly aired, we will be found lawful, just as recently the civil-rights trespassers were found (or became) lawful. In American tradition, the meaning of law is always emerging. The Government has been loath to accept the challenge, choosing instead to pick off individuals, hoping to deter. Now, however, the draft-card burners are being subpoenaed and there may be a massive showdown.

The aim of testing the law and nonviolent confrontation, trying to persuade by putting oneself on the line, is to get the Americans to make up their minds and change their minds; it is not to frighten or compel. Unfortunately, since the populace has been sluggish and complacent, occasional violence seems to be advantageous to wake people up; certainly it is mainly violent incidents that the TV and press want to notice. And naturally, resisters are frustrated by their powerlessness when, even now as I write this, our Government is killing those people. Yet I cannot accept the *putschist* use of violence, for instance, to "take over" a draft board or burn it down by a physical power play. This is unacceptable not because it is a fantasy—in a complex technology a few clever people can make a shambles—but because out of the shambles can come only the same bad world.

Nonviolent confrontation asks, "What is your real will, when you confront our resistance and have to think, feel and decide? Do you mean, in order to continue your routine, to jail so many, beat so many, investigate so many, bring police on the campus, pass panicky unconstitutional laws, invoke martial law, poison the community further?" By and large, except as an awakener, violence prevents confrontation. Attacked physically, a policeman or soldier responds routinely as a professional, with tear gas or bayonet, but the aim is to get him to think and feel as man and citizen. Confronted, he may respond routinely anyway, but hopefully he cannot continue to do so.

It is possible that the Americans do really intend the Vietnam war or don't care at all. They may be truly complacent with their standard of living, arrogant about American power, indifferent to the lapse of democracy and the militarizing of society, deaf to world outrage, callous about gooks. If this were so, we resisters would have to think in other terms, of exile or "underground." But there is evidence that we are succeeding, that we represent the general will of the body politic.

I here lay all my stress on the legitimacy of resistance. It does not follow, however, that our movement is not radical or even revolutionary, perhaps beyond what many moral resisters think. The Vietnam war is not something isolated that can just be written off. Really to get out of it—and especially the young want really to get out of it and will continue to fight for that—will require a major reconstruction of the American economy, the use of technology, the system of education, foreign relations, the structure of authority and the whole quality of American life. This year the military budget is $84 billion. More significantly, 86 per cent of the money for research and development is for military purposes. Is that the future we intend?

"Civil Disobedience Is Not Justified By Vietnam"
Irving Kristol

Has there ever been, in this country, a movement of protest so unreflective about its principles of action as the present anti-Vietnam "crusade"? I cannot offhand think of one. The kinds of discrimination and judgment that have long been the staple of moral and political philosophy seem utterly incomprehensible to it. One even encounters young people—and not-so-young people, too—who appear to think that dodging the draft is actually a form of conscientious objection! So one is perforce compelled to insist on some elementary distinctions:

(1) Civil disobedience is not a right—though it may, under certain circumstances, be an obligation. A right is a particular freedom you may exercise without penalty. An obligation is something that, in principle, you are not free to evade, regardless of penalty.

(2) Civil disobedience is always defensible—if not always practicable—when one is confronted by the unjust political regime. It *may* be defensible, in certain extreme cases, when one is confronted by the unjust action of a regime that is, on the whole, just and legitimate (i.e., deserving of our loyalty).

(3) Those who are morally committed to civil disobedience can properly claim that the government which arrests them, or the law that punishes them, is so perverse as to be without due authority. What they may *not* do in good conscience is to practice civil disobedience—and then hire a clever lawyer to argue that it wasn't in violation of the law at all, but rather the exercise of some kind of "right."

(4) Civil disobedience is to be distinguished from "dissent" at the one extreme and "resistance" at the other. Dissent assumes that lawful agitation and argument and demonstration can achieve the desired change in government policy. Civil disobedience openly breaches the law and scornfully accepts the penalty; it aims to mobilize opinion through self-sacrificial, exemplary action. Resistance may include all sorts of covert and illegal actions, and will almost certainly include the provocation and perpetration of violence where this is possible.

(5) Those who believe in "resistance" inevitably regard civil

disobedience merely as a tactic, to be employed under conditions where more militant action would be futile. In this case, civil disobedience ceases to have any moral dimension at all and is nothing but a highly organized and artfully contrived species of riot.

(6) Even were I opposed to the Administration's policy in Vietnam, which I am not, I would not regard this case as one in which civil disobedience is justified. The opportunities for dissent are obviously abundant, and even Ho Chi Minh seems to think they can be effectual. But I realize that there are some good people who feel strongly that civil disobedience is the only honorable course open to them. I would only ask of these individuals that they distinguish themselves from those who, talking bombastically of "resistance," mindlessly flirt with revolution-making. You can emulate Thoreau when confronted with the Mexican War, or Lenin when confronted with World War I. But the idea of a Leninist Thoreau is an intellectual and moral absurdity.

Part Four:

INTERPRETATION AND JUSTIFICATION

INTRODUCTION

The reader who has come this far has already had ample opportunity to assess the justifications actually offered by persons engaged in civil disobedience. What, however, is the logic of such justifications? All of the selections in this Part are designed to shed light on this difficult question. H. B. Acton's essay sets out concisely the topic of justification in politics and how, typically, its questions can be resolved and where the major difficulties will be found. As Acton sees it, the justification of disobedience is likely to take one of three major paths: the appeal to the individual's own conscience, construed as a final moral arbiter of what each person ought and ought not to do; the appeal to a "higher" or so-called "natural" law, which may not be embodied in the actual legal structure within which the individual is called upon to act; and the utilitarian appeal to the "common good" or "the greatest happiness of the greatest number." On behalf of each of these three justificatory patterns, especially the second, Acton arranges the relevant considerations and surveys the difficulties. His treatment, of course, is not exhaustive, but nothing less than several volumes of moral philosophy would suffice to do the job adequately.[1]

The essay by John Rawls (published here for the first time) is one of several over the past decade in which he has argued for the special place that "justice as fairness" plays in all our moral and, therefore, also our political and legal thinking. In this essay, he grapples with the specific problem of justifying civil disobedience within the framework of the theory of constitutional democracy. He argues in essence that appeals to the common good or the general welfare, which often seem intelligible only on purely utilitarian assumptions, must also be consistent with the demands of justice and fair play. Thus, it is possible for the prospective civil disobedient to be correct in believing that the consequences of his proposed disobedience are better than the consequences of obedience, and yet be morally wrong to commit that act, because in doing so he would act unjustly toward others. Rawls' general theory of justice, which has aroused steady interest among contemporary philosophers as well as legal and political theorists, enables him to offer what is by far the deepest philosophical analysis that civil disobedience has so far received.

Rawls enumerates four conditions of justified civil disobedience: "The standard means of redress [must] have been tried," the objects of protest must be "substantial and clear violations of justice," the dissenter must be "willing to affirm that everyone else similarly subjected to . . . injustice has the right to . . . protest . . . in a similar way," and the act of disobedience "should be rational and reasonably designed to advance the protester's aims." With some relatively minor variations, these four conditions have been advanced independently by a number of philosophers in recent discussions of the same problem.[2]

These conditions are open to a number of comments. First, while they may justify the civil disobedience of someone who is acting in a constitutional democracy and is committed to its principles, they do not necessarily solve the problem of justification under a tyranny or for someone acting in a democracy but not committed to its principles.[3] There is, therefore, no finality to these four conditions unless it can be shown that there is only one political ideology common to all dissenters and their opponents, in terms of which any conceivable justification must take place. Otherwise, the task of justification will in each case be colored by these differences. (The essay below by Bruce Pech illustrates this problem in some detail.)

Second, the four conditions might be regarded (even by Rawls) not as necessary and jointly sufficient justificatory conditions but instead as a quartet of justificatory variables. That is, we may regard an act of civil disobedience as more or less justified accordingly as the object of protest is a graver or lesser injustice, etc. This interpretation may help us to see how dissenters can disagree among themselves as to why and to what degree their acts are justified even though they agree as to what the criteria of justification are. It also explains how dissenters and their critics can disagree over the justification of a given act of disobedience even when they agree on the criteria of justification and on the relative weight to be accorded to each criterion.

Finally, one must ponder whether these conditions even if satisfied produce a *right* to disobey or the *duty* to disobey. In his essay, Rawls decides on the former but does not speak o the latter. When someone decides he ought to commit civil disobedience, we may well wonder whether this is because he believes he has the *right* to do so or whether it is because he believes he has the *duty* to do so. Most philosophers, Rawls included, would say that the first reason can never be sufficient, and surely this is correct. Some philosophers would also argue that the second reason is inapplicable in this area; while it is possible to decide that one ought to commit civil disobedience, it makes no sense to speak of having the "duty" (or being "obligated") to do so. Yet others would deny this. Michael Walzer, for instance, has recently argued that many men find themselves with such a duty because of their membership in and loyalty to dissenting groups within the larger society of which they are also members.

> . . . men have a *prima facie* obligation to honor the engagements they have explicitly made, to defend the groups and uphold the ideals to which they have committed themselves, even against the state, so long as their disobedience of laws or legally authorized commands does not threaten the very existence of the larger society or endanger the lives of its citizens. It is obedience to the state, when one has a duty to disobey, that must be justified. First explanations are owed to one's brethren, colleagues, or comrades.[4]

But even if Walzer is correct, how does it explain what Thoreau means and how he could be correct in claiming that he, too, has a "duty" to disobey? By what principles can a solitary person determine upon such a duty, especially when it involves him in breaching what is undeniably his *prima facie* duty, viz., obeying the laws of the one society of which he is, willy-nilly, a member? In fact, how can Walzer's own argument take one from what on his account is at best only a *"prima facie* obligation" to what really is one's duty? Or is all this talk of "duty" just a misleading way of saying "I ought to commit civil disobedience," with the "ought" expressive of the true finality of a decision of principle? We are on the threshold of the full range of problems in normative and anlytical ethics, and there is no possibility of trying to sketch a full answer to them within the confines of the present discussion.

Probably no injunction has proved to be more cautionary, at least in the judgment of moral philosophers since Kant, than the demand to consider what one is doing under the supposition that everyone else will do the same. This has special relevance to the civil disobedient because, as we have seen, one of the themes occasionally explicit in criticism of actual cases of civil disobedience is the challenge: "But if everyone did as you do, the consequences would be disastrous, and even you would have to admit it"; and the implication is: "Therefore, in doing as you did, you have in effect cheated, and your civil disobedience is unjustified." In the selection below from Richard Wasserstrom, this argument is developed and criticized (not, one should note, by reference to civil disobedience but to "law evasion"). Wasserstrom tries to show how a judgment of the probable conduct of others, hypothetical and subject to error as it may be, is a perfectly legitimate thing for the prospective disobedient to take into account in justifying his own conduct. Wasserstrom's argument is designed to restore typically utilitarian considerations into the evaluation of prospective conduct in a manner disallowed by Rawls' position.

The argument and analysis so far presented by the selections in this Part will seem to some to be woefully out of touch with the thinking of younger radicals on and off campus whose views, inspired by Mississippi Summer and the Free Speech Movement in Berkeley, are now heard all over the nation. The kind of argument one hears in these quarters does not take any one form. Still, the "New Left" style, though it does not necessarily consist merely of the old leftover radical arguments in disguise, is usually more Marxist in ideology and rhetoric than any of the selections so far would suggest. For these reasons, I have included the essay (specially written for this collection) of a young philosopher, Bruce Pech, which advances this style of reasoning specifically in regard to what he calls "radical disobedience." The reader of his argument may well wonder, however, whether Pech's approach to justification appears different from that of Acton, Rawls, and Wasserstrom, only because he is not willing to press his analysis further. One might even challenge him with this dilemma: Either his argument fails to be a justification of radical disobedience, because it nowhere takes into account the distinctively moral considerations of justice, the common good, equal liberty, etc., which are relevant to any conceivable justification of political conduct; or it does tacitly acknowledge their relevance, in which case the disobedience it would justify is not so "radical" as it seems and, in any case, it cannot escape confronting all the problems of the more conventional arguments.

It is not inevitable that philosophical clarification should proceed by way of or culminate in a definition. Some philosophers have argued that definitions, in general, are unobtainable unless the demands placed upon what is to count as a definition are considerably relaxed. There is, nevertheless, often considerable value in trying to give a definition to a concept, because in arguing for and against the various alternatives, one can illuminate many of the issues at stake in the subject-matter to which the term being defined applies. This is one of the ways in which philosophical analysis, a second-order inquiry, sheds light on first-order political and moral issues. It largely accounts for the steady preoccupation by philosophers since Socrates with what appear to some to be merely matters of definition. Granting, therefore, that a suitable definition of any key term is bound to be but one proposal among others, and that while it is pulled in the direction of what the writer believes to be the prevailing usage, it is also under pressure from his own particular view of the topic under discussion (in this case, the moral relation of the individual to duly constituted authority), I offer here some brief definitional though not definitive reflections.

Nothing so well registers the present confusion over civil disobedience as the self-conscious efforts to define it. Gandhi once said, "Civil disobedience is civil breach of unmoral statutory enactments";[5] this has the consequence that unjustifiable civil disobedience becomes all but inconceivable. Recently, W. H. Auden wrote, "I commit an act of civil disobedience if I deliberately break a law because I believe it to be unjust . . .";[6] this has the consequence that any lad under legal age who thinks it is morally permissible for him to drink when no one will notice it, and who does so, is committing civil disobedience. Judged by any reasonable criterion, both Gandhi's and Auden's statements are inadequate as definitions. Unfortunately, if one looks to scholars for more exact formulations (never mind the unabridged dictionaries!), one goes away no less confused. Consider the following half-dozen quotations, each offered by a professional philosopher, lawyer or political scientist:

(1) "Anyone commits an act of civil disobedience if and only if he acts illegally, publicly, nonviolently, and conscientiously with the intent to frustrate (one of) the laws, policies, or decisions of his government."[7]

(2) ". . . civil disobedience is a course of legally unauthorized conduct engaged in by relatively homogeneous groups for redress of grievances."[8]

(3) ". . . civil disobedience [is] . . . the *right,* under principles of natural or moral law, to determine which laws are just and to disobey unjust laws provided the disobedience is open and peaceable."[9]

(4) ". . . civil disobedience may be defined as an organized refusal to obey particular laws in order to secure or prevent political change by exerting direct pressure on an offending government."[10]

(5) "By an act of civil disobedience I shall mean an act of deliberate and open violation of law with the intent, within the framework of the prevailing form of government, to protest a wrong or to accomplish some betterment in the society."[11]

(6) " 'Civil disobedience' . . . [is] any act or process of public defiance of a law or policy enforced by established governmental authorities, in so far as the action is premeditated, understood by the actor(s) to be illegal or of contested legality, carried out and persisted in for limited

public ends, and by way of carefully chosen and limited means." [12]

It is an instructive exercise to assess the logic of these six statements. According to (3), civil disobedience is not an *act* but a *right*. The attempt by a nonviolent anarchist to overthrow the government cannot be civil disobedience, if (5) and (6) are correct. Nonviolence, in intention or in consequence, is not a feature of all civil disobedience as it is defined in (4) and (6). Civil disobedience by a solitary individual is clearly ruled out by (2) and (4). One could continue indefinitely. If scholars cannot agree on what civil disobedience is, how can ordinary men be expected to? What could possibly be accomplished in an attempt to justify an act of civil disobedience, when as likely as not those disputing the matter do not even understand the same thing by the same terms?

Of course, there is nothing peculiar in this. Comparable disagreement can be found over the formal definitions of almost every term central to any body of theory. It is not true that what we have here is a symptom of "persuasive definitions," peculiar and inevitable in political and moral discourse, but thankfully absent from other areas of theoretical interest. Nor is it necessary for intelligible communication and dispute that all parties agree on one and only one use of key terms. All that is required is that at each point the use be intelligible and open to further clarification.

Accordingly, there is no need for me to try to arbitrate among the above definitions, although it is tempting (not least since one of them happens to be my own). It is far more profitable to inspect more closely the properties of civil disobedience mentioned in the definitions and test each by the degree to which it captures important and recurring features of acts and campaigns of civil disobedience as these have been presented and interpreted throughout this volume. That task the reader must perform for himself.

POLITICAL JUSTIFICATION

H. B. Acton

I

The question with which our discussion commences is this. We imagine a government and its officials on the one hand, and a citizen or group of citizens on the other. The government's officers are upholding some legal ordinance, and the citizen or group of citizens are considering whether they ought or ought not to obey. We suppose, furthermore, that, at any rate for a time, the question of obedience or disobedience is being discussed in as rational a manner as is possible. The question then is: how *could* such a matter be rationally discussed between two such parties? Clearly it could not be rationally discussed if there were no prospect whatever of the issue's being brought to an agreed conclusion. Disputation that cannot lead anywhere is not rational disputation at all, but rather a sort of unorganized amusement or disguised fight like competitive boasting that comes to an end merely because one of the parties can think of nothing more to say rather than because a conclusion has been reached. When there is an argument between a citizen and his government about whether the citizen should obey or not, by reference to what sort of consideration could one party hope rationally to convince the other that

Reprinted by permission of the author and publisher from "Political Justification," in H. D. Lewis, ed., *Contemporary British Philosophy* (London: George Allen & Unwin, Ltd., 1956), pp. 21–44.

obedience or disobedience is the proper decision? We know, of course, that such arguments are seldom carried out on a purely rational plane, that, indeed, they are not intended to remain on the purely argumentative level at all. The questioning citizen will either obey or disobey, and the governmental party will terminate the discussion with an attempt at enforcement. But when these things have been done it will be possible to look back on them and consider whether they were done rightly or wrongly and why they were right if they were right or why they were wrong if they were wrong. Both parties to the discussion, we are supposing, wish to act in a way that they can *justify,* and hence our question is about the nature of justification in politics. We want to know how it is possible, when the parties concerned are a government on the one side and a citizen on the other, for the one to justify its conduct to the other, whether it be the enforcement of obedience or an act or policy of disobedience.

In modern times the question has most often been put in terms of justifying obedience to government, but when the question is put in this way there is at any rate a suggestion that obedience is in greater need of justification than disobedience is. The situation we have in mind, however, is one in which one of the parties has open to him the alternatives of obeying or disobeying, and hence, if he is to justify his conduct he must be ready to justify obedience if that is the course he decides he should adopt, or disobedience if that is the course he decides he should adopt. The presumption against obedience has been encouraged, of course, by the theory of a State of Nature in which men are supposed to live without any political superior. For the masterless condition is, in the very act of being called "natural," regarded as original and in some degree proper, so that it is the derivative civil state that is called upon to produce credentials. In fact, however, it is men who have been born in civil society and have lived their lives in it who may come, on occasion, to doubt whether they owe loyalty to the state, and therefore their position is more realistically described as one in which reasons are put forward in favour of disobedience than as one in which they ask why they should obey. The question "Why should I obey the laws of the state?" might, therefore, be understood as a question about whether there ought to be any state or government at all rather than as a call for justification in a dispute between a citizen and his government. Justifying government is a very different thing from justifying the acts of this or that government or of this or that objector. It is the latter sort of justification that I wish to consider, since it seems more reasonable to set out from a situation that sometimes arises than to raise a question which is so abstract that we cannot even see how to begin answering it.

Obedience to government is a clear enough idea—there is a law or ordinance, and those people obey it who do what is prescribed to them in it. Disobedience, however, may take a variety of forms. It may take the form of refusing to obey and of then remaining passive to receive the penalities of disobedience. It may take the form of not obeying and of endeavouring to escape the legal consequences. Or it may take the form of not obeying and of endeavouring to overthrow the government by force and to replace it by some other government. The first form of disobedience is called, curiously enough, "passive obedience," by virtue, I suppose, of the obedience given to the officers who apply the penalties. The second form of disobedience is of no interest to us in this paper, since either it is nothing but a sort of unprincipled subterfuge or else it leads to the third. The third form of disobedience is rebellion, and it is this that writers on the subject have mostly had in mind when they have considered the alternative to obeying the state authorities. I hope to show later that the first form of disobedience, that called "passive obedience," has a very important role to play in the process of political justification.

It will be noticed that in the last two paragraphs I have very briefly commented on two important features of the Whig tradition in political philosophy. Whig political philosophers have generally assumed a "natural," masterless condition from which men moved into civil society. Because of this assumption, Whigs have supposed that it is obedience rather than disobedience that needs to be justified. Whig political philosophers have also generally regarded forcible resistance rather than passive obedience as the proper counter to tyranny. I have now made the preliminary suggestion that, if we start our enquiry from the realistic situation of particular citizens in dispute with a particular government rather than from the abstract one of natural men and government in general, we shall get a more adequate idea of what political justification is.

II

"Justification," says Wittgenstein, "consists in appealing to something independent." The parties we are considering, the upholders of government on the one hand and the objector on the other, are both seeking to justify their position, are both seeking to justify, that is to say, the action they propose to take, and they both believe, therefore, that there is something they can both refer to that will somehow *show* that one course or the other is the right one. We must consider, therefore, what this independent thing can be, and wherein its independence consists.

It is natural to use the word "appeal," and to think, in the first place, of the legal notions of laws, rules, courts, and judges. Of course, when the dispute is about obedience or disobedience the appeal cannot be made to the *actual* laws, since with regard to them the judge can only counsel obedience, except in so far as the disputed ordinance may be unconstitutional and obedience is deferred until this can be established by the appropriate court. Nevertheless, when the attempt is made to carry rational discussion of the sort of issue we are considering as far as it can be carried, as much as possible of the judicial atmosphere and procedure is retained. It is a matter of "Let God be my judge" or "I must lay my case before a Higher Court than that which now has me in its power." This tendency to appeal beyond an actual court or positive law is present even when there is no dispute between government and subject, as can be seen from the frequency with which fundamental laws are regarded as of divine origin. It is only the most sophisticated governments which support their legislation by reference merely to their own fiat. In cases of dispute there is generally some attempt at putting both government and objector side by side before some common superior. If this were not done, neither governments nor objectors could take even the first step in justifying themselves, the former because they could do no more than threaten in their own name, the latter because disobedience undoubtedly is disobedience.

We are led in the first place, then, to laws which are held to bind governments no less than subjects. These laws are regarded both by the subject and the government as having authority over them. Neither party is in a position to change them. Neither party can claim to have made them. If they form part of any actual legislation, the legislator is not their creator or author but merely their transmitter. But what kind of law can this be, and how is it formulated? It does not help, except perhaps in a practical way, to say that it is divine, since either God *willed* it and it is arbitrary, else he *transmits* it and we are back where we started. It is hard to get beyond the notion of laws which no one has made and which have authority over individuals and governments. When we say that they have authority over individuals and governments we mean that individuals and governments ought to submit to them. Submitting to them is using them to guide and justify conduct, and this could not be done unless there were some awareness of them. Moral laws are, of course, the main instance of this kind of law, and, for purposes of political justification it is they, along with customary law and Natural Law, that are appealed to. Natural Law is that part of the moral law that is relevant to political or other public concerns, so that for our present purposes we have to consider customary law and Natural Law. Customary laws are, of course, different in different parts of the world, whereas Natural Law is held to be universal. Furthermore, whereas Natural Law is held to be rational in a manner that is in some degree analogous to the intuitive rationality of some logical and mathematical axioms, customary law is obviously an historical growth which cannot claim anything in the slightest degree like logical or mathematical rationality. The obviousness, to members of a traditional society, of their customary laws, is the result of training and familiarity, while the obviousness of Natural Law has been thought to indicate a moral necessity analogous to logical necessity. Now when Wittgenstein said that justification consists in appealing to something independent, he had in mind, as the independent thing, something like a railway timetable. It is only when there is such a thing to refer to that an opinion about the official time of a train or a suggestion about when it will be necessary to leave home to catch it, can be justified, and the question arises whether customary law or Natural Law could be appealed to in any such way. Is customary law or Natural Law a public object that both parties to a dispute can have, so to say, before them as a means of settling their difference?

To refer to the customs of a society is, of course, much more complicated than referring to a railway timetable, but in principle there is a certain similarity. For example, there may be written records of some of these customs, and there may be recognized experts in them who, on being consulted, will give a definite and unanimous response. Unless this is so, it is in vain that appeal is made to customary law. If the authenticity of the documents or the bona fides of the experts is doubted, and if no revised documents or purified experts are forthcoming and acceptable, then justification of this sort has become impossible. It is logically impossible for A to justify a course of action to B if B rejects the authorities to which A appeals. To withdraw confidence from the texts and their interpreters just is to withdraw from this particular mode of justification. When faith in a traditional order is breaking down, those who have lost their faith say that the defenders of the old order are irrational. By this they mean that they are appealing to rules that have no authority. The revolutionaries in such a situation, therefore, are calling upon their opponents to submit the dispute to a new tribunal. This might conceivably be the customs of some other traditional society so that one individual point of reference would be substituted for another. But it is more usual, once the traditional order has been questioned, for the new appeal to be made to the univeral system of Natural Law.

Now Natural Law is not individual and identifiable in the detailed way in which the customs of a particular society may be. It is said to be discoverable, of course, in the hearts and minds of all men, but policies of action cannot be justified by each party's proclaiming that something within him requires him to do what he is doing and the other man to do what he tells him. One's own inward conviction is not something independent that can be appealed to by *both* parties to the dispute. To refer inwards in this way may be to adopt the *arbitrary* attitude that is incompatible with justification of any kind. To this it may be replied that it is of the essence of Natural Law that each individual, looking within himself, finds the *same* principles, and that, this being so, it can *both* be found inwardly *and* serve as a common principle of justification. But how does any individual know that other men have discovered the same thing, by looking within themselves, that he has found by loking within himself? Only by comparing what they say with what he has found. Hence the existence of common principles of Natural Law written in each heart or mind can only be of practical relevance if they are also spoken or written in some common tongue. If, therefore, they are to serve as principles of justification in political disputes there must be some list of them, or some recognized custodian of them, to which common reference is made. At a time when philosopher-lawyers like Grotius or Pufendorf were held throughout Europe to be capable of formulating them in generally acceptable terms, there was still a possibility of appealing to them as to something independent of the particular whim or interest of some tyrant or fanatic. But when jurists and philosophers had each become specialists, the jurists concerning themselves almost exclusively with particular systems of positive law, and the philosophers, as Rousseau noted, striving at all costs to be original, the Natural Law, through being disregarded, ceased to serve as a source of justification, although if it came into regard once more, it might resume the office it has now relinquished.

Concrete principles of customary law, and the more abstract principles of Natural Law, have each their practical merits and defects as an independent point of reference in political justification. To appeal to the customs of a particular society is to appeal to something fairly definite. Furthermore, when such an appeal is made in a dispute between a government and a subject or group of subjects it is obvious that they both regard themselves as members of the same continuing society and hence have a common concern of a pretty concrete kind. These are the features of customary society that led Hegel to prefer it as a less abstract and less arbitrary ("subjective") court of appeal than Natural Law. When there is no single church or other universal community to proclaim it, Natural Law suffers from the two opposite defects of being, on the one hand platitudinous and therefore settling nothing, or on the other hand of being constantly added to and interpreted so that different parties appeal to, or even manufacture, different parts of it. This second defect may be illustrated by Berkeley's polemical device of supporting his defence of passive obedience by claiming that it is a precept of Natural Law. In general, Natural Law consists of rules by which actions may be condemned or merely permitted rather than rules that lead towards positive achievements. Since it is largely negative, there can be no such attachment to it on the part of individuals as exists when there is loyalty to a specific set of institutions.

A third sort of independent thing to which appeal is made in political justification is the common good or general happiness. But before I pass on to discuss this it will be useful, I think, if I linger somewhat on the notion, prominent, as I have already said, in certain forms of Natural Law theory, of appealing to practical maxims held to be revealed to the heart or mind or reason of each individual. The appeal to conscience is often regarded in this way, and Hegel, if what I have said above is correct, was not without reason in suspecting a tendency towards arbitrariness in this inward-looking procedure. Let us, therefore, consider how the appeal to conscience is associated with political justication.

III

We have imagined, it will be recalled, a dispute between a government on the one hand and a subject on the other. The latter is inclined to disobey some important legal command, and the issue is to be discussed rationally and fairly between the parties. We ask how either party could justify its decision to the other, and the form of justification we now have to consider is that known as "the appeal to conscience." It is pointed out on the one hand that such an appeal may be quite whimsical and that crimes may be committed in the name of conscience no less than in the name of liberty. This was Hegel's opinion when he remarked that Robespierre's Reign of Virtue almost immediately became an unprincipled Reign of Terror. On the other hand, however, there is something respectable and impressive about the appeal to conscience which makes us reluctant to say that there is nothing in it but arbitrary whim.

According to the *Oxford English Dictionary*, one meaning of "conscience" is "consciousness of right and wrong," and when the word is understood in this way a man is not necessarily consulting some private voice when, as we say, he searches or consults his conscience. For a man who searches his conscience is trying to make up his mind about what he ought to do, and if he says that his conscience forbids him to obey, he means that he *ought* to disobey, and if asked why, he will refer, not to any private illumination, but to the considerations that have led him to make this decision. It would take me too far from the main object of this paper if I were to discuss in detail what sort of considerations these are. Some have already been mentioned when we discussed custom and Natural Law, but there will obviously be more specific ones relating to the particular situation of the agent and the people with whom he is connected. My point here is that they are normally open to formulation and discussion. Discussion between disagreeing parties can go on until action is necessary, and at that point both parties must act on the judgement they have by then reached.

It should be observed that each party may think that the other is right in opposing him. Let us suppose that A has decided that he ought to refuse obedience, and that B has decided that it is his duty to secure A's arrest in the event of A's doing this. It is quite possible that A thinks that B ought to arrest him and that B thinks that A ought to disobey. A, for example, may be a political leader who has told his followers that a certain measure should be disobeyed if it becomes law, and the measure may have become law and have been disobeyed already by some of A's followers. In such circumstances (which it would be tedious to elaborate) it might be A's duty to disobey even though he now recognizes that he ought not to have urged this in the first place, and B might agree that A ought to disobey though he believes it is his own duty to proceed against A for it. In such a situation, the conflict of the different people's duties is by no means a sign of arbitrariness. Indeed, the fact that each recognizes that the other ought to oppose him shows that both parties are guided by a similar view of the same system of social relationships within which they occupy different positions.

The next case to be considered is that in which one or both of the parties thinks that the other party is *not* doing what is right. Let us suppose, for example, that A thinks he ought to disobey and that B thinks that A ought to obey. B may nevertheless also think that A is quite sincere in holding his mistaken view and in endeavouring to pursue his wrong course of action. B might come to think, therefore, that A's false view of his duty being what it is, A ought to disobey. In such a case, B is able to consider A's duty from A's point of view, to contemplate the circumstances that A considers, and to see that if they were as A thought they were, then it *would* be A's duty to do what A now (mistakenly) thinks is right. This leads us to a most important step. For we now say: "*If* A had been aware of such and such, and had realized the relevance of this or that moral rule, then he would have seen that he ought to have done X; but the matter appeared differently to him at the time, and he therefore did right to follow his own conscience." In these circumstances B may hold that A ought to follow his own conscience rather than to do what B has rightly told him to do. The case we considered in the last paragraph was of one individual recognizing that another ought to oppose him because of this other man's situation and the duties involved in it. The case we are now considering is of one individual recognizing that another man ought to oppose him because of this other man's sincerely held but false view of what his duty is. The essence of this second case is that a man ought to follow his own conscience rather than what someone else tells him to do when these two things come into conflict.

We must next consider, therefore, what it would be for someone to do what someone else told him to do instead of following his own conscience. The case we are considering is that in which A is doing what he has decided he ought to do notwithstanding B's arguments to the contrary. For this to happen, A must have *made up his mind* that he ought to disobey. If he is to do what B tells him to do rather than what his conscience tells him to do, he must have made up his mind he ought to disobey and must decide to obey notwithstanding this. That is to say, when the time for action comes he must fail to do what he is quite sure he ought to have done. He must therefore have been *tempted* in some way. In the case we are considering, in which B is an officer of the government, it is possible that A obeys him against his conscience out of fear. Or he may have been attracted by personal liking for him, or by general respect for his authority, or he might merely have been lazy, since conformity is generally the more immediately comfortable course. But once A has decided he ought to disobey he has also decided that submission to any of these or to any similar temptations would be wrong. For example, if he has decided that he ought to disobey notwithstanding his friendship for B, then if he allows this friendship to influence him into obedience, it must be, in his own eyes, a *reprehensible* act of friendship that he performs. It will be seen that we must distinguish here between a man's making up his mind what his duty is and then being tempted not to perform it, and his not being able to make up his mind or his making it up and then changing it. Thus, two of the temptations I have just mentioned, that of friendship and that of respect for authority, might not always be temptations in the way in which fear and laziness are. For A might first think he ought to disobey and then, when he considers his friendship for B or the many achievements of the government that B is serving, he may hesitate and finally conclude that, after all, these weigh the balance in favour of obedience.

There is, I think, a rather important conclusion to be drawn from this. If there is to be a clear case of anyone's acting against his conscience, he must have, so to say, a *definite* conscience, and must be, if not *absolutely* convinced, then at any rate pretty sure, of the direction in which his duty lies. When a man's moral situation is complicated (as is very often the case in political affairs) he may hesitate between different courses and finally take the course he does, not from any strong conviction of its rightness, but because events force *some* action upon him and this action seems at any rate not to be wrong. We might say that in such cases his conscience approves a *range* of actions or does not strongly disapprove of any single member of that range, so that to go against his conscience would be to go against this whole range. If so, then *following* his conscience would not be any very definite thing, but would involve a conviction of what ought *not* to be done along with doubts about the positive course. This indicates that in very complicated political situations it may be most misleading to suggest that there is any positive course that is a matter of conscience for any of the parties concerned, although it will always be possible to imagine actions which it would be wrong for any of them to perform. In such situations, honourable men may decide on a course because *some* decision *must* be taken and this one is not wrong.

Nevertheless, if someone *is* convinced that a particular course is his duty, then that is the course *he* ought to pursue. It is this proposition that has seemed to some philosophers to make conscience a variable and personal affair and to suggest that a man's duty is what he *thinks* is his duty. On the one hand it seems obvious that if a man thinks he ought to pursue a certain course, then that is the course he ought to pursue, and yet, on the other hand, it seems shocking to suggest that a man's duty just is what he *thinks* it is. Attempts have been made to resolve this conflict by distinguishing between subjective and objective duty, but it seems to me that the matter can be dealt with more convincingly in the following way. In the first place, as we have seen, a man does not have to look within himself for some purely private guide in order to find what it is that he thinks is his duty. He has to consider the situation in which he must act, relevant principles of behaviour, probable consequences of this or that course, other people's expectations, and so on. He may find it hard to decide what he ought to do, and if action is forced upon him there may not be any single action which his conscience prescribes. In such circumstances he may well take other people's advice, or even be persuaded or bullied by them, without acting contrary to his conscience, since on this matter his conscience is not formed or definite. In such a case, his duty to do what he thinks is his duty, is his duty to act cautiously and without fanaticism on a course that he is quite prepared to find is not the right one after all. But if, on the other hand, a man has come to a *definite* conclusion that he ought to act in a certain way, then this is the *only* way he can act in without going against his conscience.

There is a sense of "think" in which it merely indicates that a view is actually held by someone, as in the sentence: "He thinks that the Etruscans originally came from Asia Minor." There is another sense of "think" in which it indicates that the man who is said to think something is aware that his view is not certainly true, as in the sentence: "He thinks that the Etruscans originally came from Asia Minor but is by no means dogmatic about it." There is a third sense of "think" in which someone who knows that someone else is in error may express this by saying, with emphasis on the main verb: "That is what he *thinks*," or by saying some such thing as: "He *thinks* that Napoleon was born in France." In the sense of "think" in which it refers to someone's actual moral belief, a man could not possibly do his duty without doing what he thinks is his duty, for there is nothing else that a man intent on doing his duty *could* do. In the sense of "think" in which it indicates hesitation on the part of the person who is said to be thinking, no *definite* conscience can be said to exist, so that "It is his duty to do what he thinks is his duty" means that it is his duty to do one of a certain range of actions, that he will not do wrong if he does any one of them, and that he will do wrong if he does none of them. In the sense of "think" in which it indicates that the man who is said to think is wrong, "It is his duty to do what he thinks is his duty" means: "He has a wrong view about what his duty is, but since he can only act on or against the view he actually has, then from the moral point of view he will do better to act on his wrong view than to be tempted away from it by laziness or self-interest or by some other non-moral consideration." The dictum, therefore, that a man's duty is to do what he *thinks* is his duty, is not, when properly understood, either sceptical or nihilistic. It emphasizes that moral action is conscious action, and that conscious action is necessarily performed in the light of circumstances as they appear to the agent. It emphasizes, furthermore, that it is possible to make mistakes about what one ought to do without those mistakes being morally reprehensible, however unfortunate they may be in other respects.

It will be seen, therefore, that when we consider an action from the point of view of conscience we always consider it from the point of view of the person who performs it. No one can have a conscience about what someone else does—unless, indeed, he has induced this other person to do whatever it is that he has done. Talk about conscience, therefore, is necessarily about how an act or course of action accords or fails to accord with the agent's view of what he ought to have done. It follows from this that if one man knows what another man's conscience tells him to do, and if this, if done, would lead to actions which conflict with what the first man's conscience tells *him* to do, then the first man may both approve the actions of the other man and at the same time conscientiously oppose them. How does this affect the matter when the first man is an agent of the government and the second man is a conscientiously disobedient subject? Justification cannot be merely in terms of one's own inner tribunal. If it is to be distinguishable from an arbitrary fiat or egotistic coup there must be something independent to appeal to. But when consciences clash in the fundamental way I have just been describing, what is there to appeal to? There may be nothing but the rule that it is better for a man to follow his own conscience even though, in the view of other people, it is a wrong conscience (what Aquinas calls a *conscientia errans*), than for him to follow any course that does not have the sanction of his conscience. This rule, by itself, can do very little to lead to practical agreement between the parties who appeal to it. It can lead them to respect one another, but if they are to co-operate practically they must both of them be able to appeal to something more definite and concrete than the personally centered principle of merely following conscience whatever it may be.

There are some consequences of this that seem to me to be rather important for political philosophy. If two parties are to accept and act on the principle that a man ought to follow his own conscience whether it be right or wrong, each must be able to ascertain what the other party's conscience is. It is notorious that in complex political circumstances this is very difficult and that in consequence they give rise to a good deal of suspicion and cynicism. If this is to be lessened—it can hardly be possible to allay it altogether—a man who is appealing to an idiosyncratic or minority conscience must have some means of showing that it is indeed to his conscience that he is making his appeal. He can only do this by the consistency of his behaviour in relation to the peculiar principles he professes and, more particularly, by his sticking to them when this results in his personal disadvantage. This is why I said above that "passive obedience" has an important part to play in the process of political justification. Those who disobey the laws are often endeavouring to further their own personal ends or to oust others from positions of power and prestige, but when disobedience is accompanied by submission to legal penalties the distinction between ambition and personal integrity is marked as closely as it can be. It may be marked, also, by the hardships which a revolutionary is prepared to undergo in his unpopular cause, but who knows what daydreams of an ultimate refined vengeance sustain him? The distinction is marked too, though somewhat less drastically, by the convention of some parliaments that a minster resigns if some important policy or prediction of his comes to nought. The failure may be due to no serious fault on his part, and he may be the most suitable person to retrieve the situation, but he resigns in order to demonstrate that his own career is of less real concern to him than is the successful performance of the duties of his office. If a statesman thinks that the public good requires him to play the part of a trimmer, he runs the risk of obloquy and can at the best hope for no more than an ambiguous epitaph. Trimming, however high-minded it may be in a particular series of events, debases the political currency by increasing the difficulties of distinguishing between what is genuine and what is counterfeit.

I said above that when each party to a political dispute allows that the other is following his conscience, each will respect the other. Now this respect is something over and above the respect that consists in paying attention to the rights of others. The respect I am now calling attention to arises from a recognition that the individual who is respected is doing his duty as he sees it, and involves more, therefore, than a mere readiness to respect his rights. A question, here, for political philosophers concerns how, in what sort of action, one party can manifest his recognition that his opponent is following his conscience. There is no space to pursue this very far, but we may note that this sort of respect does not necessarily issue in leniency or indulgence, whether by government to subject or subject to government, since it is one thing to recognize that someone else is doing his duty and quite another to change one's own view of what one's own consists in. Indeed, an extreme readiness to give way before the moral challenge of others may, by making the profession of moral challenger an easy one, increase the occasions on which conscience is the cover for ambition. It is obvious that the sort of language the parties use in addressing one another is most important, and that abuse and contempt are quite incompatible with the recognition that the other party is following his conscience. The general point I should like to make here is that if this sort of respect is to be possible, fixed modes of manifesting it must exist; there must be etiquettes or rituals which all the parties understand and use. These may, of course, change, but if in some excess of radicalism they are abolished, then justification in terms of conscience becomes quite impossible.

What has just been said, I think, throws some light on the nature of the liberal political ideal. Liberalism arose, in part, out of the struggle for religious toleration, in the course of which such men as Bayle and Locke appealed to the principle that it is wrong to require an individual to subscribe to religious principles that produce no conviction in him. Bayle argued that penalties against the profession of particular religious beliefs ignored that "the first and most indispensable of our obligations is that of never acting against the inspiration of conscience," and Locke wrote that "No way whatsoever that I shall walk in against the dictates of my conscience will ever bring me to the mansions of the blessed." Now if what Bayle and Locke wrote and what I have just said is correct, it may follow that it is the duty of the persecutor to follow his persecuting conscience, though he should also respect the conscience of the religious dissenter by whatever means this sort of respect is exercised. It will certainly be the duty of the dissenter to undergo punishment or to go to some other country rather than to profess a religion that he believes is false. Thus the principle of respect for conscience cannot, on its own, provide a rule by which conflicting policies may be judged. Its inability in this respect is (or would be were it possible) still further increased when it is suggested that different people may act conscientiously in terms of opposed moral codes. Moral tolerance raises greater difficulties than religious tolerance does, and I am inclined to believe that the liberal principle of toleration is of little practical importance unless it is associated with more definite rules such as are comprised in Natural Law. We may ask, in this connection, whether there are rules of conduct which could not possibly function as principles of conscience. No one, for example, could be conscientiously wicked, in the sense of ascertaining what would be wrong for him to do and then deliberately doing it just because it was wrong. This is impossible because we mean by "following conscience" the attempt to do what the agent believes is right. Could a man, then, make lying, or murder, a principle of conscience? He would have to believe that it was right for him to deceive other people, not only occasionally, but regularly, and that it was right for him to take the lives of innocent non-combatants. It is difficult to take at all seriously the idea that someone who is at all capable of thinking in terms of doing what is right should regard it as a matter of conscience that he should follow a rule of deception or assassination. The case of the Thugs (or Thags) of India is often cited in this connection, but the fact that they gave only a part of their loot to their goddess Kali and kept most of it for themselves suggests that the *Encyclopaedia Britannica* is correct in describing them as "a confederacy of professional assassins." Kant was substantially right when he said that "in the case of natural laws there can be no innocent errors." Conscience is so incongruous with systematic violation of Natural Law that we tend to believe that someone who claims conscience for such violations is either mad or a pretender. Moral tolerance, therefore, can only extend to such moral differences as do not conflict with the basic moral principles. Authenticity has no claim to respect (although it may be admired as an animal or other natural object is admired) unless it is consistent with these principles.

IV

I have said that a third independent thing that is appealed to in political justification is the common good or general happiness. The phrase "common good," of course, is part of the vocabulary of Natural Law theorists, but when this system fell into disrepute the idea arose that the general happiness was something more definite which could be appealed to with greater prospect of agreement. Indeed, Bentham and J. S. Mill believed that if the utilitarian criterion was used, it would enable scientific methods to be employed in matters of government and facilitate social agreement thereby. Obedience or disobedience, or any other disputed social decision, would be justified by appealing to the knowledge that one course rather than the other would in fact lead to the greatest happiness. Bentham, with his belief that money could be used as an instrument for measuring happiness just as thermometers are used for measuring temperatures, thought that this would be a simpler thing to do than it has in fact proved to be. In the last hundred years such things as statistics of death and disease, of output, incomes and consumption, along with the device of the retail price index, have been used in the hope that they would do what Bentham had hoped would be done with the money measure. Disputes about rights, it was thought, are as insoluble as the disputes of metaphysicians, and would be rendered obsolete, as metaphysics has been, by use of scientific methods.

This is a view that deserves a great deal more examination than it usually gets either from its supporters or opponents, and here I can only call attention to one or two fundamental points.

It will be noticed in the first place that stress is laid on the importance of ascertaining which course of conduct will in fact lead to the general happiness of the society in question. But the attempt to find out the most effective means of carrying out the policy it is desired to carry out is relevant not only to the utilitarian system of justification but also to the others I have mentioned, since *any* course that is undertaken is the better for being carried out in the light of the best available knowledge. It is not this aspect of scientific utilitarianism, therefore, that needs our attention here, but that part of it that concerns the end to be aimed at and its more or less accurate estimation.

In the second place, then, let us consider the end to be achieved. There are two features of it that need examination, its measurability on the one hand, and its singleness or individuality on the other.

As to the first, the utilitarian aim has been to secure as long life as possible along with as little disease and as little poverty as possible. The measurable content of happiness thus consists in longevity, health and the consumption of goods. Now it is obvious that there are many things besides these that are prized and form part of happiness. Some of these extra things, such as sport and artistic enjoyment, can be submitted to some sort of quantitative treatment, by such methods as enumerating the members of sports clubs or of books purchased or plays produced. Others, such as the happiness to be gained in love and friendship, do not seem to be amenable to this sort of treatment at all, and yet make up a large part of what is most satisfying in the lives of happy people. Why, then, should there be so much stress on the measurable aspects of happiness? Partly, no doubt, just because they *are* measurable in a fashion and so *can* provide *some* sort of basis for comparison. (We are all familiar with the method of justifying an educational policy in terms of money spent or buildings put up.) But it would be a mere irrational obsession with measurability to deny the existence or importance of those parts of happiness that cannot be measured. Another reason, no doubt, is that life, health and the consumption of (at least some) goods are conditions of there being any happiness at all. But why should we be asked to judge the whole happiness of a society in terms of what are so obviously only a part of it? I believe that there is only one answer to this that has any plausibility, namely, that it is believed that the standard enjoyments that all can have ought to be given priority over the more refined pleasures of which many people may be incapable. If this is so, then the measurable happiness criterion is not an independent one, but depends upon a view about just distribution and just timing which may or may not be correct but which must be judged in terms of rights and duties and other terms of traditional morality and Natural Law.

In conclusion something must be said about the singleness or individuality of the end referred to when appeal is made to the common good or general happiness. It cannot be doubted that when there are important disputes within a society, those who are sincerely aiming at a right solution regard the appeal to the common good as relevant and necessary. But what is this common good, and how can it be referred to in the process of political justification? The word "common" in the phrase "common good," and the word "general" in the phrase "general happiness," are clearly meant to contrast, in some way, with what is peculiar or particular. When individuals or groups are opposed to one another and wish to justify their case rationally, it will not constitute such a justification if each appeals to his *own* good. Hence "common" cannot refer to some range of personal interests that every individual member of the society has—if it did our liability to service could never be more than limited. Perhaps, then, the appeal, in such circumstances, is to a rule that applies to all in the way that moral rules do. If so, it must be to a rule that concerns the society as a whole as well as each individual in it. Following out this line of thought, we can conceive of such rules as the following. "All the members of this society are, together, more important than any single member of it." "No individual or group within this society has a right to ignore the rights and interests of the rest." "We all have a duty to try to maintain our society as a whole, even to the extent of risking personal extinction." It seems to me that it is this sort of rule, with a reference to a *particular* society, that is appealed to in political justification. Furthermore, justification is by reference to a society rather than by reference to a number of individuals. I suppose it is true that the existence or survival of many individuals is more important than the existence or survival of one individual, though some might question this, and in any case it is difficult to be sure that the convincingness of the proposition is not due merely to the arithmetical truth that many are more than one. But the appeal to the common good seems to presuppose loyalty to a society that continues in being longer than does the membership of any set of contemporary individuals. Other principles of Natural Law, such as those about promises or gratitude, apply to any man anywhere. But the duty to have regard to the common good is different from these, and has some kinship with the older mode of justification by reference to the customs of a given society. The difference is that, whereas the appeal to custom was to fairly fixed rules of behaviour, the appeal to the common good in modern times involves reference to institutions that are known to be changing. This would be as uncertain as an appeal to a judge who could change the law whenever he wished, were it not that many of the changes are in accordance with aims that are shared and promoted by most members of the society. Even so, political justification in a modern society is a much less definite process than it was in earlier times, since the common good to which appeal is made is so much more volatile.

THE JUSTIFICATION OF CIVIL DISOBEDIENCE

John Rawls

I. Introduction

I should like to discuss briefly, and in an informal way, the grounds of civil disobedience in a constitutional democracy. Thus, I shall limit my remarks to the conditions under which we may, by civil disobedience, properly oppose legally established democratic authority; I am not concerned with the situation under other kinds of government nor, except incidentally, with other forms of resistance. My thought is that in a reasonably just (though of course not perfectly just) democratic regime, civil disobedience, when it is justified, is normally to be understood as a political action which addresses the sense of justice of the majority in order to urge reconsideration of the measures protested and to warn that in the firm opinion of the dissenters the conditions of social cooperation are not being honored. This characterization of civil disobedience is intended to apply to dissent on fundamental questions of internal policy, a limitation which I shall follow to simplify our question.

Originally presented at the meetings of the American Political Science Association, September 1966. Some revisions have been made and two paragraphs have been added to the last section. Copyright © 1968 by John Rawls.

II. The Social Contract Doctrine

It is obvious that the justification of civil disobedience depends upon the theory of political obligation in general, and so we may appropriately begin with a few comments on this question. The two chief virtues of social institutions are justice and efficiency, where by the efficiency of institutions I understand their effectiveness for certain social conditions and ends the fulfillment of which is to everyone's advantage. We should comply with and do our part in just and efficient social arrangements for at least two reasons: first of all, we have a natural duty not to oppose the establishment of just and efficient institutions (when they do not yet exist) and to uphold and comply with them (when they do exist); and second, assuming that we have knowingly accepted the benefits of these institutions and plan to continue to do so, and that we have encouraged and expect others to do their part, we also have an obligation to do our share when, as the arrangement requires, it comes our turn. Thus, we often have both a natural duty as well as an obligation to support just and efficient institutions, the obligation arising from our voluntary acts while the duty does not.

Now all this is perhaps obvious enough, but it does not take us very far. Any more particular conclusions depend upon the conception of justice which is the basis of a theory of political obligation. I believe that the appropriate conception, at least for an account of political obligation in a constitutional democracy, is that of the social contract theory from which so much of our political thought derives. If we are careful to interpret it in a suitably general way, I hold that this doctrine provides a satisfactory basis for political theory, indeed even for ethical theory itself, but this is beyond our present concern.[1] The interpretation I suggest is the following: that the principles to which social arrangements must conform, and in particular the principles of justice, are those which free and rational men would agree to in an original position of equal liberty; and similarly, the principles which govern men's relations to institutions and define their natural duties and obligations are the principles to which they would consent when so situated. It should be noted straightway that in this interpretation of the contract theory the principles of justice are understood as the outcome of a hypothetical agreement. They are principles which would be agreed to if the situation of the original position were to arise. There is no mention of an actual agreement nor need such an agreement ever be made. Social arrangements are just or unjust according to whether they accord with the principles for assigning and securing fundamental rights and liberties which would be chosen in the original position. This position is, to be sure, the analytic analogue of the traditional notion of the state of nature, but it must not be mistaken for a historical occasion. Rather it is a hypothetical situation which embodies the basic ideas of the contract doctrine; the description of this situation enables us to work out which principles would be adopted. I must now say something about these matters.

The contract doctrine has always supposed that the persons in the original position have equal powers and rights, that is, that they are symmetrically situated with respect to any arrangements for reaching agreement, and that coalitions and the like are excluded. But it is an essential element (which has not been sufficiently observed although it is implicit in Kant's version of the theory) that there are very strong restrictions on what the contracting parties are presumed to know. In particular, I interpret the theory to hold that the parties do not know their position in society, past, present, or future; nor do they know which institutions exist. Again, they do not know their own place in the distribution of natural talents and abilities, whether they are intelligent or strong, man or woman, and so on. Finally, they do not know their own particular interests and preferences or the system of ends which they wish to advance: they do not know their conception of the good. In all these respects the parties are confronted with a veil of ignorance which prevents any one from being able to take advantage of his good fortune or particular interests or from being disadvantaged by them. What the parties do know (or assume) is that Hume's circumstances of justice obtain: namely, that the bounty of nature is not so generous as to render cooperative schemes superfluous nor so harsh as to make them impossible. Moreover, they assume that the extent of their altruism is limited and that, in general, they do not take an interest in one another's interests. Thus, given the special features of the original position, each man tries to do the best he can for himself by insisting on principles calculated to protect and advance his system of ends whatever it turns out to be.

I believe that as a consequence of the peculiar nature of the original position there would be an agreement on the following two principles for assigning rights and duties and for regulating distributive shares as these are determined by the fundamental institutions of society: first, each person is to have an equal right to the most extensive liberty compatible with a like liberty for all; second, social and economic inequalities (as defined by the institutional structure or fostered by it) are to be arranged so that they are both to everyone's advantage and attached to positions and offices open to all. In view of the content of these two principles and their application to the main institutions of society, and therefore to the social system as a whole, we may regard them as the two principles of justice. Basic social arrangements are just insofar as they conform to these principles, and we can, if we like, discuss questions of justice directly by reference to them. But a deeper understanding of the justification of civil disobedience requires, I think, an account of the derivation of these principles provided by the doctrine of the social contract. Part of our task is to show why this is so.

III. The Grounds Of Compliance With An Unjust Law

If we assume that in the original position men would agree both to the principle of doing their part when they have accepted and plan to continue to accept the-benefits of just institutions (the principle of fairness), and also to the principle of not preventing the establishment of just institutions and of upholding and complying with them when they do exist, then the contract doctrine easily accounts for our having to conform to just institutions. But how does it account for the fact that we are normally required to comply with unjust laws as well? The injustice of a law is not a sufficient ground for not complying with it any more than the legal validity of legislation is always sufficient to require obedience to it. Sometimes one hears these extremes asserted, but I think that we need not take them seriously.

An answer to our question can be given by elaborating the social contract theory in the following way. I interpret it to hold that one is to envisage a series of agreements as follows: first, men are to agree upon the principles of justice in the original position. Then they are to move to a constitutional convention in which they choose a constitution that satisfies the principles of justice already chosen. Finally they assume the role of a legislative body and guided by the principles of justice enact laws subject to the constraints and procedures of the just constitution. The decisions reached in any stage are binding in all subsequent stages. Now whereas in the original position the contracting parties have no knowledge of their society or of their own position in it, in both a constitutional convention and a legislature, they do know certain general facts about their institutions, for example, the statistics regarding employment and output required for fiscal and economic policy. But no one knows particular facts about his own social class or his place in the distribution of natural assets. On each occasion the contracting parties have the knowledge required to make their agreement rational from the appropriate point of view, but not so much as to make them prejudiced. They are unable to tailor principles and legislation to take advantage of their social or natural position; a veil of ignorance prevents their knowing what this position is. With this series of agreements in mind, we can characterize just laws and policies as those which would be enacted were this whole process correctly carried out.

In choosing a constitution the aim is to find among the just constitutions the one which is most likely, given the general facts about the society in question, to lead to just and effective legislation. The principles of justice provide a criterion for the laws desired; the problem is to find a set of political procedures that will give this outcome. I shall assume that, at least under the normal conditions of a modern state, the best constitution is some form of democratic regime affirming equal political liberty and using some sort of majority (or other plurality) rule. Thus it follows that on the contract theory a constitutional democracy of some sort is required by the principles of justice. At the same time it is essential to observe that the constitutional process is always a case of what we may call imperfect procedural justice: that is, there is no feasible political procedure which guarantees that the enacted legislation is just even though we have (let us suppose) a standard for just legislation. In simple cases, such as games of fair division, there are procedures which always lead to the right outcome (assume that equal shares is fair and let the man who cuts the cake take the last piece). These situations are those of perfect procedural justice. In other cases it does not matter what the outcome is as long as the fair procedure is followed: fairness of the process is transferred to the result (fair gambling is an instance of this). These situations are those of pure procedural justice. The constitutional process, like a criminal trial, resembles neither of these; the result matters and we have a standard for it. The difficulty is that we cannot frame a procedure which guarantees that only just and effective legislation is enacted. Thus even under a just constitution unjust laws may be passed and unjust policies enforced. Some form of the majority principle is necessary but the majority may be mistaken, more or less willfully, in what it legislates. In agreeing to a democratic constitution (as an instance of imperfect procedural justice) one accepts at the same time the principle of majority rule. Assuming that the constitution is just and that we have accepted and plan to continue to accept its benefits, we then have both an obligation and a natural duty (and in any case the duty) to comply with what the majority enacts even though it may be unjust. In this way we become bound to follow unjust laws, not always, of course, but provided the injustice does not exceed certain limits. We recognize that we must run the risk of suffering from the defects of one another's sense of justice; this burden we are prepared to carry as long as it is more or less evenly distributed or does not weigh too heavily. Justice binds us to a just constitution and to the unjust laws which may be enacted under it in precisely the same way that it binds us to any other social arrangement. Once we take the sequence of stages into account, there is nothing unusual in our being required to comply with unjust laws.

It should be observed that the majority principle has a secondary place as a rule of procedure which is perhaps the most efficient one under usual circumstances for working a democratic constitution. The basis for it rests essentially upon the principles of justice and therefore we may, when conditions allow, appeal to these principles against unjust legislation. The justice of the constitution does not insure the justice of laws enacted under it; and while we often have both an obligation and a duty to comply with what the majority legislates (as long as it does not exceed certain limits), there is, of course, no corresponding obligation or duty to regard what the majority enacts as itself just. The right to make law does not guarantee that the decision is rightly made; and while the citizen submits in his conduct to the judgment of democratic authority, he does not submit his judgment to it.[2] And if in his judgment the enactments of the majority exceed certain bounds of injustice, the citizen may consider civil disobedience. For we are not required to accept the majority's acts unconditionally and to acquiesce in the denial of our and others' liberties; rather we submit our conduct to democratic authority to the extent necessary to share the burden of working a constitutional regime, distorted as it must inevitably be by men's lack of wisdom and the defects of their sense of justice.

IV. The Place of Civil Disobedience in a Constitutional Democracy

We are now in a position to say a few things about civil disobedience. I shall understand it to be a public, nonviolent, and conscientious act contrary to law usually done with the intent to bring about a change in the policies or laws of the government.[3] Civil disobedience is a political act in the sense that it is an act justified by moral principles which define a conception of civil society and the public good. It rests, then, on political conviction as opposed to a search for self or group interest; and in the case of a constitutional democracy, we may assume that this conviction involves the conception of justice (say that expressed by the contract doctrine) which underlies the constitution itself. That is, in a viable democratic regime there is a common conception of justice by reference to which its citizens regulate their political affairs and interpret the constitution. Civil disobedience is a public act which the dissenter believes to be justified by this conception of justice and for this reason it may be understood as addressing the sense of justice of the majority in order to urge reconsideration of the measures protested and to warn that, in the sincere opinion of the dissenters, the conditions of social cooperation are not being honored. For the principles of justice express precisely such conditions, and their persistent and deliberate violation in regard to basic liberties over any extended period of time cuts the ties of community and invites either submission or forceful resistance. By engaging in civil disobedience a minority leads the majority to consider whether it wants to have its acts taken in this way, or whether, in view of the common sense of justice, it wishes to acknowledge the claims of the minority.

Civil disobedience is also civil in another sense. Not only is it the outcome of a sincere conviction based on principles which regulate civic life, but it is public and nonviolent, that is, it is done in a situation where arrest and punishment are expected and accepted without resistance. In this way it manifests a respect for legal procedures. Civil disobedience expresses disobedience to law within the limits of fidelity to law, and this feature of it helps to establish in the eyes of the majority that it is indeed conscientious and sincere, that it really is meant to address their sense of justice.[4] Being completely open about one's acts and being willing to accept the legal consequences of one's conduct is a bond given to make good one's sincerity, for that one's deeds are conscientious is not easy to demonstrate to another or even before oneself. No doubt it is possible to imagine a legal system in which conscientious belief that the law is unjust is accepted as a defense for noncompliance, and men of great honesty who are confident in one another might make such a system work. But as things are such a scheme would be unstable; we must pay a price in order to establish that we believe our actions have a moral basis in the convictions of the community.

The nonviolent nature of civil disobedience refers to the fact that it is intended to address the sense of justice of the majority and as such it is a form of speech, an expression of conviction. To engage in violent acts likely to injure and to hurt is incompatible with civil disobedience as a mode of address. Indeed, an interference with the basic rights of others tends to obscure the civilly disobedient quality of one's act. Civil disobedience is nonviolent in the further sense that the legal penalty for one's action is accepted and that resistance is not (at least for the moment) contemplated. Nonviolence in this sense is to be distinguished from nonviolence as a religious or pacifist principle. While those engaging in civil disobedience have often held some such principle, there is no necessary connection between it and civil disobedience. For on the interpretation suggested, civil disobedience in a democratic society is best understood as an appeal to the principles of justice, the fundamental conditions of willing social cooperation among free men, which in the view of the community as a whole are expressed in the constitution and guide its interpretation. Being an appeal to the moral basis of public life, civil disobedience is a political and not primarily a religious act. It addresses itself to the common principles of justice which men can require one another to follow and not to the aspirations of love which they cannot. Moreover by taking part in civilly disobedient acts one does not foreswear indefinitely the idea of forceful resistance; for if the appeal against injustice is repeatedly denied, then the majority has declared its intention to invite submission or resistance and the latter may conceivably be justified even in a democratic regime. We are not required to acquiesce in the crushing of fundamental liberties by democratic majorities which have shown themselves blind to the principles of justice upon which justification of the constitution depends.

V. The Justification of Civil Disobedience

So far we have said nothing about the justification of civil disobedience, that is, the conditions under which civil disobedience may be engaged in consistent with the principles of justice that support a democratic regime. Our task is to see how the characterization of civil disobedience as addressed to the sense of justice of the majority (or to the citizens as a body) determines when such action is justified.

First of all, we may suppose that the normal political appeals to the majority have already been made in good faith and have been rejected, and that the standard means of redress have been tried. Thus, for example, existing political parties are indifferent to the claims of the minority and attempts to repeal the laws protested have been met with further repression since legal institutions are in the control of the majority. While civil disobedience should be recognized, I think, as a form of political action within the limits of fidelity to the rule of law, at the same time it is a rather desperate act just within these limits, and therefore it should, in general, be undertaken as a last resort when standard democratic processes have failed. In this sense it is not a normal political action. When it is justified there has been a serious breakdown; not only is there grave injustice in the law but a refusal more or less deliberate to correct it.

Second, since civil disobedience is a political act addressed to the sense of justice of the majority, it should usually be limited to. substantial and clear violations of justice and preferably to those which, if rectified, will establish a basis for doing away with remaining injustices. For this reason there is a presumption in favor of restricting civil disobedience to violations of the first principle of justice, the principle of equal liberty, and to barriers which contravene the second principle, the principle of open offices which protects equality of opportunity. It is not, of course, always easy to tell whether these principles are satisfied. But if we think of them as guaranteeing the fundamental equal political and civil liberties (including freedom of conscience and liberty of thought) and equality of opportunity, then it is often relatively clear whether their principles are being honored. After all, the equal liberties are defined by the visible structure of social institutions; they are to be incorporated into the recognized practice, if not the letter, of social arrangements. When minorities are denied the right to vote or to hold certain political offices, when certain religious groups are repressed and others denied equality of opportunity in the economy, this is often obvious and there is no doubt that justice is not being given. However, the first part of the second principle which requires that inequalities be to everyone's advantage is a much more imprecise and controversial matter. Not only is there a problem of assigning it a determinate and precise sense, but even if we do so and agree on what it should be, there is often a wide variety of reasonable opinion as to whether the principle is satisfied. The reason for this is that the principle applies primarily to fundamental economic and social policies. The choice of these depends upon theoretical and speculative beliefs as well as upon a wealth of concrete information, and all of this mixed with judgment and plain hunch, not to mention in actual cases prejudice and self-interest. Thus unless the laws of taxation are clearly designed to attack a basic equal liberty, they should not be protested by civil disobedience; the appeal to justice is not sufficiently clear and its resolution is best left to the political process. But violations of the equal liberties that define the common status of citizenship are another matter. The deliberate denial of these more or less over any extended period of time in the face of normal political protest is, in general, an appropriate object of civil disobedience. We may think of the social system as divided roughly into two parts, one which incorporates the fundamental equal liberties (including equality of opportunity) and another which embodies social and economic policies properly aimed at promoting the advantage of everyone. As a rule civil disobedience is best limited to the former where the appeal to justice is not only more definite and precise, but where, if it is effective, it tends to correct the injustices in the latter.

Third, civil disobedience should be restricted to those cases where the dissenter is willing to affirm that everyone else similarly subjected to the same degree of injustice has the right to protest in a similar way. That is, we must be prepared to authorize others to dissent in similar situations and in the same way, and to accept the consequences of their doing so. Thus, we may hold, for example, that the widespread disposition to disobey civilly clear violations of fundamental liberties more or less deliberate over an extended period of time would raise the degree of justice throughout society and would insure men's self-esteem as well as their respect for one another. Indeed, I believe this to be true, though certainly it is partly a matter of conjecture. As the contract doctrine emphasizes, since the principles of justice are principles which we would agree to in an original position of equality when we do not know our social position and the like, the refusal to grant justice is either the denial of the other as an equal (as one in regard to whom we are prepared to constrain our actions by principles which we would consent to) or the manifestation of a willingness to take advantage of natural contingencies and social fortune at his expense. In either case, injustice invites submission or resistance; but submission arouses the contempt of the oppressor and confirms him in his intention. If straightway, after a decent period of time to make reasonable political appeals in the normal way, men were in general to dissent by civil disobedience from infractions of the fundamental equal liberties, these liberties would, I believe, be more rather than less secure. Legitimate civil disobedience properly exercised is a stabilizing device in a constitutional regime, tending to make it more firmly just.

Sometimes, however, there may be a complication in connection with this third condition. It is possible, although perhaps unlikely, that there are so many persons or groups with a sound case for resorting to civil disobedience (as judged by the foregoing criteria) that disorder would follow if they all did so. There might be serious injury to the just constitution. Or again, a group might be so large that some extra precaution is necessary in the extent to which its members organize and engage in civil disobedience. Theoretically the case is one in which a number of persons or groups are equally entitled to and all want to resort to civil disobedience, yet if they all do this, grave consequences for everyone may result. The question, then, is who among them may exercise their right, and it falls under the general problem of fairness. I cannot discuss the complexities of the matter here. Often a lottery or a rationing system can be set up to handle the case; but unfortunately the circumstances of civil disobedience rule out this solution. It suffices to note that a problem of fairness may arise and that those who contemplate civil disobedience should take it into account. They may have to reach an understanding as to who can exercise their right in the immediate situation and to recognize the need for special constraint.

The final condition, of a different nature, is the following. We have been considering when one has a right to engage in civil disobedience, and our conclusion is that one has this right should three conditions hold: when one is subject to injustice more or less deliberate over an extended period of time in the face of normal political protests; where the injustice is a clear violation of the liberties of equal citizenship; and provided that the general disposition to protest similarly in similar cases would have acceptable consequences. These conditions are not, I think, exhaustive but they seem to cover the more obvious points; yet even when they are satisfied and one has the right to engage in civil disobedience, there is still the different question of whether one should exercise this right, that is, whether by doing so one is likely to further one's ends. Having established one's right to protest one is then free to consider these tactical questions. We may be acting within our rights but still foolishly if our action only serves to provoke the harsh retaliation of the majority; and it is likely to do so if the majority lacks a sense of justice, or if the action is poorly timed or not well designed to make the appeal to the sense of justice effective. It is easy to think of instances of this sort, and in each case these practical questions have to be faced. From the standpoint of the theory of political obligation we can only say that the exercise of the right should be rational and reasonably designed to advance the protester's aims, and that weighing tactical questions presupposes that one has already established one's right, since tactical advantages in themselves do not support it.

VI. Conclusion: Several Objections Considered

In a reasonably affluent democratic society justice becomes the first virtue of institutions. Social arrangements irrespective of their efficiency must be reformed if they are significantly unjust. No increase in efficiency in the form of greater advantages for many justifies the loss of liberty of a few. That we believe this is shown by the fact that in a democracy the fundamental liberties of citizenship are not understood as the outcome of political bargaining nor are they subject to the calculus of social interests. Rather these liberties are fixed points which serve to limit political transactions and which determine the scope of calculations of social advantage. It is this fundamental place of the equal liberties which makes their systematic violation over any extended period of time a proper object of civil disobedience. For to deny men these rights is to infringe the conditions of social cooperation among free and rational persons, a fact which is evident to the citizens of a constitutional regime since it follows from the principles of justice which underlie their institutions. The justification of civil disobedience rests on the priority of justice and the equal liberties which it guarantees.

It is natural to object to this view of civil disobedience that it relies too heavily upon the existence of a sense of justice. Some may hold that the feeling for justice is not a vital political force, and that what moves men are various other interests, the desire for wealth, power, prestige, and so on. Now this is a large question the answer to which is highly conjectural and each tends to have his own opinion. But there are two remarks which may clarify what I have said: first, I have assumed that there is in a constitutional regime a common sense of justice the principles of which are recognized to support the constitution and to guide its interpretation. In any given situation particular men may be tempted to violate these principles, but the collective force in their behalf is usually effective since they are seen as the necessary terms of cooperation among free men; and presumably the citizens of a democracy (or sufficiently many of them) want to see justice done. Where these assumptions fail, the justifying conditions for civil disobedience (the first three) are not affected, but the rationality of engaging in it certainly is. In this case, unless the costs of repressing civil dissent injures the economic self-interest (or whatever) of the majority, protest may simply make the position of the minority worse. No doubt as a tactical matter civil disobedience is more effective when its appeal coincides with other interests, but a constitutional regime is not viable in the long run without an attachment to the principles of justice of the sort which we have assumed.

Then, further, there may be a misapprehension about the manner in which a sense of justice manifests itself. There is a tendency to think that it is shown by professions of the relevant principles together with actions of an altruistic nature requiring a considerable degree of self-sacrifice. But these conditions are obviously too strong, for the majority's sense of justice may show itself simply in its being unable to undertake the measures required to suppress the minority and to punish as the law requires the various acts of civil disobedience. The sense of justice undermines the will to uphold unjust institutions, and so a majority despite its superior power may give way. It is unprepared to force the minority to be subject to injustice. Thus, although the majority's action is reluctant and grudging, the role of the sense of justice is nevertheless essential, for without it the majority would have been willing to enforce the law and to defend its position. Once we see the sense of justice as working in this negative way to make established injustices indefensible, then it is recognized as a central element of democratic politics.

Finally, it may be objected against this account that it does not settle the question of who is to say when the situation is such as to justify civil disobedience. And because it does not answer this question, it invites anarchy by encouraging every man to decide the matter for himself. Now the reply to this is that each man must indeed settle this question for himself, although he may, of course, decide wrongly. This is true on any theory of political duty and obligation, at least on any theory compatible with the principles of a democratic constitution. The citizen is responsible for what he does. If we usually think that we should comply with the law, this is because our political principles normally lead to this conclusion. There is a presumption in favor of compliance in the absence of good reasons to the contrary. But because each man is responsible and must decide for himself as best he can whether the circumstances justify civil disobedience, it does not follow that he may decide as he pleases. It is not by looking to our personal interests or to political allegiances narrowly construed, that we should make up our mind. The citizen must decide on the basis of the principles of justice that underlie and guide the interpretation of the constitution and in the light of his sincere conviction as to how these principles should be applied in the circumstances. If he concludes that conditions obtain which justify civil disobedience and conducts himself accordingly, he has acted conscientiously and perhaps mistakenly, but not in any case at his convenience.

In a democratic society each man must act as he thinks the principles of political right require him to. We are to follow our understanding of these principles, and we cannot do otherwise. There can be no morally binding legal interpretation of these principles, not even by a supreme court or legislature. Nor is there any infallible procedure for determining what or who is right. In our system the Supreme Court, Congress, and the President often put forward rival interpretations of the Constitution. Although the Court has the final say in settling any particular case, it is not immune from powerful political influence that may change its reading of the law of the land. The Court presents its point of view by reason and argument; its conception of the Constitution must, if it is to endure, persuade men of its soundness. The final court of appeal is not the Court, or Congress, or the President, but the electorate as a whole. The civilly disobedient appeal in effect to this body. There is no danger of anarchy as long as there is a sufficient working agreement in men's conceptions of political justice and what it requires. That men can achieve such an understanding when the essential political liberties are maintained is the assumption implicit in democratic institutions. There is no way to avoid entirely the risk of divisive strife. But if legitimate civil disobedience seems to threaten civil peace, the responsibility falls not so much on those who protest as upon those whose abuse of authority and power justifies such opposition.

THE OBLIGATION TO
OBEY THE LAW   *(abridged)*

Richard A. Wasserstrom

. . . One . . . argument against ever acting illegally, and the most common argument advanced, goes something like this: The reason why one ought never to disobey the law is simply that the consequences would be disastrous if everybody disobeyed the law. The reason why disobedience is never right becomes apparent once we ask the question, "But what if everyone did that?"

Consider . . . the case of the doctor who has to decide whether he is justified in performing an illegal abortion. If he only has a prima facie duty to obey the law it looks as though he might justifiably decide that in this case his prima facie obligation is overridden by more stringent conflicting obligations. Or, if he is simply a utilitarian, it appears that he might rightly conclude that the consequences of disobeying the abortion law would be on the whole and in the long run less deleterious than those of obeying. But this is simply a mistake. The doctor would inevitably be neglecting the most crucial factor of all, namely, that in performing the abortion he was disobeying the law. And imagine what would happen if everyone went around disobeying the law. The alternatives are obeying the law and general disobedience. The choice is between any social order and chaos.

Reprinted, by permission of the author and publisher, from "The Obligation to Obey the Law," *U.C.L.A. Law Review,* X (May 1963), pp. 790–797. Copyright © U. C. L. A. Law Review, 1963.

Such an argument, while perhaps overdrawn, is by no means uncommon.[1] Yet, as it stands, it is an essentially confused one. Its respective claims, if they are to be fairly evaluated, must be delineated with some care.

At a minimum, the foregoing attack upon the possibility of justified disobedience might be either one or both of two radically different kinds of objection. The first, which relates to `the consequences of an act of disobedience, is essentially a *causal* argument. The second questions the *principle* that any proponent of justified disobedience invokes. As to the causal argument, it is always relevant to point out that any act of disobedience may have certain consequences simply because it is an act of disobedience. Once the occurrence of the act is known, for example, expenditure of the state's resources may become necessary. The time and energy of the police will probably be turned to the task of discovering who it was who did the illegal act and of gathering evidence relevant to the offense. And other resources might be expended in the prosecution and adjudication of the case against the perpetrator of the illegal act. Illustrations of this sort could be multiplied, no doubt, but I do not think either that considerations of this sort are very persuasive or that they have been uppermost in the minds of those who make the argument now under examination. Indeed, if the argument is a causal one at all, it consists largely of the claim that any act of disobedience will itself cause, to some degree or other, general disobedience of all laws; it will cause or help to cause the overthrow or dissolution of the state. And while it is possible to assert that any act of disobedience will tend to further social disintegration or revolution, it is much more difficult to see why this must be so.

The most plausible argument would locate this causal efficacy in the kind of example set by any act of disobedience. But how plausible is this argument? It is undeniable, of course, that the kind of example that will be set is surely a relevant factor. Yet, there is nothing that precludes any proponent of justified disobedience from taking this into account. If, for example, others will somehow infer from the doctor's disobedience of the abortion law that they are justified in disobeying *any* law under *any* circumstances, then the doctor ought to consider this fact. This is a consequence —albeit a lamentable one—of his act of disobedience. Similarly, if

others will extract the proper criterion from the act of disobedience, but will be apt to misapply it in practice, then this too ought
to give the doctor pause. It, too, is a consequence of acting. But
if the argument is that disobedience would be wrong even if no
bad example were set and no other deleterious consequences likely,
then the argument must be directed against the principle the doctor appeals to in disobeying the law, and not against the consequences of his disobedience at all.

As to the attack upon a principle of justified disobedience, as
a principle, the response "But what if everyone disobeyed the law?"
does appear to be a good way to point up both the inherent inconsistency of almost any principle of justified disobedience and
the manifest undesirability of adopting such a principle. Even if
one need not worry about what others will be led to do by one's
disobedience, there is surely something amiss if one cannot consistently defend his right to do what one is claiming he is right
in doing.

In large measure, such an objection is unreal. The appeal to
"But what if everyone did that?" loses much, if not all, of its persuasiveness once we become clearer about what precisely the "did
that" refers to. If the question "But what if everyone did that?"
is simply another way of asking "But what if everybody disobeyed
the law?" or "But what if people generally disobeyed the laws?"
then the question is surely quasi-rhetorical. To urge general or indiscriminate disobedience to laws is to invoke a principle that, if
coherent, is manifestly indefensible. It is equally plain, however,
that with few exceptions such a principle has never been seriously
espoused. Anyone who claims that there are actions that are both
illegal and justified surely need not be thereby asserting that it
is right generally to disobey all laws or even any particular law.
It is surely not inconsistent to assert both that indiscriminate disobedience is indefensible and that discriminate disobedience is
morally right and proper conduct. Nor, analogously, is it at all
evident that a person who claims to be justified in performing an
illegal action is thereby committed to or giving endorsement to the
principle that the entire legal system ought to be overthrown or
renounced. At a minimum, therefore, the appeal to "But what if
everyone did that?" cannot by itself support the claim that one
has an absolute obligation to obey the law—that disobeying the
law can never be truly justified.

There is, however, a distinguishable but related claim which merits very careful attention—if for no other reason than the fact that it is so widely invoked today by moral philosophers. The claim is simply this: While it may very well be true that there are situations in which a person will be justified in disobeying the law, it is surely not true that disobedience can ever be justified solely on the grounds that the consequences of disobeying the particular law were in that case on the whole less deleterious than those of obedience.[2]

This claim is particularly relevant at this juncture because one of the arguments most often given to substantiate it consists of the purported demonstration of the fact that any principle which contained a proviso permitting a general appeal to consequences must itself be incoherent. One of the most complete statements of the argument is found in Marcus Singer's provocative book, *Generalization in Ethics:*

> Suppose, . . . that I am contemplating evading the payment of income taxes. I might reason that I need the money more than the government does, that the amount I have to pay is so small in comparison with the total amount to be collected is that the government will never miss it. Now I surely know perfectly well that if I evade the payment of taxes this will not cause others to do so as well. For one thing, I am certainly not so foolish as to publicize my action. But even if I were, and the fact became known, this would still not cause others to do the same, unless it also became known that I was being allowed to get away with it. In the latter case the practice might tend to become widespread, but this would be a consequence, not of my action, but of the failure of the government to take action against me. Thus there is no question of my act being wrong because it would set a bad example. It would set no such example, and to suppose that it must, because it would be wrong, is simply a confusion. . . . Given all this, then if the reasons mentioned would justify me in evading the payment of taxes, they would justify everyone whatsoever in doing the same thing. For everyone can argue in the same way—everyone can argue that if he breaks the law this will not cause others to do the same. The supposition that this is a justification, therefore, leads to a contradiction.
>
> I conclude from this that, just as the reply "Not everyone will do it" is irrelevant to the generalization argument, so is the fact that one knows or believes that not everyone will do the same; and that, in particular, the characteristic of knowing or believing that one's act will remain exceptional cannot be used to define a class

of exceptions to the rule. One's knowledge or belief that not every-one will act in the same way in similar circumstances cannot there-fore be regarded as part of the circumstances of one's action. One's belief that not everyone will do the same does not make one's cir-cumstances relevantly different from the circumstances of others, or relevantly different from those in which the act is wrong. Indeed, on the supposition that it does, one's circumstances could never be specified, for the specification would involve an infinite regress.[3]

Singer's argument is open to at least two different interpreta-tions. One quite weak interpretation is this: A person cannot be morally justified in acting as he does unless he is prepared to ac-knowledge that everyone else in the identical circumstances would also be right in acting the same way. If the person insists that he is justified in performing a certain action because the consequences of acting in that way are more desirable than those of acting in any alternative fashion, then he must be prepared to acknowledge that anyone else would also be justified in doing that action when-ever the consequences of doing that action were more desirable than those of acting in any alternative fashion. To take Singer's own example: A person, *A,* could not be morally justified in evad-ing the payment of his taxes on the grounds that the consequences of nonpayment were *in his case* more beneficial, all things con-sidered, than those of payment, unless *A* were prepared to acknowl-edge that any other person, *X,* would also be justified in evading his, *i.e., X*'s taxes, if it is the case that the consequences of *X*'s nonpayment would in *X*'s case be more beneficial, all things con-sidered, than those of payment. If this is Singer's point, it is, for reasons already elaborated, unobjectionable.[4]

But Singer seems to want to make a stronger point as well. He seems to believe that even a willingness to generalize in this fashion could not justify acting in this way. In part his argument appears to be that this somehow will permit everyone to justify nonpayment of taxes; and in part his argument appears to be that there is a logical absurdity involved in attempting to make the likelihood of other people's behavior part of the specification of the relevant consequences of a particular act. Both of these points are wrong. To begin with, on a common sense level it is surely true that the effect which one's action will have on other people's behavior is a relevant consideration. For as was pointed out earlier, if *A* determines that other people will be, or may be, led to evade *their* taxes even when the consequences of nonpayment will in their cases be less beneficial than those of payment, then this is a consequence of *A*'s action which he must take into account and attempt to balance against the benefits which would accrue to society from his nonpayment. Conversely, if for one reason or another *A* can determine that his act of nonpayment will not have this consequence, this, too, must be relevant. In this sense, at least, other people's prospective behavior is a relevant consideration.

More importantly, perhaps, it is surely a mistake—although a very prevalent one in recent moral philosophy—to suppose that permitting a general appeal to consequences would enable everyone to argue convincingly that he is justified in evading his taxes. Even if I adopt the principle that everyone is justified in evading his taxes whenever the consequences of evasion are on the whole less deleterious than those of payment, this in no way entails that I or anyone else will always, or ever, be justified in evading my taxes. It surely need not turn out to be the case—even if no one else will evade his taxes—that the consequences will on the whole be beneficial if I succeed in evading mine. It might surely be the case that I will spend the money saved improvidently or foolishly; it might very well be true that the government will make much better use of the money. Indeed, the crucial condition which must not be ignored and which Singer does ignore is the condition which stipulates that the avoidance of one's taxes in fact be optimific, that is, more desirable than any other course of conduct.

The general point is simply that it is an empirical question— at least in theory—what the consequences of any action will be. And it would surely be a mistake for me or anyone else to suppose that that action whose consequences are most pleasing to me—in either the short or long run—will in fact be identical with that action whose consequences are on the whole most beneficial to society. Where the demands of self-interest are strong, as in the case of the performance of an unpleasant task like paying taxes, there are particular reasons for being skeptical of one's conclusion that the consequences of nonpayment would in one's own case truly be beneficial. But once again there is no reason why there might not be cases in which evasion of taxes would be truly justified, nor is there any reason why someone could not consistently and defensibly endorse nonpayment whenever these circumstances were in fact present.

There is one final point which Singer's discussion suggests and which does appear to create something of a puzzle. Suppose that I believe that I am justified in deliberately trespassing on an atomic test site, and thereby disobeying the law, because I conclude that this is the best way to call attention to the possible consequences of continued atmospheric testing or nuclear war. I conclude that the consequences of trespassing will on the whole be more beneficial than any alternative action I can take. But suppose I also concede—what very well may be the case—that if everyone were to trespass, even for this same reason and in the same way, the consequences would be extremely deleterious. Does it follow that there is something logically incoherent about my principle of action? It looks as though there is, for it appears that I am here denying others the right to do precisely what I claim I am right in doing. I seem to be claiming, in effect, that it is right for me to trespass on government property in order to protest atomic testing only if it is the case that others, even under identical circumstances, will not trespass. Thus, it might be argued, I appear to be unwilling or unable to generalize my principle of conduct.

This argument is unsound, for there is a perfectly good sense in which I am acting on a principle which is coherent and which is open to anyone to adopt. It is simply the principle that one is justified in trespassing on government property whenever—among other things—it happens to be the case that one can say accurately that others will not in fact act on that same principle. Whether anyone else will at any given time act on any particular principle is an empirical question. It is, to repeat what has already been said, one of the possible circumstances which can be part of the description of a class of situations. There is, in short, nothing logically self-contradictory or absurd about making the likelihood of even identical action one of the relevant justifying considerations. And there is, therefore, no reason why the justifiability of any particular act of disobedience cannot depend, among other things, upon the probable conduct of others. . . .

RADICAL DISOBEDIENCE AND ITS JUSTIFICATION

Bruce Pech

A presupposition underlying most current discussion of civil disobedience is that acts falling under this definition are undertaken within a framework of legal and political institutions to which the disobedient admits he owes allegiance. That is, while the disobedient, for a variety of reasons, may choose to violate certain laws, he recognizes the legitimacy of the state or society within the jurisdiction of which his violation is committed. It is with respect to this presupposition that many of the difficulties arising from attempts to justify acts of civil disobedience are both framed and resolved, for, speaking generally, the criteria in terms of which acts of civil disobedience may be justified turn upon the assumption that the role of civil disobedience is the promotion of justice and reform *within* just such an existing structure of legitimate legal and political institutions. From this assumption follow such criteria as "cheerfully accepting the consequences of acts of civil disobedience,"[1] describing justifiable civil disobedience as a "recognized procedure for challenging law or policy and obtaining a court determination thereof,"[2] the common emphasis on an inversely proportional relationship between the justifiability of disobedience and the degree to which a society embodies functional democratic institutions, the belief that disobedience cannot be justified when the disobedient has failed to take advantage of all avenues of due process in seeking redress, and other, similar prescriptions.

Recent events in the anti-war and "Black Power" movements, however, have cast doubt upon the adequacy of this conception of justifiable civil disobedience, for the presupposition that disobedients recognize and consent to the legitimacy of the authority they have chosen to defy can no longer, in many instances, be granted. Frequently, contemporary disobedients challenge not only a particular law or practice, but, explicitly or implicitly, the authority of a given state to make, enforce, or tolerate certain laws or practices. They conceive of themselves as radicals, seeking to bring about fundamental or qualitative changes in the existing social order and in the underlying values upon which they believe it to rest—a goal which they maintain to be significantly different from the mere promulgation of reforms within the established structure of society. The analysis of society in terms of which they frame their programs may take a number of forms including anarchism, Marxism of one variety or another, racial nationalism or the rather ambiguous ideological theses characteristic of the "New Left."

With the possible exception of anarchism, today more or less irrelevant as a political doctrine, the common element in these analyses is a "class" or "interest-group" explanation of social, political, and economic relationships. Upon this interpretation, one distinguishable interest-group in a society (defined with respect to such fundamental characteristics as race or economic function) dominates the whole, employing the manifold instruments of its authority to further its own interests and to obstruct the realization of the actually or supposedly contradictory interests of other, less powerful interest-groups. The instruments of authority accessible to and employed by the dominant group include the state, both in kind and with respect to particular political institutions, the legal system, again both in kind and with respect to particular laws, the prevailing economic ideology, and societal values of both an operational sort and those traditional values in terms of which the state articulates its claim to legitimacy. Also of significance are those less formal but equally effective powers accessible through control of such belief-shaping agencies as the schools and the mass media. It follows from this analysis that democratic structures, even if they are free of formal imperfections, do not create conditions of equality with respect to the determination of laws, policies, and practices. Nor do they tend to ameliorate inequities in the distribution of wealth, of real if not nominal political power, or of the social status accorded to the various interest-groups. On the contrary, such putatively democratic institutions as exist act to reinforce the influence of the dominant group by appearing to legitimize its possession and exercise of the instruments of its authority. Formally, for example, the effectively rigid two-party system, electoral mechanisms, and legislative practices in the United States work to the advantage of some interest-groups—perhaps even, generally speaking, a socio-economic class—and to the disadvantage of others while, informally, these dominant groups are able to manipulate schools and the mass media to create and popularize a mythology attesting to the legitimacy of the institutions and practices through which they act to maintain their superior position. This mythology serves also to foster the belief that values and ideologies contrary to the interests of the dominant group are contrary to the interests of the entire society. In this manner, the dominant group seeks both to extend the sway of an ideology favorable to its own interests to other groups and to blind these other groups to ideologies more appropriate to the realization of their real interests.

Disobedients who adhere to this interpretation of society conceive of themselves as representatives or allies of the dominated interest-groups, dedicated to overcoming the obstacles which prevent the realization of their interests both within the body politic and within the group itself. They consider the members of the group with which they align themselves to be effectively and of necessity disenfranchised, and, therefore, they reject the laws and institutions of the state as illegitimate with respect to that group. Their disobedience (and their other politically relevant activities), therefore, play a twofold role. On the one hand, they are engaged in an active struggle against the exploitative practices of the dominant group. On the other hand, they seek to articulate the real interests of their own group. This does not merely mean publicizing its plight in an effort to convince society as a whole of the justice of its demands (although they may make such representations), but attempting to counteract the mythologies which sustain the superiority of the dominant group, and, further, to forge a self-consciousness of the subordinate group's own real interests by explicating the character and etiology of its exploitation. That is, to paraphrase Mills on Marx, to bring about a transformation from a "class-in-itself" to a "class-for-itself."[3]

This analysis has two crucial implications for civil disobedience. In the first place, as dominant groups act to exploit and oppress dominated groups, members or allies of the dominated group place their loyalty to it above any loyalty to the heterogenous society in which it exists. The legitimacy of the institutions and laws of that society is granted only when they tend to further the interests of the dominated group—or, at the very least, when they do not act primarily as instruments of the interests of the dominant group. This is characteristic, for example, of the "Black Power" movement regarded both as a social and political force within the American state and as an ally of non-white "third world" revolutionary movements. In the second place, the effort to create a "class-for-itself" entails a redirection of the appeal of disobedience. Instead of addressing grievances to the entire society through its institutionalized avenues of due process and redress, the disobedient seeks to enhance his group's self-awareness and political sophistication. Again, one may cite as examples the "Black Power" movement and, to some extent, recent activities within the white "New Left."

Acts of disobedience grounded in these convictions serve, in whole or part, a threefold purpose.

1) They may be provocative, i.e., they may tend to disrupt the normal functioning of the state, provoking the dominant interest group into a display of coercion which cannot be reconciled with the values or ideals upon which it bases its claims that existing social, political, and economic institutions are legitimate. This disclosure of hypocrisy is intended to weaken the persuasiveness of these claims within the dominated group and among members of other interest-groups who are potential allies of the dominated group.

2) They may promote group self-awareness by exposing the manner in which it is exploited and identifying the group responsible for its exploitation. This acts, in turn, to further unify the dominated group.

3) They may forcefully articulate the demands of the dominated group to other groups and to the dominant group, demonstrating

that the dominated group, having become aware of the actuality and the causes of its exploitation, refuses to remain quiescent or merely supplicative.

It is noteworthy that in terms of this analysis, the value of disobedience is assessed largely as a matter of strategy and tactics. And, not infrequently, such an assessment is carried out within a unique historical perspective—a perspective in which certain fundamentally objective conditions are perceived as rendering success possible, likely, or inevitable for the efforts of the dominated group to achieve its ends. Disobedience is understood to be a tactic (among others) of midwifery, and the criteria with respect to which it must be justified turn upon its efficacy in facilitating the realization of the group's interests. While moral issues may be of the greatest concern to the individuals engaged in this form of disobedience, their relevance to the question of its justification is seriously qualified by tactical considerations. It follows, moreover, that the statutory illegality of an act, a judgment made by the dominant group through its legal apparatus, is only rarely germane to questions of justification as they are understood by disobedients themselves.

It may, of course, be inquired why such activities are to be distinguished from those conventionally characterized as revolutionary. Clearly, by most standards, activities which are predicated upon a denial of the legitimacy of an existing social order tend to eventuate in violence and insurrection. However, while such consequences may follow from the form of disobedience in question, they are entailed by neither the analysis nor the intentions of the disobedients. As was suggested earlier, the ultimate goal of radical disobedience is not the usurpation of all political, social, or economic power. To the contrary, even when disobedience is of the provocative sort, the provocation acts to call attention to the inherent inadequacy of legally constituted avenues of redress and to the discrepancy between the values espoused by the body politic and the manner in which the government acts to promote or enforce the domination of one group by another. Recognition of these two facts assists, in turn, in educating and uniting the dominated group, in the acquisition of allies from other groups, and in notifying the dominant group that the dominated group no longer requests, but demands the liberty and resources essential to furthering its own interests. While, for example, the orthodox Marxian model of class struggle insists that the proletariat seize control of the state, society, and economy through a violent, revolutionary confrontation with the bourgeois, the model in terms of which radical disobedience is understood and justified is essentially both pluralistic and egalitarian. Such disobedience is premised upon the belief that the conflicts between interest-groups can only be resolved if no one group is in a position to exploit, dominate, or control another in those matters which affect their vital interests. The illegitimacy of the laws, the institutions, or the practices of any one group with respect to another follows directly from a violation of this premise—and a society in which such violations form part of the essential fabric of socio-political and socio-economic relationships is, until they are remedied, illegitimately constituted. Theoretically at least, this point of view is flexible enough to be consistent with the constraints imposed on the possibilities of social change by contemporary social realities. Radical disobedience does not seek to bring about a violent revolutionary confrontation, but to consolidate a base of power within a society and to employ this power to promote a more fundamental and far-reaching program of social change than is conceivable if the apparatus of exploitation and domination controlled by the dominant interest group is granted the legitimacy to which it lays claim. The justification of radical disobedience rests, of necessity, upon the validity of the analysis of society outlined in this paper, upon its tactical value, and upon its adherence to the twofold ideal it seeks to realize—equality within a pluralistic society.

REFERENCES

Preface

1. See Staughton Lynd, ed., *Nonviolence in America: A Documentary History* (New York, 1966); Peter Mayer, ed., *The Pacifist Conscience* (New York, 1966); Lillian Schlissel, ed., *Conscience in America: A Documentary History of Conscientious Objection in America 1757–1967* (New York, 1968); Mulford Q. Sibley, ed., *The Quiet Battle: Writings on the Theory and Practice of Nonviolent Resistance* (New York, 1963); and Arthur and Lila Weinberg, eds., *Instead of Violence* (Boston, 1965).

Part I

Introduction

1. According to Walter Harding, ed., *The Variorium Civil Disobedience* (New York, 1967), p. 59. In his correspondence, Thoreau referred to his lecture under the title, "The Rights and Duties of the Individual in Relation to Government"; see F. B. Sanborn, ed., *Familiar Letters of Henry David Thoreau* (Boston, 1894), p. 185. When it was first published, in Elizabeth Peabody, ed., *Aesthetic Papers* (Boston, 1849), it carried the title, "Resistance to Civil Government." The version of the essay which is reprinted below is the one he prepared shortly before his death and published in *A Yankee in Canada with Anti-Slavery and Reform Papers* (Boston, 1866), pp. 123–51; it has been checked for accuracy against the variorum text prepared by Professor Harding and the punctuation modified at several places to conform to current usage.
2. These and other details of Thoreau's civil disobedience may be found in Harding, *op. cit.*, and in his biography, *The Days of Henry Thoreau* (New York, 1965).
3. George Woodcock, *Civil Disobedience* (Toronto, 1966), p. 3.
4. Mohandus K. Gandhi, *Non-Violent Resistance* (New York, 1961), p. 3.
5. Mortimer Adler, "Is There a Jurisprudence of Civil Disobedience?" *Illinois Continuing Legal Education*, V (1967), p. 96.
6. Evan Jahos, in "Symposium on Civil Disobedience," *New Jersey State Bar Journal* (Fall, 1965), p. 1380. Substantially the same charge has been made by Charles E. Whittaker, "The Dangers of Mass Disobedience," *Reader's Digest* (Dec. 1965), pp. 121–24.
7. See, for Socrates' defense of disobeying the edict of the Thirty Tyrants and his refusal to resist his own death sentence, though he regarded it as unjust, Plato's dialogues *Apology* and *Crito*, respectively.
8. See Harding, *op. cit.*, p. 59, and a letter to this editor from Walter Harding, Feb. 29, 1968.
9. See his essays, "A Plea for Captain John Brown" and "The Last Days of John Brown," both of which he reprinted alongside "Civil Disobedience" in *A Yankee in Canada*.
10. Gandhi, *op. cit.*, pp. 4, 60.
11. Martin Oppenheimer and George Lakey, *A Manual for Direct Action* (Chicago, 1965), p. 112.

12. Harry Kalven, *Civil Disobedience* (Santa Barbara, 1966), p. 27.
13. Richard Wasserstrom, in *Civil Disobedience* (Santa Barbara, 1966), p. 18. He adds, ". . . every act of civil disobedience is an attempt at civic education . . ." (p. 19).
14. Emma Goldman, "Anarchism: What it Really Stands For," reprinted in Staughton Lynd, ed., *Nonviolence in America* (New York, 1966), p. 126.
15. Lewis F. Powell, Jr., "A Lawyer Looks at Civil Disobedience," *Washington & Lee Law Review*, XXIII (1966), p. 230.
16. Gandhi, *op. cit.*, p. 142.
17. Charles E. Whittaker, "The Effects of Planned Mass Disobedience of Our Laws," *F. B. I. Law Enforcement Bulletin*, XXXV (Sept. 1966), p. 12.
18. Abe Fortas, *Concerning Dissent and Civil Disobedience* (New York, 1968), p. 63.
19. Heinz Eulau, "Wayside Challenger: Some Remarks on the Politics of Henry David Thoreau," reprinted in Sherman Paul, ed., *Thoreau: A Collection of Critical Essays* (Englewood Cliffs, 1962), p. 118.

Part II

Introduction

1. See, for a general discussion, Martin Luther King, Jr., *Stride Toward Freedom* (New York, 1958).
2. See especially Arthur Waskow, *From Race-Riot To Sit-In* (New York, 1966), pp. 225 ff., and Howard Zinn, *SNCC: The New Abolitionists* (Boston, 1965).
3. Lewis F. Powell, Jr., "A Lawyer Looks at Civil Disobedience," *Washington & Lee Law Review*, XXIII (1966), p. 217. The opposite position is taken, however, by former Justice Charles Whittaker; see Charles E. Whittaker and William Sloan Coffin, Jr., *Law, Order and Civil Disobedience* (Washington, D.C., 1967), pp. 9–10.
4. Martin Luther King, Jr., "Showdown for Non-Violence," *Look* (April 16, 1968), p. 23.
5. Burke Marshall, "The Protest Movement and the Law," *Virginia Law Review*, LXXI (1965), p. 794.
6. The theory is a logical corollary of Holmes' oft-quoted statement, ". . . a legal duty . . . is nothing but a prediction that if a man does or omits certain things he will be made to suffer in this or that way by judgement of the court . . ."; Oliver Wendell Holmes, *Collected Legal Papers* (Boston, 1920), p. 169.
7. F. L. Shuttlesworth and N. H. Smith, "The Birmingham Manifesto," reprinted in Staughton Lynd, ed., *Nonviolence in America* (New York, 1966), p. 458.
8. C. C. J. Carpenter *et al.*, "Letter to Martin Luther King, Jr.," reprinted in H. M. Bishop and S. Hendel, eds., *Basic Issues of American Democracy* (New York, 1965), p. 287.
9. Martin Luther King, Jr., *Stride Toward Freedom* (New York, 1960), p. 72.
10. *Ibid.*, p. 41.
11. M. L. King, Jr., *Why We Can't Wait* (New York, 1964), p. 71, in general, chapters 4 and 6.
12. *Congressional Record*, April 24, 1964, p. 8967.

13. See, e.g., R. B. McKay, "Racial Protest, Civil Disobedience, and the Rule of Law," *N.Y.U. Arts and Sciences* (Winter 1964-5), pp. 1-9; Charles L. Black, Jr., "The Problem of the Compatibility of Civil Disobedience with American Institutions of Government," *Texas Law Review,* XLIII (1965), pp. 492-506; and Archibald Cox, "Direct Action, Civil Disobedience, and the Constitution," in *Civil Rights, the Constitution and the Courts* (Cambridge, 1967), pp. 2-29.

14. See, e.g., Herbert Brownell, "Civil Disobedience—A Lawyer's Challenge," *American Criminal Law Quarterly,* III (Fall 1964), pp. 27-32; Morris Liebman, "Civil Disobedience—A Threat to Our Law Society," *American Bar Association Journal,* LI (July 1965), pp. 645-47; Charles Rice, "Civil Disobedience: Formula for Chaos," *Alabama Lawyer,* XXVII (1966), pp. 248-79.

15. M. L. King, Jr., "Showdown for Non-Violence," *op. cit.,* pp. 24, 25. See also the scholarly survey provided by Mulford Q. Sibley, "Direct Action and the Struggle for Integration," *Hastings Law Journal,* XVI (1965), pp. 351-400.

William L. Taylor, "Civil Disobedience: Observations on the Strategies of Protest"

1. M. K. Gandhi, "The Origins of Satyagraha Doctrine," in Mulford Q. Sibley, ed., *The Quiet Battle* (New York 1963), p. 43.

2. Martin Luther King, Jr., "The Time for Freedom Has Come," in Sibley, *op. cit.,* pp. 300, 303.

3. See, e.g., Poe v. Ullman, 367 U.S. 497 (1961); United Public Workers v. Mitchell, 330 U.S. 75 (1947).

4. See e.g., Taylor v. La., 370 U.S. 154 (1962); Garner v. La., 368 U.S. 157 (1961); cf. Dresner v. Tallahassee, 375 U.S. 136 (1963). See also Politt, "Dime Store Demonstrations," *Duke L. J.,* p. 315 (1960).

5. Congress did enact the Civil Rights Act of 1964 which *inter alia* declared a right to equal treatment at places of public accommodation.

6. See Boynton v. Va., 364 U.S. 454 (1960); Henderson v. United States, 339 U.S. 816 (1950); Mitchell v. United States, 313 U.S. 80 (1941); N.A.A.C.P. v. St. Louis-San Francisco Ry., 297 I.C.C. 335 (1955); Keys v. Carolina Coach Co., 64 M.C.C. 769 (1955); 49 Stat. 558 (1935), as amended, 54 Stat. 924 (1940), 49 U.S.C. § 316(d) (1958).

7. Baldwin v. Morgan, 251 F.2d 780 (1958); United States v. U.S. Klans, 194 F. Supp. 897 (M.D. Ala. 1961).

8. See 49 C.F.R. Pt. 180a.

9. Edwards v. So. Carolina, 372 U.S. 235 (1963).

10. Inter'l Brotherhood of Teamsters v. Wohl, 315 U.S. 769 (1942) (picketing); Thornhill v. Ala., 310 U.S. 88 (1940) (picketing); Fruit and Vegetable Packers & Warehousemen v. N.L.R.B., 308 F.2d 311 (1962) (picketing). But see Burr v. N.L.R.B., 321 F.2d 612 (1963); Tally v. Cal., 362 U.S. 60 (1960) (distribution of handbills); Jamison v. Tex., 318 U.S. 413 (1943) (distribution of handbills); Schneider v. State, 308 U.S. 174 (1939) (handbills); Lovell v. Griffin, 303 U.S. 444 (1938) (handbills).

11. *The New York Times,* Jan. 14, 1964, p. 25; *The New York Times,* Dec. 31, 1963, p. 1.

12. *Ibid.,* July 16, 1963, p. 1.

13. *Ibid.,* Feb. 28, 1968, p. 14.

14. *Ibid.,* Mar. 7, 1964, p. 1.

15. Martin Luther King, Jr. "The Time for Freedom Has Come," in Sibley, *op. cit.,* p. 303.

16. M. K. Gandhi, *Non-Violent Resistance* (1961), p. 175.

17. It should be noted that a claim that public schools are operated in an unconstitutional manner may well be a defense to a prosecution for violation of compulsory education laws. In the matter of Skipwith, 180 N.Y.S.2d 852 (Dom. Rel. Ct. N.Y.C. (1958)).

18. United States v. United Mine Workers, 330 U.S. 258 (1947).

19. See Thomas v. Collins, 323 U.S. 516 (1945); see also *In re* Green, 369 U.S. 689 (1962); *Ex parte* George, 371 U.S. 72 (1962); United States v. United Mine Workers, 330 U.S. 258, 270 (1947) (dissenting opinion).

20. See Norris-LaGuardia Act, 47 Stat. 70 (1932); 29 U.S.C. sec. 101 (1958).

21. H. D. Thoreau, "Civil Disobedience and Non-Violent Resistance," in Silbey, *op. cit.,* p. 27.

Part III

Introduction

1. "Handbook on Nonpayment of War Taxes," published by Greenleaf Books for the Peacemaker Movement, 3rd edition, 1967 (mimeo.), p. 31.

2. *The New York Times,* January 31, 1968, p. 40.

3. See Norman Thomas, *Conscientious Objector in America* (New York, 1925); Mulford Sibley and Paul Jacobs, *Conscription of Conscience* (Ithaca, 1952); and Lillian Schlissel, ed., *Conscience in America* (New York, 1968).

4. For a full account of this voyage, see Albert Bigelow, *The Voyage of the Golden Rule* (New York, 1959). Subsequent efforts by others, sailing in *Phoenix* and *Everyman,* were also interrupted by the Coast Guard on the high seas; see Earle Reynolds, *The Forbidden Voyage* (New York, 1961), and *The New York Times,* May 28, 1962, p. 2.

5. See his essays, "Civil Disobedience," *New Statesman,* February 17, 1961, pp. 245–46; and "On Civil Disobedience," given as a lecture in 1961 and published in Arthur and Lila Weinberg, eds., *Instead of Violence* (Boston, 1965), pp. 51–57. See also David Boulton, ed., *Voices From the Crowd: Against the H-Bomb* (London, 1964). L. J. Macfarlane, "Disobedience and the Bomb," *Political Quarterly,* XXXVII (1966), pp. 366–77, provides a full review of C.N.D. and its use of direct action against nuclear weapons in Britain.

6. See particularly his books, *Common Sense and Nuclear Warfare* (London, 1959), *Has Man a Future?* (London, 1962), *Unarmed Victory* (London, 1963), and *War Crimes in Vietnam* (London, 1967).

7. B. Russell, "Civil Disobedience," *op. cit.,* p. 246.

8. See "Declaration Concerning the Right of Insubordination in the Algerian War," *Evergreen Review,* IV (Nov.–Dec. 1960); and also "Letters and Comments: On Civil Disobedience and the Algerian War," *Yale Review,* L (Spring 1961), pp. 462–88.

9. See Benjamin Spock, "Vietnam and Civil Disobedience," *Humanist,* XXVIII (Jan.–Feb. 1968), pp. 3–7.

10. This argument has been advanced in various ways in a series of articles by Harrop Freeman: "A Remonstrance for Conscience," *Univ. of Pennsylvania Law Review,* CVI (1958), pp. 806–30; "Civil Disobedience, Law and Democ-

racy," *Law in Transition Quarterly*, III (1966), pp. 13–44; "The Case for the Disobedient," *Hastings Law Journal*, XVII (1966), pp. 425–38; "The Right of Protest and Civil Disobedience," *Indiana Law Journal*, XLI (1966), pp. 228–55; and in *Civil Disobedience* (Santa Barbara, 1966), pp. 2–10. It has been criticized by J. J. Farraher, "The National Laws and Conscience-Based Claims in Relation to Legitimate State Expectations," *Hastings Law Journal*, XVII (1966), pp. 439–53.

11. Precisely what responsibilities, if any, a citizen not in uniform or under military orders has to resist his government in order to avoid implication in "crimes against peace," "war crimes," and "crimes against humanity," as defined in the "Nuremberg Principles" formulated by the International Law Commission and affirmed by the General Assembly of the United Nations on December 11, 1946, remains obscure. See, however, Guenter Lewy, "Superior Orders, Nuclear Warfare and the Dictates of Conscience," *American Political Science Review*, LV (1961), pp. 3–23; Harrop Freeman, "The Case for the Disobedient," *op. cit.*, pp. 427–29; and *In the Name of America* (New York, 1968), a comprehensive documentation of the United States' military conduct in South Vietnam, arranged according to the relevant international law governing land and aerial warfare.

12. Among other valuable discussions of civil disobedience prompted by the Vietnam conflict, mention should be made here of John C. Bennett, "The Place of Civil Disobedience," *Christianity and Crisis*, XXVII (1967), pp. 299–302; Robert McAfee Brown, "In Conscience, I Must Break the Law," *Look*, October 31, 1967, pp. 48–52; Staughton Lynd *et al.*, "Selective Conscientious Objection," *Worldview*, X (February 1967), pp. 4–11; (March 1967), pp. 4–10; Quentin L. Quade, "Civil Disobedience and the State," *worldview*, X (November 1967), pp. 4–9; Michael Walzer *et al.*, "Symposium: Civil Disobedience and 'Resistance'," *Dissent*, XV (Jan.–Feb. 1968), pp. 13–25; and Ronald Dworkin, "On Not Prosecuting Civil Disobedience," *The New York Review of Books*, X (June 6, 1968), pp. 14–21.

Part IV

Introduction

1. On natural law, see Sidney Hook, ed., *Law and Philosophy* (New York, 1964), Part II; and M. R. MacGuigan, "Civil Disobedience and Natural Law," *Catholic Lawyer*, XI (1965), pp. 118–29.

On conscience, see C. D. Broad, "Conscience and Conscientious Action," reprinted in his *Ethics and the History of Philosophy* (London, 1952), pp. 244–62; Gilbert Ryle, "Conscience and Moral Convictions," reprinted in M. MacDonald, ed., *Philosophy and Analysis* (Oxford, 1954), pp. 156–65; H. D. Lewis, "Obedience to Conscience," *Mind*, LIV (1945), pp. 227–53; J. F. M. Hunter, "Conscience," *Mind*, LXXII (1963), pp. 309–34; and D. O. Thomas, "Obedience to Conscience," *Proceedings of the Aristotelian Society*, LXIV (1964), pp. 243–58.

On utilitarianism, see David Lyons, *Forms and Limits of Utilitarianism* (Oxford, 1965); and Jan Narveson, *Morality and Utility* (Baltimore, 1967).

On political philosophy in general, see S. I. Benn and R. S. Peters, *The Principles of Political Thought* (New York, 1965); Brian Barry, *Political Argument* (London, 1965); and J. R. Lucas, *The Principles of Politics* (Oxford, 1966).

2. See Stuart M. Brown, Jr., "Civil Disobedience," *Journal of Philosophy*, LVIII (1961), pp. 676 ff.; Carl Cohen, "Civil Disobedience and the Law," *Rutgers Law Review*, XXI (1966), pp. 12–16; Morris Keeton, "The Morality of Civil Disobedience," *Texas Law Review*, XLIII (1965), pp. 511–22; Irving Thalberg, "Philosophical Problems of Civil Disobedience," *Scientia*, CI (1966), pp. 6 ff.; and Rudolph H. Weingartner, "Justifying Civil Disobedience," *Columbia University Forum*, IX (Spring 1965), pp. 42 ff.

3. See David Spitz, "Democracy and the Problem of Civil Disobedience," *American Political Science Review*, XLVIII (1954), pp. 386–403; Franz Neumann, "On the Limits of Justifiable Disobedience," in his *The Democratic and Authoritarian State* (Glencoe, 1958), pp. 149–59; and Guenter Lewy, "Resistance to Tyranny: Treason, Right or Duty?", *Western Political Quarterly*, XIII (1960), pp. 581–95.

4. Michael Walzer, "The Obligation to Disobey," *Ethics*, LXXVII (1967), p. 171.

5. Mohandus K. Gandhi, *Non-Violent Resistance* (New York, 1961), p. 3.

6. W. H. Auden, *The New York Times Magazine*, February 4, 1968, p. 20.

7. H. A. Bedau, "On Civil Disobedience," *Journal of Philosophy*, LVIII (1961), p. 661; cf. Weingartner, *op. cit.*, p. 39; and Cohen, *op. cit.*, p. 3.

8. John W. Riehm, "Civil Disobedience—A Definition," *American Criminal Law Quarterly*, III (1964), p. 12; cf. J. L. LeGrand, "Nonviolent Civil Disobedience and Police Enforcement," *Journal of Criminal Law, Criminology, and Police Service*, LVIII (1967), p. 343.

9. Lewis F. Powell, Jr., "A Lawyer Looks at Civil Disobedience," *Washington & Lee Law Review*, XXIII (1966), p. 215.

10. Anthony De Crespigny, "The Nature and Methods of Non-Violent Coercion," *Political Studies*, XII (1964), p. 263ff.

11. Keeton, *op. cit.*, p. 508.

12. Christian Bay, "Civil Disobedience: Prerequisite for Democracy in Mass Society," in David Spitz, ed., *Political Theory and Social Change* (New York, 1967), p. 166.

John Rawls, "The Justification of Civil Disobedience"

1. By the social contract theory I have in mind the doctrine found in Locke, Rousseau, and Kant. I have attempted to give an interpretation of this view in: "Justice as Fairness," *Philosophical Review* (April, 1958); "Justice and Constitutional Liberty," *Nomos*, VI (1963); "The Sense of Justice," *Philosophical Review* (July 1963). [Ed. note. See also "Distributive Justice," in Peter Laslett and W. G. Runciman, eds., *Philosophy, Politics and Society* (1967).]

2. On this point see A. E. Murphy's review of Yves Simon's *The Philosophy of Democratic Government* (1951) in the *Philosophical Review* (April, 1952).

3. Here I follow H. A. Bedau's definition of civil disobedience. See his "On Civil Disobedience," *Journal of Philosophy* (October, 1961).

4. For a fuller discussion of this point to which I am indebted, see Charles Fried, "Moral Causation," *Harvard Law Review* (1964).

5. For a presentation of this view to which I am indebted, see A. M. Bickel, *The Least Dangerous Branch* (Indianapolis, 1962), especially Chapters 5 and 6.

Richard A. Wasserstrom, "The Obligation to Obey the Law"

1. Socrates, for instance, supposes that were he to escape he might properly be asked: "[W]hat are you about? Are you going by an act of yours to over-turn us—the laws and the whole state, as far as in you lies? Do you imagine that a state can subsist and not be overthrown, in which the decisions of law have no power, but are set aside and overthrown by individuals?" Plato, *Crito.* Analogous arguments can be found in, for example: John Austin, *The Province of Jurisprudence Determined* (London, 1954), pp. 52–53. Hobbes, *Leviathan,* ch. XV; David Hume, *A Treatise of Human Nature,* bk. III, pt. II, 3, 6, 8, 9; Stephen Toulmin, *An Examination of the Place of Reason in Ethics* (Cambridge, 1950), p. 151.

2. This is a particular illustration of the more general claim that for one reason or another utilitarianism cannot be a defensible or intelligible moral theory when construed as permitting one's moral obligation to do any parti-cular action to be overridden by a direct appeal to the consequences of per-forming that particular action. For recent statements of the claim see, *e.g.,* Patrick Nowell-Smith, *Ethics* (Baltimore, 1953); John Rawls, "Two Concepts of Rules," *Philosophical Review,* LXIV (1955), reprinted in F. A. Olafson, ed., *Society, Law, and Morality* (Englewood Cliffs, 1961), p. 420; Marcus Singer, *Generalization in Ethics* (New York, 1961), pp. 61–138, 178–216; Toulmin, *op. cit.,* pp. 144–65; Harrison, "Utilitarianism, Universalisation, and Our Duty To Be Just," *Proceedings* of the Aristotelian Soc'y, LIII (1952–53), pp. 105–134.
   For some criticisms of this restriction on utilitarianism see, *e.g.,* Wasserstrom, *The Judicial Decision* (Stanford, 1961), pp. 118–37. But see H. L. A. Hart, "Book Review," *Stanford Law Review,* XIV (1962), pp. 924–926.

3. Singer, *op. cit.,* pp. 149–50.

4. Neither Singer nor I have adequately refuted the confirmed ethical egoist who insists that he is prepared to generalize but only in the sense that *X's* nonpayment is justified if, and only if, the consequences of *X's* nonpayment would in *X's* case be more beneficial to *A* than those of payment. This is a problem which surely requires more careful attention than it typically re-ceives. It will not do simply to insist that the egoist does not understand ordinary moral discourse. Instead, what must be demonstrated are the re-spects in which the egoist's position is an inherently unjust one. But to make this showing is beyond the scope of this article.

Bruce Pech, "Radical Disobedience and Its Justification"

1. Bayard Rustin, in *Civil Disobedience* (Santa Barbara, 1966), p. 11.
2. Harrop A. Freeman, in *op. cit.,* p. 5
3. C. Wright Mills, *The Marxists* (New York, 1962), p. 87.

NOTES ON
THE CONTRIBUTORS

H(arry) B(urrows) Acton is Professor of Moral Philosophy at the University of Edinburgh and the author of *The Illusion of the Epoch: Marxism-Leninism as a Philosophical Creed* (1955) and *What Marx Really Said* (1967).

Hugo Adam Bedau is Professor of Philosophy at Tufts University, and editor of *The Death Penalty in America* (1964).

Albert Bigelow, painter and architect, has been active in leadership with the American Friends Service Committee and has written *The Voyage of the Golden Rule* (1959).

Richard M. Boardman, a graduate of Antioch College, has been active with the Chicago Area Draft Resistance (CADRE).

Noam Chomsky is Professor of Modern Languages and Linguistics at Massachusetts Institute of Technology, and author of *Syntactic Structures* (1957), *Aspects of the Theory of Syntax* (1965), and other volumes.

Carl Cohen is Associate Professor of Philosophy at the University of Michigan at Ann Arbor, and the editor of *Communism, Fascism, and Democracy* (1962).

Lewis S. Feuer is Professor of Sociology at the University of Toronto, author of *Psychoanalysis and Ethics* (1955), *Spinoza and the Rise of Liberalism* (1958), *The Scientific Intellectual* (1963), and has edited *Marx & Engels: Basic Writings on Politics and Philosophy* (1959).

Paul Goodman, lecturer, social critic, and educator, is the author of many books analyzing contemporary American culture, including *Growing Up Absurd* (1960), *Utopian Essays and Practical Proposals* (1962), *Compulsory Mis-Education* (1964), *People or Personnel* (1965), and *Like a Conquered Province* (1967).

Tom Jarrell matriculated in 1965 at New College (Sarasota, Florida). Recently, he has been living and writing in Cambridge, Massachusetts.

Martin Luther King, Jr. (1929–1968), recipient of the Nobel Prize for Peace (1964), was pastor of the Dexter Avenue Baptist Church in Montgomery, Alabama, President of the Southern Christian Leadership Conference, and author of *Stride Toward Freedom* (1956), *Why We Can't Wait* (1964), and *Where Do We Go From Here?* (1967).

Irving Kristol is editor-in-chief of Basic Books, Inc., and co-editor of *The Public Interest.*

Milton Mayer has lectured in Europe and America for the American Friends Service Committee, is author of *They Thought They Were Free* (1955), *What Can a Man Do?* (1964), and is on the faculty at the University of Massachusetts in Amherst.

A(braham) J(ohannes) Muste (1885–1967) was born in Holland, ordained to the Presbyterian ministry, and active in organizing and directing the peace work of such groups as the War Resisters League, Fellowship of Reconciliation, Peacemakers, and the Committee for Nonviolent

Action. His writings have been collected in *The Essays of A. J. Muste* (1967).

Herbert L. Packer is Professor of Law at Stanford University Law School and is the author of *Ex-Communist Witnesses* (1961).

Bruce Pech is a graduate of Tufts University and a graduate student in philosophy.

John Rawls, Professor of Philosophy at Harvard University, has taught on the faculties at Princeton, Cornell, M.I.T., and is the author of several influential essays in moral and political philosophy.

Bertrand Russell, winner of the Nobel Prize for Literature (1950), is the author of several score of volumes, including *German Social Democracy* (1896), *Justice in War-Time* (1916), *The Practice and Theory of Bolshevism* (1920), *Freedom and Organization 1814–1914* (1934), *Authority and the Individual* (1949), *Human Society in Ethics and Politics* (1954), *Has Man a Future?* (1962), and *War Crimes in Vietnam* (1967). In recent years he has devoted most of his energies to the Bertrand Russell Peace Foundation in London.

Bernard G. Segal is a senior partner in the law firm of Schnader, Harrison, Segal, and Lewis in Philadelphia, and a recent president of the American College of Trial Lawyers.

William L. Taylor is staff director for the United States Commission on Civil Rights.

Harrison Tweed is a senior partner in the law firm of Milbank, Tweed, Hadley, and McCloy in New York, and chairman of the Council of the American Law Institute.

Louis Waldman is a partner in the law firm of Waldman and Waldman in New York.

Richard A. Wasserstrom, Professor of Law and Philosophy at University of California at Los Angeles Law School, was formerly Dean of the College of Arts and Sciences of Tuskegee Institute, and is the author of *The Judicial Decision* (1961).

Harris L. Wofford, Jr. is president of the New York State University College at Old Westbury, Long Island, and was formerly Associate Director of the Peace Corps, Professor of Law at the University of Notre Dame Law School, and legal adviser to the U.S. Civil Rights Commission.

Charles E. Wyzanski, Jr. is United States District Judge for Massachusetts and author of *The New Meaning of Justice* (1965).

INDEX